Slave Breeding

UNIVERSITY PRESS OF FLORIDA

Florida A&M University, Tallahassee
Florida Atlantic University, Boca Raton
Florida Gulf Coast University, Ft. Myers
Florida International University, Miami
Florida State University, Tallahassee
New College of Florida, Sarasota
University of Central Florida, Orlando
University of Florida, Gainesville
University of North Florida, Jacksonville
University of South Florida, Tampa
University of West Florida, Pensacola

# Slave Breeding

## Sex, Violence, and Memory in African American History

GREGORY D. SMITHERS

University Press of Florida

Gainesville · Tallahassee · Tampa · Boca Raton

Pensacola · Orlando · Miami · Jacksonville · Ft. Myers · Sarasota

17  16  15  14  13  12    6  5  4  3  2  1

A record of cataloging-in-publication data is available from the Library of Congress.
ISBN 978-0-8130-4238-1

University Press of Florida
15 Northwest 15th Street
Gainesville, FL 32611-2079
http://www.upf.com

For my teacher, Clarence E. Walker.
Thank you.

# CONTENTS

# FIGURES

# ACKNOWLEDGMENTS

In the course of writing this book, I received insights, criticisms, and suggestions from some wonderfully generous scholars. I am particularly indebted to my "best man," Brian Behnken. Brian's own work will change our understanding of the civil rights movement, and I am eternally grateful to him for taking time away from his work to give his detailed and careful reading of much of this book. I also extend my gratitude to David Barber, Trevor Burnard, Rebecca Fraser, Alan Gallay, Kwasi Konadu, Peter Onuf, Ben Schiller, Carolyn Strange, Kathleen Wilson, and Michael Ondaatje, all of whom pushed me to think through various portions of my analysis. Special acknowledgment is owed to the brilliant Steven Deyle for the support he has offered to this project over the years. I thank you all for your counsel and take full responsibility for any shortcomings in the analysis that follows. Finally, I'd like to extend my appreciation to Meredith Morris-Babb, the director at the University Press of Florida, for her continued support of this book.

I'd also like to acknowledge one very important person. To Paul Spickard, one of the most generous and kindhearted individuals I've had the good fortune to meet, I thank you for your guidance over many years. Paul has supported my career for some time. For his mentorship, and the example he sets as a creative and original historian, I extend my deepest gratitude.

Thanks also go to the University of Aberdeen and the Library Company of Philadelphia for providing financial support. This support enabled me to complete portions of the research for this book. I would also like to extend my thanks to the History Department and the Centre for Cultural History at the University of Aberdeen for allowing me to present portions of my research. The feedback I received from these events helped to clarify my thinking on some critical areas of my analysis. And to Andrew MacKillop, my "mentor" during my time at the University of Aberdeen, I am grateful for the time you took to listen to me talk about the subject matter contained in this book over many strong libations. You are a patient and very collegial man indeed.

I owe a special word of acknowledgment and thanks to my colleague and friend, Clarence E. Walker. I would not have written this book had Professor Walker not instilled in me long ago the importance of reading widely, researching thoroughly, and unflinchingly analyzing history's more unpleasant events and people. Professor Walker's guidance as a teacher, his willingness to suffer (and at times, not to suffer) my impudence, and his generosity and good humor have played a major role in making me the scholar I am today. I would like to thank him for all that he has done for me and hope that he accepts this book as a token of my appreciation.

Finally, and most important, I want to thank the three most treasured people in my life: Brooke, Gwyneth, and Simone. To my wife, Brooke Newman, words do not adequately express the depth of my appreciation for your love, support, and comfort. Brooke is my harshest critic and strongest supporter; without her, this book would not have been written. Finally, a special message to my daughters, Gwyneth and Simone: please continue to be adorable—at all hours of the day and night!

# Introduction

"My marster . . . started out wid two 'omen slaves and raised 300 slaves." So testi-fied John Smith, a 108-year-old former slave who was interviewed by a Works Project Administration employee in the late 1930s. Smith's testimony was as sensational as it was disturbing. He recalled that "Short Peggy" and "Long Peggy," the two women his master "started out wid," were prized for their fe-cundity. The sexual exploitation that Smith claimed these women experienced led to the reproduction of slaves who enriched Smith's master through their labor or sale. But Smith also insisted that the exploitation of enslaved women like "Short Peggy" and "Long Peggy" resulted in the master appointing them to positions of authority among fellow slaves. Smith explained, "Long Peggy, a black 'oman, wuz boss ob de plantation. Marster freed her atter she had 25 chil-luns. Just think o' dat," Smith concluded, "raisin' 300 slaves wid two 'omen. It sho' is de truf, do' [though]."[1]

Smith's memories of slave "raisin'" served to highlight the sexual exploitation that formed a critical part of many former slaves' memories of nineteenth-cen-tury bondage in the American South. Slave breeding, as coercive, often violent, reproductive practices were known among the enslaved and their descendants, structured African American historical, ethnographic, and cultural understand-ings of black life in the United States.[2] As former slaves like Smith recalled dur-ing the depths of the Great Depression, slave masters selected women who were purported to be particularly fecund. These women were to reproduce, or breed, future generations of slaves. As Smith remembered, "Long Peggy's" status among her fellow slaves rested on her master's assessment of her as an efficient breeder of slaves. Indeed, her master predicated her future freedom on the birth and survival of her twenty-fifth child. Perhaps this was why Smith "never married befo' de war," aware, as many slaves were, that a history of vio-lent sexual exploitation meant that "Nobody married on marster's plantation."[3]

Smith's recollections, idiosyncratic as they may appear, force us to dig deeper into the historical significance of coercive and violent forms of reproductive sex during slavery. They also invite us to consider the implications that such memories have for the social and cultural context in which slavery was (and is) remembered. Reading Smith's account, one is confronted with insights into how former slaves and their descendants imagined the moral worldview that once anchored the daily life of the slave master, the plantation overseer, and the slave trader. Smith's master, Haywood Smith, "wuz a preacher" and was reportedly "good to all us niggers."[4] What, then, are we to make of Smith's memories of slave breeding? How do we make sense of a God-fearing man—a preacher—like Haywood Smith, apparently encouraging slave-breeding practices and allowing men like Tom Bridgers, the "master's overseer," to have "160 chilluns by niggers"?[5] Does the sexual violence conveyed in such recollections reveal the real motive for why slave owners like Haywood Smith "wuz good to all us niggers"? And what do oral histories of this nature teach us about African American understandings of gender and sexual relations, to say nothing of the significance of family in black culture?[6] These are not easy questions to answer.

Indeed, John Smith's memories reveal as much as they obscure. Filtered through decades of personal experiences—ranging from memories of the "whippin' pos'" on the slave plantation, the uncertainty of the Civil War, Jim Crow segregation, and the terror of lynch mobs—Smith's narrative of slave breeding paints a picture of southern slavery that was brutally exploitative one minute and seemingly nurturing the next.[7] These seeming contradictions in Smith's "remembered history" were echoed in the memories of many other former slaves. Slave-breeding practices, they insisted, should not be dismissed, marginalized, or ignored in American history. They spoke to the immoral essence of slavery. This, as Smith remembered it, was "de truf" of slavery.

This book tells the story of "de truf" of slave breeding from the perspectives of multiple generations of African Americans. Like all histories, this one is a subjective "truth." Focusing primarily on the nineteenth and twentieth centuries, the following chapters explore how black Americans defined, constructed, and used memories of slave breeding to structure historical narratives about sexual violence, explore the connections between life and death in American society, and discuss the importance of family in African American history. Slave breeding is therefore a phrase with broad interpretive significance in black American culture. It refers to more than the reproduction of human beings; it is a malleable narrative shorthand in which social norms, cultural values, and historical consciousness can be "bred," or learned, over time. In other words, the use of "breeding" in African American articulations of "slave breeding" refers to two connected issues. First, slave breeding constitutes a narrative focal point that reveals how racial violence and sexual coercion have shadowed African American reproductive practices since slavery. Second, slave breeding functions as an historical trope that allows black Americans to contextualize contemporary acts of racial and sexual violence against an exceptionally brutal historical backdrop.

Professional historians generally define slave breeding in much narrower terms. The most commonly used methodological approach to understand slave breeding is economic. Economic historians Robert Fogel and Stanley Engerman set the standard for the empirical analysis of slave breeding with their groundbreaking book *Time on the Cross* (1974). They argued that slave breeding required the slave master's systematic "interference in the normal sexual habits of slaves to maximize fertility through such devices as mating women with especially potent men." It is unclear whose standards of "normal sexual habits" Fogel and Engerman were referring to, but on the matter of slave breeding they found no demographic or economic evidence to indicate that "interference" ever occurred.[8]

Similarly, historian John Boles argued in his seminal *Black Southerners* (1984) that "there is no reliable evidence that slave owners as a general practice interfered with the sex lives of slaves so as to maximize reproduction."[9] Boles based his argument on empirical data found in plantation records, the transaction of slave sales, and census statistics. Like many historians of his generation who addressed the question of slave breeding, Bowles did not pause to question the validity or accuracy of these sources of historical "proof" when it came to slave breeding. While we should not ignore economic and demographic data, it is important to keep in mind that the details, experiences, and emotions of human life are rarely found on the bottom line of a slave ship's manifest or a plantation owner's account book. Sources of this nature often make it difficult to grapple in detail with the violent sexual encounters that accompanied slavery and expressed "complex, dynamic power relations." Such is the case with slave breeding in American history writing.[10]

The economic definition has become so entrenched in the American historical profession that efforts to correct it are met with hostility, disbelief, or a combination of the two. In the course of researching and writing this book I have encountered these reactions. I have repeatedly been told, mainly by white, senior, male historians, that slave breeding was not "real," that the sources used to claim it was "de truf"—the writings of nineteenth-century abolitionists, memoirs by former slaves, and oral histories—are so skewed and biased that there is no possibility that such practices ever "actually happened." In other words, there is assumed to be such a lack of tangible written, economic, and/ or commercial evidence to prove empirically that slave breeding ever occurred that to pursue this topic would be like trying to transform a figment of one's imagination into something verifiably "real."

## Memory, Culture, and Slave Breeding

Historical perspective and scholarly methodologies have thus played a major role in the way slave breeding is understood in American history. Since the abolition of the international slave trade to the United States in 1808, generation after generation of black Americans have discussed slave breeding as a reality of life in the slave South. In contrast, post–Civil War historians found that they could not describe slave breeding as a reality of southern life after reviewing the archival documents of plantation owners, overseers, and slave traders. That the creation and preservation of these documents were the products of plantation bookkeeping (and, it bears emphasizing, the empirical sleight of hand involved in double-entry bookkeeping), subject to the gendered and racial perspectives of their creators and of the archivists who filed them away for later reference, has long been overlooked when the topic of slave breeding crops up. Indeed, these sources shaped, and continue to shape, our historical perceptions of what is, and is not, historically important.

As all historians know, archival documentation is the scaffold upon which we build our analyses. The absence of verifiable *evidence* often means there is not a reliable story to be told, or at least not a story that the historian feels comfortable telling without slipping into the world of popular history and fiction writing—and, dare it be said, becoming an author of books that reach audiences outside the academy. For much of the twentieth century, this meant that the histories about African Americans, Native Americans, immigrants, and women were left untold, or only partially told, and the scholars who told them were "ghettoized," as several historians have commented to me, in women's or ethnic "studies" departments.[11]

Despite a dearth of written and archival sources, analysis of subaltern histories has flourished since the 1960s and 1970s. Indeed, if the historian of slavery hopes to get at the emotions and feelings of enslaved men, women, and children, he or she is often forced to compensate for a lack of archival documentation by drawing from non-literate sources and the theoretical insights of scholars outside the historical profession. Social, economic, and political historians often complain that incorporating non-literate sources and theoretical insights diminishes the ability of the historian to craft "objective" narratives based on verifiable evidence—on the "truth." However, one need only turn to the pages of economic or agricultural history books and scholarly journals to realize just how theory-driven empirical, evidence-based history can be. When economic historians turn to topics like sex and reproduction during slavery, the author(s) squeeze data (that is, "evidence" valued as "factual") into predetermined economic models. These models allow the economic historian of slavery to conveniently deploy the benign language of "rational utility" and "natural increase" to describe economic motives and fluctuations in slave population size.[12] No topic more clearly demonstrates these interpretive tensions and methodological myopia than slave breeding, a topic that historians, particularly economic historians, usually dismiss. As John Musgrave, the "list owner" of ILGALLT-L, an online history forum hosted by *Rootsweb*, reported in July 2000, "slave breeding is a controversial subject. I've talked to historians who laugh at the possibility."[13]

As a historian devoted to the interdisciplinary study of race, gender, and sexuality, I am familiar with the type of condescension Musgrave experienced. Too often, academic historians use tactics—highlighting a misplaced comma, emphasizing an incorrectly typed statistic, alleging intentional errors in transcription, or disparaging the use of theoretical insights and non-literate sources—that seek both to discredit historians of subaltern histories and to marginalize the individuals and groups these scholars write about. Examples of this abound. On September 1, 2011, for instance, renowned historian Peter Wood advertised the arrival of a new book, *The Jefferson-Hemings Controversy: Report of the Scholars Commission*. Edited by Robert F. Turner, the book contains chapters by senior historians that, in general, discredit recent analyses of the sexual affair between Thomas Jefferson and his slave Sarah "Sally" Hemings, an affair that produced at least one child. In particular, the contributors to *The Jefferson-Hemings Controversy* criticize the efficacy of DNA evidence—calling it "junk science"—and discredit leading scholars in this field. Most notably, Annette Gordon-Reed is targeted for some sustained and biting criticism. Gordon-Reed's work on the Jefferson-Hemings affair has added invaluable new insights into the historical significance of race and sexuality in the founding of the American republic.[14] That *The Jefferson-Hemings Controversy* devotes so much attention to Gordon-Reed's work reflects the impact she has had on historical writing, and how some historians are displeased with this influence.

Most of the attacks made on Gordon-Reed's scholarship by the contributors to *The Jefferson-Hemings Controversy* are petty. Peter Wood's insistence that the contributors to *The Jefferson-Hemings Controversy* "seek the facts of the particular case" is therefore belied by the tenor of the volume. In the introduction, for instance, a lament for the professional demise of writer Brad Vice and historian Michael Bellesiles—for plagiarism and fabrication of evidence, respectively— contextualizes an extraordinarily vitriolic attack on Gordon-Reed. It is alleged, for instance, that while the careers of Vice and Bellesiles were torpedoed by allegations of plagiarism and the fabrication of evidence, Gordon-Reed "has apparently paid no price for what appear to be equally if not more serious transgressions against accepted standards of professional behavior."[15] Under the pretense of "objective," fact-finding history, the contributors to *The Jefferson-Hemings Controversy* attempt to choke off debate about a topic that they find particularly uncomfortable.[16]

*Slave Breeding*, then, comes with a warning: it deals with a very uncomfortable topic. It does so by exploring how multiple generations of African Americans have used the trope of slave breeding to emphasize the brutalities of slavery and its violent legacies. Few narrative tropes in African American culture are as powerfully evocative as slave breeding. It is a trope that has conveyed, and continues to convey, a sense of the trauma, endurance, and adaptive skills that black Americans have needed to live under slavery and to envision how they might begin to prosper in the wake of that brutal regime's demise.

From the antebellum era to the present day, African American memories of slave-breeding practices have been part of the "vernacular" history of slavery. By "vernacular history" I refer to understandings of the past that are often invisible to "mainstream" Americans and professional historians. To borrow from literary scholar Robert O'Meally, vernacular histories include "aspects of the American experience that do not get told in any other way" than in art, theater, oral narratives, self-published memoirs, song, or dance.[17] Slave breeding is just such a vernacular history. It allows us to begin to understand how these memories foster historical understandings of sexual violence, capture the connection between life and death in a racially structured society, and highlight the importance of family. As with the production of all memories and historical writing, this was, and continues to be, an active, creative process in black culture. It is a process that can be set in motion by a word, an image, a phrase, a song, a dance, or a story.

The trope of slave breeding provides African Americans with a well of "deep" memories.[18] That is, slave breeding focuses narratives about slavery on its brutalities and its legacy—the racial violence associated with the sexual assault of black domestics, race riots and lynchings, and challenges to family and community stability since the Thirteenth Amendment to the Constitution abolished slavery in 1865. Thus, African Americans have nurtured narratives about slave breeding in political speeches and autobiographies of the nineteenth century; in abolitionist propagandizing; in religious sermons; in oral histories, political testimonies, and folklore; and in plays, movies, and literary fiction. Historically, these sources have engaged with the broader American culture in which they were produced and became part of black America's historical and political discourse in slavery and freedom.

Since the passage of the Civil Rights and Voting Rights Acts in 1964 and 1965, Americans have become hyper-aware of topics like slave breeding and the legacy of slavery in American society. In general, most Americans try to avoid such topics, but on occasion avoidance is no longer an option. This was the case in 1988 when Jimmy "the Greek" Snyder, a sportscaster for CBS television, attempted to explain why African American athletes dominated professional sports in the United States. Snyder remarked, "The slave owner would breed his big Black with his big woman so that he would have a big Black kid." Snyder concluded, "The Black is a better athlete to begin with because he was bred to be that way."[19] The editors of *Jet* magazine referred to Snyder's remarks as a "slur" against black athletes.[20] Executives at CBS television agreed and terminated the network's association with the controversial sportscaster.

Some fifteen years after Snyder's ill-fated remarks, a similar set of comments inflamed media and public opinion once again. In 2003, then manager of the Chicago Cubs baseball team, Dusty Baker, reignited debate over the link between black athletes, slavery, and racial inheritance. Baker asserted, "I like playing in the heat. Most Latin people and minority people do. You don't find too many brothers from New Hampshire or Maine, right? We were brought over here because we could work in the heat—isn't that history?"[21] Coming from a well-known and likable black celebrity, Baker's comments reflected a shared history of racial consciousness. Where Snyder's remarks were interpreted as a "slur" by many blacks because they implied that African American athletes achieve success only through their genetic inheritance, Baker spoke to the idea of black American success being achieved against a historical backdrop of intense racism. And lurking in the subtext of Baker's comments was an allusion to one of the most profound forms of human exploitation in black historical memory: the coerced, often violent, selection of Africans and African Americans to be slaves because of their perceived physical attributes.

The biological selection that Baker alluded to reflects the active ways in which black Americans articulate and rearticulate memories of slave breeding in contemporary culture. In September 2009, for example, en route from my temporary home in New Haven, Connecticut, to the nearby airport, my shuttle driver asked me what I do for a living. I offered up a generic answer—"I'm a historian of U.S. history, slavery mainly"—upon which he stated: "You know, they bred slaves." What followed was the retelling of a deeply moving family history that began in slavery and slave breeding in Louisiana. I asked if he thought his family history with slave breeding warranted "reparations" from the federal government. He responded, not unlike the civil rights activists of the 1950s and 1960s, that it did not, that black people simply needed the government to pass and police laws that would allow African Americans to rise on their own merits. What struck me about this encounter was the matter-of-fact nature with which this particular gentleman, a working-class black man with no investment in academic artifice or historiographical debates, related his family history.

I have encountered similarly direct statements about slave breeding from black scholars and authors of fiction. For instance, Elizabeth Nunez has "Anna," the central character in her novel *Anna-in-Between*, accuse slave owners of breeding slaves for profit. I asked Nunez about this scene and the inspiration behind it. She stated that for her, stories of slave breeding "came inseparable from the stories I heard about slavery. I never questioned it. It seemed the obviously horrible thing slave owners would do, like Washington using his slaves' teeth to have dentures made for himself. Supposedly, he paid them for their teeth, but I often wondered if the slave had the option of not selling their teeth to him." I followed this question by asking Nunez if she thinks "slave breeding is something that occupies a popularly accepted part of the African American and Afro-Caribbean writer's historical memory." To this question she replied, "Yes, I do. It's a central part of any discussion on the state of black families and the absence of fathers in the lives of children."[22]

Zakes Mda's evocative novel *Cion* (2007) also grapples with the memory of slave breeding. Mda, a literary scholar and novelist at Ohio University, sets

*Cion* in rural Ohio. Here he explores the origins and implications of mixed-race Americans. In *Cion*, racial mixing has very brutal origins indeed. On a fictional plantation in Fredericksburg, Virginia, the Fairfield family operates a slave-breeding plantation. Historians often insist that for slave breeding to have occurred there must have existed some sort of science and/or strict management to the system. This is not the case in *Cion*. Mda writes that the "breeding process was not formalized or planned in any scientific manner. Children happened when they did and were sold just before they reached their teens." Indeed, the violence associated with interracial sex and slave-breeding practices on the Fairfield plantation evokes distressing images. Inbreeding is common, as are "binge parties" in which young men from nearby colleges join David Fairfield, the son of plantation owner Charles Fairfield, in indulging their addictions for "black pussy."[23] I asked Mda about the inspiration for the portrayal of such sexual violence. He responded that his "initial source for slave breeding was J. A. Rogers' *Sex and Race: A History of White, Negro and Indian Miscegenation in the Two Americas*." Mda noted that as an "organic historian," the largely self-trained Rogers was "not highly regarded by the academy." So, to flesh out his portrayal of slave breeding, and the inspiration for the Fairfield plantation, Mda did some archival research, finding "some of the letters and articles by the Virginia lawyer [and slave owner] George Fitzhugh enlightening on the subject."[24]

These stories are striking for their narrative synergy. The blunt, matter-of-fact nature of the knowledge narrated and the connection between historical wrongs and twentieth- and twenty-first-century racial questions and anxieties give such narratives their "deep" meaning. These stories belong to an African American culture and oral tradition that incorporates memories of slave breeding into what Thomas Abercrombie refers to as "social memory." Social memory is an active and creative process in which "people constitute themselves and their social formations in communicative actions and interactions, making themselves by making rather than inheriting their pasts."[25] In this sense, the political, social, historical, and popular narratives of slave breeding that black Americans have woven into, and out of, their understanding of slavery since the nineteenth century demands serious scholarly attention.

For slaves, former slaves, and the descendants of slaves, slave breeding buttresses memories of the violent sexual exploitation of African American women, the abuse and sale of enslaved children, and the hegemonic white majority's seeming power to define the parameters of life and death for black Americans.

During slavery, the progeny of the coercive sexual mating between enslaved couples, or the sexual manipulation—including what we would understand today as rape—of slave women by white men (and, on occasion, black men), was, and continues to be, remembered by African Americans as a source of wealth for slave owners and slave traders. But as I noted above, slave breeding is much more than this. In the different forms of memory produced by black people since the nineteenth century, slave breeding became critical to historical explanations of the racial and sexual objectification of black bodies; of the distortion of ideals regarding gender roles between black men and black women; of the fragile nature of black family life; and of the need for African Americans to craft narratives that make sense of the brutal ways in which life can be conceived and snuffed out—for instance, through interracial rape and lynchings—in a racist society.

### History, the Historian, and Slave Breeding in American Culture

As the above discussion suggests, slave breeding occupies an inglorious and contested place in the American historical imagination. Professional historians are certainly a long way from reaching a consensus on this topic. As we have seen, Fogel and Engerman became the standard-bearers for the economic historian's narrow approach to slave breeding in the 1970s. But a competing narrative also existed in the 1970s. This alternative approach to slave breeding emerged with the rise of the "new social history" of the 1960s and 1970s. Practitioners of this brand of history took a broader, more critical approach to the analysis of slave breeding than scholars engaged in economic history. Most notably, Alfred H. Conrad and John R. Meyer, as well as Herbert Gutman and Richard Sutch, insisted that efforts to breed slaves in the upper South for sale in the slave states of the lower South did indeed exist. In a famous 1976 essay, Gutman and Sutch defined slave breeding as "any practice of the slave master intended to cause the fertility of the slave population to be higher than it would have been in the absence of such interference."[26] Although Gutman backtracked on the impact of slave breeding on black family life in *The Black Family in Slavery and Freedom* (1977), in collaboration with Sutch, Gutman argued that slave-breeding practices included rewards such as more comfortable living quarters, better and greater quantities of food, and/or a lightened workload.[27] Scholars with a more rigid approach to economic and demographic history dismiss such arguments. They look at the data on slave reproduction, births, deaths, and sales and do not believe slave-breeding practices were a reality of plantation life. For example, Barry Higman, a historian of West Indian slavery, argues that "the broader definition of [slave] breeding has little value as a means of distinguishing the manipulation of fertility in slave and free societies, and there seems to be little gained from pursuing this debate."[28]

Despite Higman's attempt to shut down historical debate about slave breeding, scholars do still engage the topic. In his compelling *Becoming Southern* (1995), Christopher Morris details how "Judge Alexander Covington and his nephew Edmund left Natchez," Mississippi, and established a new plantation on "2000 acres in the south end of Warren County, near the Big Black River."[29] Here, Morris explains, the Covingtons developed a business strategy that allowed them to cultivate an image of themselves as planter elites. This strategy was "to raise young negroes," rather than crops. Morris contends that the Covingtons' desire to "raise young negroes" locked "masters *and* slaves [into a] shared interest in slave family formation." Whereas slaves longed for stable and emotionally supportive families, slave masters like the Covingtons valued slave families because they "had much to gain by attempting to increase the birth rate of their slaves, and so they endeavored to do just that." Evidently the Covingtons were a smashing success at such endeavors, as neighbors testified that they "succeeded very well in raising young negroes."[30]

Intimate human relations, as the literary scholar Saidiya Hartman observes, can involve "brutal power and authority" and do not necessarily encompass consensual physical and emotional encounters.[31] They often involve great degradation that, not coincidentally, leaves little empirical evidence in the archives that professional historians usually consult.[32] Methodological agility is therefore necessary when surveying the different cultural and historical contexts through which the topic of slave breeding has been filtered. This is because debate about the utility, much less the existence, of slave breeding has circulated throughout the Atlantic world in various genres since the late eighteenth century.

To begin to understand the circulation of this information, a brief historical overview is necessary. According to the sociologist Eddie Donoghue, Denmark became the first European power to explicitly propose a scheme for the breeding of slaves. In 1791 the Danish Committee for Improving the Organization of the Slave Trade in the West Indian Islands and the Guinea Coast established what Donoghue calls a "blueprint" for breeding African slaves.[33] British slave interests shared the Danish preoccupation with breeding slaves at a time when the abolition of imported slaves from West Africa to the British Caribbean appeared imminent. Britons with an interest in Caribbean slavery expressed a mixture of views about slave breeding. While historians remain divided over whether slave breeding was practiced on a large scale in the British Caribbean, evidence suggests that both British parliamentarians and West Indian slave owners and overseers were increasingly focused on slave reproduction after the 1780s and 1790s. These were decades in which British abolitionists raised their voices in unison against the transatlantic slave trade, prompting some with an investment in Caribbean slavery to look to other means to ensure a steady supply of slave labor.[34] As Sampson Wood, the manager of Newton Estate, reported in 1797, "I encourage their [the slaves'] breeding as much as I can."[35]

In the United States, slaveholders took a keen interest in these European debates. This interest was reflected in travel writing, contemporary histories, plantation manuals, and agricultural publications such as De Bows Review. In 1787, for example, John Lang, a white farmowner living in disputed territory between Georgia and the Creek Nation, lost his twelve-year-old slave girl to Creek Indian warriors. Long intended to use Lucy to reproduce slaves for his farmstead. Evidently, the Creek slave master who took possession of Lucy had similar ideas, as she eventually became a grandmother while still enslaved in the Creek Nation.[36] Other lurid stories of reproduction abound. In 1800 the African American writer William T. Alexander argued in his History of the Colored Race in America that "slave breeding for gain . . . deliberately and systematically pursued, appears to be among the latest devices and illustrations of inhumanity."[37] Travel writers also added to nineteenth-century discourse about the existence of slave breeding. William Faux, an English farmer and amateur travel writer, published in 1823 a revealing account of life in the American South. Faux described his travels through the United States and introduced readers to a South Carolinian by the name of Patrick Duncan. According to Faux, Duncan knew "a young gentleman, who once bought a negro wench, the only slave he ever purchased; but, at his death, his heirs divided 70 slaves amongst them, all her offspring and posterity, during a period of only 35 years."[38] Frederick Law Olmstead, a northerner who made several trips to the South, also observed the practice of slave breeding. In A Journey in the Seaboard Slave States in the Years 1853–1854 (1856) and A Journey to the Back Country (1861), Olmstead argued that slave breeding was profitably practiced in portions of "Delaware, Maryland, Virginia, North Carolina, Kentucky, and Missouri," in addition to South Carolina, where the climate was mild and the management of slaves was profitably geared toward increasing rates of human reproduction.[39]

By the antebellum period, slave breeding had become a topic of intense debate at virtually every level of American culture and society. Within the private correspondence of slave owners and in the public instructions given to plantation overseers, masters liberally dispensed advice on how best to encourage successful "breeding" practices.[40] Take the South Carolina planter James Henry Hammond, who gave explicit instructions to overseers on how to encourage "marriage" and ensure the good health of pregnant slave women and young children. While the law did not recognize slave "marriages," slave owners such as Hammond encouraged the union between enslaved men and women because it had the potential to increase the slave population, and thus, the profits of the master. "Marriage is to be encouraged," Hammond's instructions read, "as it adds to the comfort, happiness and health of those who enter upon it, besides ensuring a greater increase." Every effort was thus made on Hammond's plantation to ensure the survival of newborn slave children. "Pregnant women, at 5 mos, are put in the sucklers [breast-feeding women's] gang. No plowing or lifting must be required of them." While pregnant women on the plantation had their manual labor reduced during the latter stages of pregnancy, breast-feeding women were charged with the important task of ensuring the health and well-being of the infant slaves. Hammond instructed that "sucklers are not required to leave their houses until sun-rise, when they leave their children at the children's house before going to the field. The period of suckling is 12 ms. Their work lies always within 1/2 mile of the quarter. They are required to be cool before commencing to suckle—to wait 15 minutes, at least, in summer, after reaching the children's house before nursing."[41] Such clear directions indicate some slave owners' desire for, if not a sophisticated medical understanding of, the reproduction of the slave population and the breeding of nominally healthy slaves.

Hammond was not alone among slave owners in encouraging slave reproduction.[42] On his Virginia plantation, Pharsalia, William Massie purchased slave women who, according to the family records, played important roles as breeders. The slave women "Judy," "Milly," "Sally," "Rachel," "Sukey," "Matilda," and "Hannah" all feature prominently in Massie plantation records because they were considered particularly fecund bearers of slave children.[43] The Massie family recorded births and monitored the mothering skills of enslaved women. For example, the slave woman "Lizzie" gave birth to a son, "Gabriel," on June 21, 1856. However, a subsequent entry records that "Gabriel was murdered right out by his mothers [sic] neglect and barbarous cruelty on the 22 Sept 1857."

The monitoring of slave mothers, whom planters assumed lacked nurturing "instincts" and possessed deficient mothering skills, was regularly practiced at Pharsalia. That said, "Marriage" was also encouraged among the enslaved at Pharsalia, just as it was on Hammond's plantation. But neither Hammond nor the Massie family promoted "marriage" out of any heartfelt concern for the emotional well-being of the enslaved. Instead, slave "marriages" were designed to maximize the efficiency and profitability of the Massie and Hammond plantations. Such practices reminded slaves of who was in control, who oppressed them, and who had the power to assent to the creation of life, or to define the terms on which a slave's life ended.[44]

The defenders of antebellum slavery denied accusations that slaves were sexually exploited or that they reproduced children for the slave owner's commercial gain. Instead, slavery's apologists asserted that slave owners acted with compassion and patriarchal concern for the enslaved. For example, the Barbour County Agriculture Society of Alabama attempted to contradict a growing wave of abolitionist opposition to slavery when it reported in 1846 that because the slave is a valuable piece of property, "we can readily conceive how strongly the motive of the master in taking good care of the slave, and thus extending the time of his usefulness."[45] It was therefore a simple matter of economic self-interest that motivated the slave owner to ensure the good health of his "crop" of slaves and to ensure that the slave's life as a productive laborer (or reproducer of new slaves) continued for as long as possible. However, this, according to the proslavery lobby, was not slave breeding; it merely reflected the paternalism that governed the slave owner's economic decisions and actions on behalf of his slaves.[46]

Slave owners persisted throughout the antebellum period with this type of self-deception, treating and "managing" the "Negro" with a view to increasing their "cheerfulness." If this meant that the rate of slave reproduction increased, all the better. It did not mean, however, that efforts were being made to select and biologically engineer future generations of slaves. For example, the winning entry in the 1851 "Planter-Prize Essay" competition in Georgia instructed readers that "females, during a state of pregnancy should be exempt from all labor that would have a tendency to injure them, such as lifting heavy burdens, fencing, plowing, &c., and for several weeks previous to confinement they should be required to perform no outdoor labor."[47]

Despite persistent denials, all of this advice amounted to a desire—in rhetoric, if not in scientific know-how—on the part of slave-owning and slave-trading interests to maximize profits through exploitative labor regimes and reproductive practices. To borrow a phrase from Karl Marx and Friedrich Engels, slave breeding involved the "naked self-interest" and "callous 'cash payment'" between slave traders, buyers, and masters for slaves who would breed prodigiously and work efficiently.[48] Indeed, some recent historical scholarship has suggested that the commodification of sex among the enslaved, and the offspring they produced, highlighted the most brutal aspect of the "chattel principle" in the slave South, a principle that, as chapter 1 demonstrates, a growing army of abolitionists and free-labor, free-soil politicians systematically critiqued after the 1830s.[49]

From an African American perspective, it might be acknowledged that slaves shared with the master an "interest in slave family formation," but their motives for doing so were based on an entirely different set of objectives. It is at this point that the trope of slave breeding casts new light on the debates about black families that persist into the twenty-first century. Since the 1960s, historical analysis has exhibited great sensitivity to nuances in slave family formation. This work has grown in volume and sophistication since the publication of Daniel Patrick Moynihan's *The Negro Family: A Case for National Action* (1965). The "Moynihan Report," as it came to be known, built on early-twentieth-century analyses by black scholars like W. E. B. Du Bois and E. Franklin Frazier. Like these black scholars, Moynihan identified the roots of black poverty and family dislocation in slavery. Specifically, Moynihan detailed a tangled web of pathology that he argued resulted from the matriarchal nature of black families.[50]

Since the publication of *The Negro Family*, a plethora of historical monographs have raised serious questions about Moynihan's conclusions. The following passages provide a brief summation of how some of the most prominent historians of the late twentieth and early twenty-first centuries have addressed the topics of the slave family and the sexual exploitation of African American women. This overview should provide some basic historical background from which to contextualize the following discussions of slave breeding and the relationship of slave breeding to black families.

Since the late 1970s, the idea that African Americans were passive victims of enslavement has come under sustained revision. Historians such as Herbert Gutman, Eugene Genovese, George Rawick, and John Blassingame focused our attention away from the slave master and on the "world the slave's made."[51] To be sure, these historians had their disagreements, but most tended to agree that the slave possessed an *agency* of his or her own. Gutman's *The Black Family in Slavery and Freedom, 1750–1925* (1977) explored this agency by focusing on how black families struggled to endure slavery and strove to carve out lives of dignified independence after slavery's demise. Notably absent from his analysis were references to slave breeding, a topic Gutman explored in detail with Richard Sutch just one year prior to the publication of *The Black Family in Slavery and Freedom*. However, given the growing emphasis that historians placed on the *agency* of historically marginalized peoples, this omission should not come as a surprise. Gutman wanted to destroy Moynihan's thesis by emphasizing strong family bonds and highlighting the ways in which African American people cultivated a strong spirit and independence of action that neither slavery nor Jim Crow segregation could extinguish.

The figure of the black matriarch as a source of strength, as opposed to being the focal point of family pathology, did not attract serious historical attention until the 1980s. One book in particular, Deborah Gray White's *Ar'n't I a Woman?* (1985) changed the way historians think about slavery and gender. While not losing sight of black women's agency, White offered nuanced insights into the context in which that agency was exercised. For example, White did not shy away from contextualizing black female agency against a historical backdrop in which sexual and reproductive abuses were not uncommon. "Slave masters," White argued, "wanted adolescent girls to have children, and to this end they practiced a passive, though insidious kind of breeding."[52] Faced with such exploitative practices, White's enslaved women actively cultivated supportive emotional bonds with fellow slaves and developed strategies that proved vital in navigating the inhumanity associated with the commodification of their sexuality and the implications this had for their families.

When former slave women looked back on their experiences in slavery during the late nineteenth and early twentieth centuries, they often appeared to speak openly about many aspects of slave life, except sexual abuse or the threat of sexual violence. Historian Darlene Clark Hine refers to this as the "cult of dissemblance," a phrase that defines the "behavior and attitudes of Black women that created the appearance of openness and disclosure but actually shielded the truth of their inner lives and selves from their oppressors."[53] Hine's formulation has produced a rethinking of black women's history. Recent works by Michelle Mitchell, Lisa Materson, and Danielle McGuire reflect how historians have paid much greater attention to how Hine's concept of dissemblance enables us to understand the "politics of respectability" that black women helped to cultivate for over a century after the Civil War.[54]

If talk of slave breeding was ever muted, it was usually done so in the presence of whites and in adherence to the "cult of respectability." Uppermost in the minds of African American people was a determination to shield family and friends from the types of racist and sexist stereotypes that black women struggled to combat throughout the twentieth century. Elsa Barkley Brown has written about these efforts, arguing that after slavery the "family and the concept of the community of family offered a unifying thread that bound African Americans together."[55] Black women were instrumental in sewing these threads of family and community together, often forming the backbone of the churches and community organizations that institutionalized the family in African American culture—that is, making it a focal point of church and social organizations' activities—and helped its members deflect racist and sexist stereotypes that began in slavery.[56]

The following chapters will take up these issues in more detail. It is important to note, however, that even before slavery became a memory, black women struggled against sexual violence, worried about children being torn from them, and grappled with the uncertainty of "abroad marriages" (marriages in which husband and wife resided on different plantations). Historians such as Ann Malone and Brenda Stevenson have chronicled these experiences. While the incidences of matrifocal families varied over time and space, the existence of single-parent matriarchal "households" did not prevent slaves from actively working to create stable, nurturing families. Under slavery, though, "family," much less "community," was tenuous. As a result, the notion of "family" was far more variegated than the imposition of a nuclear family model allows.[57] As Stevenson argues, slaves wanted to forge enduring relationships, to marry whomever they wanted, and to control their own sexual activity and reproductive lives. Irrespective of how adaptable slaves attempted to make their "family" and "community," enslaved African Americans recognized that when their master forced them to "marry" another slave, the intent behind that union seemed obvious: to breed slaves.[58]

Historian Marie Schwartz has taken up the issue of childbirth and breeding slaves in her research. In *Birthing a Slave* (2006) she focuses on the history of medicine and gender, arguing that plantation management in the antebellum South centered on the "struggle for domination centered on women's bodies."[59] She insists that slave owners from Thomas Jefferson—who believed that "a woman who brings a child every two years [is] more profitable than the best man of the farm"[60]—to the paternalists of nineteenth-century America aimed to purchase slave women who were "good breeders," invest money in the medical care of physically attractive childbearing women, and act as matchmakers to both increase reproductive rates and "improve the stock."[61] As Schwartz argues, and the following chapters of this book demonstrate, the African American representation of the antebellum plantation as a breeding farm produced memories and historical narratives that intentionally characterized slavery as an inhuman institution in which sexual exploitation was commonplace, in which families were torn apart, and where the violent ways in which black life was created and/or brutally ended were emphasized.[62]

Connecting disparate threads of memory has long been viewed as a valid cultural enterprise in black America. Such connections not only narrate the past but impute meaning to the present. Feminist scholar Patricia Hill Collins, for example, connects the history of slave breeding and the "actual breeding of 'quadroons and octoroons' during slavery" with the pornographic representation of black Americans after slavery. Collins argues that America's history of "racism and sexism" is grounded in the antebellum exploitation of slave women as potential "breeders" and in the postbellum objectification of black female sexuality.[63]

Since the civil rights movement, black women have seemingly cast aside the "cult of dissemblance" and openly expressed indignation for slave breeding. For example, Josephine Carson presents an image of slavery in which slaves were "made to work fields and to breed more marketable pounds of chattel by the plantation stud or his master."[64] The African American journalist Jill Nelson has written similarly damning condemnations of slavery's exploitation. Focusing on black men, Nelson argues that during slavery the "purpose [of the black man was] to work the field and function as a plantation stud, producing slaves, or objects of ridicule."[65]

More recently, the legal scholar Pamela Bridgewater has placed the enduring legacy of slave breeding in African American life in a legal context. Bridgewater argues that slave breeding "was an integral component of the North American slave trade."[66] She contends that slave owners used two methods to increase slave reproduction: a system of rewards and punishments, not unlike the freedom that was allegedly promised to "Long Peggy" after the birth of her twenty-fifth child; or a system of coercion and sexual abuse, such as the master or white overseer "raping" an enslaved woman. In her book *Breeding a Nation* (2009), the depth of Bridgewater's analysis comes into full view. She presents a bold argument, contending that the abolition of the international slave trade to the United States in 1808 meant that the economic and political structure (and survival) of the South had relied on slave breeding. When Congress eventually debated the Thirteenth Amendment after the Civil War, lawmakers understood that ending slavery and giving black people their freedom would end the forced reproduction of black babies on southern plantations.[67]

The work of late-twentieth- and early-twenty-first-century feminist scholars, along with recent histories of slavery and interracial sexuality, have given voice to an alternative definition of slave breeding that was long muted by the narrow definitions offered by economic and social historians. By eschewing the "list history"—or the narration of one event occurring after another—that generations of predominantly (white) male economic and social historians have used to dismiss accusations of slave breeding, scholars such as Bridgewater force us to reflect more deeply on what history is, what constitutes valid historical documentation, and how important subjective factors are in analyzing archival sources and representing historical "truth."[68] This book aims to build on this endeavor.

In the six chapters that follow, I explore the history and memory of slave breeding from the perspectives of nineteenth-century abolitionists;[69] Lost Cause mythologizers and late-nineteenth- and early-twentieth-century historians;[70] early-twentieth-century black playwrights; former slaves in the late 1930s; black scholars and civil rights leaders between the end of World War I and the modern civil rights movement; and in the literature, films, and folktales by and about African Americans. As a whole, the chapters in this book problematize white America's hegemonic hold over the retelling of American history and of slavery's place in that history. Through different intellectual and cultural genres, we will see how African American memories of slave breeding expose the tension between "vernacular" interpretations of the past and professional historical narratives. These tensions are important because they force readers to grapple with a history that "white folks don't like to hear about."[71] This book will therefore challenge readers. Ultimately, however, it is my hope that *Slave Breeding* results in a richer, deeper, and more complex understanding of the importance of slave breeding in African American history and memory.

# 1

## American Abolitionism and Slave-Breeding Discourse

From at least the 1770s and 1780s, anti-slavery groups in Britain and North America began coordinating political attacks on international slavery. Initially focused on abolishing the international slave trade, by the turn of the nineteenth century anti-slavery activists paid increased attention to sensational claims about slave-breeding practices in the Caribbean and mainland North America. The anti-slavery focus on slave breeding intensified in the United States during the 1830s and 1840s, reaching a crescendo in the 1850s as black and white abolitionists deployed sensational and sentimental rhetoric to attack the slave South. As one of the most important literary genres of the eighteenth and nineteenth centuries, sentimentalism was particularly important to abolitionist representations of slave breeding. Sentimental literature set out to appeal to the reader's moral senses. The goal of the author was to awaken one's feelings and emotions for a given subject. One need only skim through nineteenth-century newspapers to see how often the word "horror" appears to describe audience or reader reaction to descriptions of the more lurid abuses of slavery.[1] As Victoria Bynum observes of abolitionist descriptions of slavery, "Most white Americans were too horrified by tales of racial violence and lust to question their veracity."[2] In this sense, sentimental literature increasingly became politically and morally charged during the nineteenth century.[3] African American authors thus recognized the value of sentimental language in political discourse. As literary scholar Valerie Smith observes, black abolitionists like Frederick Douglass and Harriet Jacobs used the conventions of sentimental literature to undermine the cultural and socioeconomic structures that buttressed slavery.[4]

Abolitionists defined slave breeding as the coercive reproduction of new generations of slave laborers for sale and resale. They added that slave-breeding practices highlighted the immoral commodification of reproductive sexuality in Caribbean and North American plantation societies. It was impossible to talk about slave breeding, abolitionists maintained, without also discussing the emotional and physical abuse that slave-breeding schemes had on enslaved women, the anguish such practices caused when a husband, a wife, and/or children were separated and sold away from family, and the violence and exploitative power that the slave-owning and slave-trading classes exercised over enslaved people.

African American memories and representations of slave breeding began taking shape in this politically charged atmosphere and era of cultural sentimentalism. But before we delve into an analysis of these memories and representations it is important to begin with a comparative overview of anti-slavery and abolitionist discourse from which these representations entered popular and political culture at the end of the eighteenth century. The representation of slave-breeding practices ultimately coalesced around a general moral aversion to physical and emotional brutality in bourgeois culture during the 1840s and 1850s. Starting from this historical context allows us to do three things. First, we can reassess the political writings, speeches, and slave testimonies that refer to slave breeding prior to the outbreak of the Civil War. Second, we can develop a clearer picture of the relative importance that abolitionists placed on slave-breeding allegations in their commentaries on compromise politics over slavery and debate about slavery's westward extension during the antebellum decades. Finally, by analyzing the public accusations of slave breeding we begin to appreciate the importance that black and white abolitionists placed on the images associated with sexual exploitation, racial violence, and family separation. By the antebellum era, black abolitionists in particular focused on slave breeding as a key motivating factor for the violence experienced in slavery, particularly the abuses endured by enslaved women and their families. These representations gave the voiceless millions of enslaved people an important role in anti-slavery politics. While black abolitionist spokespeople shared with white abolitionist colleagues a determination to prevent slavery's westward extension, black spokespeople used slave-breeding imagery to emphasize the slaves' suffering, demand the immediate abolition of slavery, and insist on the importance of legal equality for all Americans. Thus, the images of slave breeding that black abolitionists contributed to abolitionist discourse provided a less politically abstract rationale for slavery's immediate end and emphasized either firsthand experiences or eyewitness accounts that white abolitionists could only recite.[5]

## Anglo-American Abolitionism and Slave Breeding

In recent decades, historians have detailed the emergence and development of transalantic abolitionism after the 1770s and 1780s.[6] There exist scores of excellent historical accounts of the British abolitionist movement, the narrative of which is well known.[7] It is worth emphasizing, however, that slavery and the international slave trade were phenomenally profitable components of the British Empire's economy during the last third of the eighteenth century. Historian Philip Morgan gives us a sense of just how important slavery was to the British Empire, arguing that between 1780 and 1810 the British trade in slaves amounted to some eighty thousand "shackled Africans" per year. It was in this context, and against seemingly insurmountable political and imperial odds, that British abolitionists attacked the Empire's interest in slavery and precipitated its decline.[8] Indeed, British abolitionists were so successful in transforming Britain's political discourse about the international slave trade that British parliamentarians sitting within the hallowed halls of the House of Commons began to hear predictions of the consequences of its sudden demise, long before an act to abolish the slave trade was passed into law. With the flow of slaves from Africa to the British Caribbean halted, British parliamentarians listened to lurid predictions of Caribbean planters developing an "interest to keep up the slaves by breeding, if possible."[9]

Alarming predictions of slave breeding in the British Caribbean became an increasingly common part of British debate about slavery during the first third of the nineteenth century. This was because abolitionists had been so successful in abolishing the transatlantic slave trade that late-eighteenth-century predictions became early-nineteenth-century reports of Caribbean plantation owners and overseers boasting of the success of their "breeding" schemes. Adam Hochschild observes that the operators of the Codrington Plantation in Barbados claimed to have increased its slave population following the abolition of the British slave trade in 1807 thanks to "breeding" schemes.[10] The great leader of British abolitionism, William Wilberforce, could not ignore these reports. He explained the unintended consequences of the British slave trade's abolition by suggesting that only after the abolition of the international slave trade would "men . . . apply their minds in earnest to effect the establishment of the breeding system."[11]

But "men" turning their minds to something does not always mean they will meet success. Much of the historical debate about slave breeding in the

Caribbean is in reality a story of the trials and failures of Caribbean planters to stimulate reproduction among enslaved populations.[12] Nonetheless, failure did not prevent British plantation owners from urging their overseers to implement practices designed to encourage the rapid increase in the slave labor force. On the Georgia Estate in Jamaica, for example, plantation owner Thomas Gordon received word from his overseers in the 1820s and 1830s that consistent increases in slave population size were unattainable. In account ledgers that list slave births and deaths alongside those for livestock, Gordon could read for himself the failure of efforts to stimulate slave reproduction. Over the course of the 1820s and 1830s slight increases in the slave population were recorded. However, by the 1830s things changed dramatically. From 1832 to 1833, for instance, the number of adult slaves of reproductive age decreased from 168 to 154. Illness, disease, death, rebellions, and runaways, in addition to the use of contraceptives among the enslaved, may account for the drop in the adult population and a decline in the number of newborn and infant children.[13]

However, the intent behind efforts to stimulate slave reproduction in the Caribbean during the early nineteenth century was what truly alarmed abolitionists, and is an aspect of historical writing on abolitionism that remains underdeveloped. The British experience demonstrated to black and white abolitionists in the United States that the abolition of the international slave trade had the potential to give rise to slave-breeding schemes. This was something abolitionists were forced to grapple with from the early years of the American republic. In this sense, American abolitionists had much to learn from the experiences of their British counterparts if they wanted to abolish slavery by root and branch and to perpetuate their own version of bourgeois sexual morality and monogamous marriage practices.

During the late colonial and Revolutionary eras in British North America, American abolitionists and lawmakers shared a preference for a gradual approach to the abolition of slavery in which former slave owners would receive financial compensation for the loss of their chattel. This was the path taken by the northeastern and mid-Atlantic colonies and states during the late eighteenth and early nineteenth centuries. As in Britain, American abolitionists tended to be non-slaveholding, highly educated elites. By 1831, however, the year that William Lloyd Garrison's abolitionist newspaper *The Liberator* appeared for the first time, American abolitionist discourse changed dramatically. While happy that the international slave trade to the United States ended, in theory, in 1808, American abolitionists recognized the political battles that were tied to land

and slaves in the early republic. The reproduction of the United States' enslaved millions, and the labor they performed on southern plantations, drove an international web of finance, manufacturing, and trade. The global economy of the nineteenth century, abolitionists insisted, was driven by the exploitation of the slave's reproductive and physical labor.[14]

In this context, American abolitionists demanded an immediate end to the internal slave trade and slavery in the United States.[15] Abolishing the international slave trade to the United States became simply a starting point for ending a critically important cog in the American and Atlantic world economies: slavery and the internal slave trade in the American republic. Garrison's language in the January 1831 edition of *The Liberator,* in which he pronounced that "I will not equivocate," prefaced the forceful tenor of immediate abolitionist rhetoric in the decades prior to the Civil War.[16] Key figures in shaping abolitionist discourse during the antebellum era, such as Garrison and Susan B. Anthony, and African Americans like Frederick Douglass and Harriet Jacobs, gave abolitionist rhetoric a radical edge that drowned out those antebellum voices espousing a gradual end to slavery. One of the defining aspects of radical abolitionism's rhetoric after the 1830s was its use of imagery designed to shock, disgust, and inspire ordinary Americans into demanding an immediate end to southern slavery, lest its train of moral evils extend from the Atlantic to the Pacific Coast. This became especially the case during the 1850s, when, as historian David Lightner demonstrates, abolitionists and anti-slavery scholars raised their voices against slave trading and slave-breeding practices to a fever pitch.[17] Horrific tales of slave breeding became a staple of this radicalized rhetoric, more than it had been in British abolitionist discourse. Audiences at anti-slavery meetings and readers of abolitionist newspapers thus confronted graphic stories of "the cruelty and turpitude of slave-breeding and slave-exporting" in the American South.[18]

## The Emergence of Slave-Breeding Discourse

Since at least the publication of Ronald Walters's important and thought-provoking analysis of abolitionist uses of sexual imagery in an *American Quarterly* essay in 1973, the interwoven histories of race, gender, and sexuality have received increasingly sophisticated historical analysis in the field.[19] The scholarship of Walters and subsequent historians has highlighted how antebellum abolitionists became increasingly vociferous in expressing their anxiety about the vice, licentiousness, and immorality that slavery fostered in the American

South. In articulating their anxieties about the immorality of slavery, antebellum abolitionists touched upon the tension between Enlightenment and post-Enlightenment concepts of individual choice, liberal ideals of legal equality, and notions of collective virtue in a territorially expanding American republic. Historians have still not fully explored the historical significance of the links between republican settler colonial expansion and the ways in which abolitionists characterized the southern section of the republic as "one great Sodom," a sexually charged imagery that abolitionists used to highlight their anxiety about the moral nature of a future continental republic.[20] Abolitionists therefore charged that slave-owning and slave-trading interests were compromising the delicate balance between liberal notions of legal equality and republican notions of collective virtue that ideally bound the states in union.[21] The rhetorical use of slave breeding became an evocative narrative device in helping American abolitionists make these points.

Abolitionist anxiety about western expansion and the intellectual tension between nineteenth-century liberal individualism and republican virtue dominated anti-slavery discourse in the early republic. As we will see, abolitionists expressed this tension in increasingly sentimental and sensational terms during the antebellum decades. What remained consistent in anti-slavery and abolitionist discourse throughout the late eighteenth century and into the nineteenth was the fear that the slave South's economic development and drive for new territories was connected to coercive human reproductive practices.[22] Destroy slavery and the slave-breeding practices that sustained the internal slave trade would wither and die, abolitionists maintained.

The deployment of a discernible slave-breeding discourse owed much to the writings and speeches of black abolitionists during the late eighteenth and early nineteenth centuries. From Phillis Wheatley's poetry at the end of the eighteenth century to Frederick Douglass's tireless protests against the "peculiar institution" in antebellum America, former slaves and free blacks engaged in abolitionist discourse and opposed the aggressive pro-slavery lobby in the South. Thus, detailed references to slave-breeding practices grew in regularity and narrative coherence as black and white abolitionists added new narrative layers of sentimentality and sensational accusations about sexual exploitation.[23]

As early as the 1760s and 1770s, formerly enslaved men and women spoke candidly about the types of sexual abuses that antebellum abolitionists would ultimately weave into narratives about slave breeding. Former slave women, for example, wrote about sexual coercion and violence, and the acute feelings of despair that an enslaved mother experienced when her infant died suddenly or was forcibly removed from her through sale. In 1773 the former New England slave and poet Phillis Wheatley spoke for other enslaved mothers when she wrote about the anguish caused by the death of a child:

> No more the flow'ry scenes of pleasure rise,
> Nor charming prospects greet the mental eyes;
> No more with joy we view that lovely face,
> Smiling, disportive, flush'd with ev'ry grace.
>
> The tear of sorrow flows from ev'ry eye;
> Groans answer groans, and sighs to sighs reply!
> What sudden pangs shot thro' each aching heart!
> When, Death! Thy messenger dispatch'd his dart!
> Thy dread attendants, all-destroying Pow'r,
>
> Hurry'd the infant to his mortal hour.[24]

Death provided finality to the separation of mother from child. Sale, on the other hand, perpetuated the deepest and most enduring of "agonizing feelings" for the mother of an enslaved child.[25] Sojourner Truth, who famously met suspicion about her sex by asserting that "her breasts had suckled many a white babe," recalled the struggles of enslaved families to maintain "the chain of family affection." Maintaining bonds of kinship was an ongoing struggle for enslaved family members who were "widely scattered" by the internal slave trade.[26]

The testimony of former slaves played an instrumental role in the emergence of a powerful slave-breeding discourse. In the early republic, "eyewitness" accounts and participant testimonies emphasized sexual abuse, violence, and family separation through sale. Prior to the 1830s, however, black and white abolitionists had not yet found the language necessary to wed these disparate violations into a coherent slave-breeding narrative that challenged the pro-slavery lobby and the rhetoric of "compromise politics" over slavery's extension. As former slaves continued to add their voices to anti-slavery protests, non-slaveholding Americans were slowly forced to confront slavery's physical and emotional impact on African American mothers, husbands, and children in the South.[27] By the early nineteenth century, then, African American leaders, writers, and orators refused to separate the politics of slavery from the personal and degrading dimensions associated with slavery's daily rhythms. Reflecting on how masters manipulated slave marriages, Solomon Bayley, a former Delaware slave, recalled his distress after being "carried from my wife and children, and from my natural place, and from my chance for freedom."[28] Bayley's words reveal much about how former slaves were increasingly connecting unrelated narrative threads about family, law, and freedom into a coherent anti-slavery discourse.

By the second decade of the nineteenth century, abolitionists believed it was both politically expedient and morally necessary to expose the sexual abuses that enslaved women were reportedly experiencing. For example, Henry Watson, an African American abolitionist, joined a growing chorus of sensational abolitionist attacks on slavery. Watson insisted that his former master "was one of those proud Virginians whose principal business was to raise slaves for the market."[29] Watson, who was born into slavery in 1813, described slavery as a "fiery ordeal" and the commercial exploitation of slave reproduction as a "bitter cup." While there existed an economic motive to slave breeding in Virginia, Watson recalled that some masters were as vicious as wild animals toward their slaves. Mistresses, too, could be cruel and "take delight in torturing" their slaves. According to Watson, neither his master nor his mistress saw their cruel behavior as contrary to their economic interests.[30] Indeed, some slaves might have been selected and used to "raise" new generations of chattel, but Watson's use of irony revealed that the "animals" in this process were the slave masters and mistresses. According to Watson, "the slaveholder watches every movement of the slave, and if he is downcast or sad,—in fact, if they are in any mood but laughing and singing, and manifesting symptoms of perfect content at heart,—they are said to have the devil in them, which is the common term; and they are often whipped or sold for their supposed wicked intentions."[31] Watson thus described for readers a classic example of psychological projection and behavioral transference. He insisted that the adjectives used to describe the slave—such as "devil," "beast," or "wicked intentions"—actually characterized the psychological and behavioral habits of the white slave owner and slave-trading classes in the South.

Watson's characterization of slavery was one that black women were all too aware of. Prominent black female abolitionists such as Sojourner Truth, Margaretta Forten, Susan Paul, and the African American Quakers Sarah and Grace Douglass all attempted to highlight slavery's licentious excesses. Many of these women had been free for several generations and went on to work closely with radical white abolitionists such as Garrison during the antebellum era.[32] Black abolitionist women believed, as the Douglass sisters believed, that their cause was "the cause of God."[33] Indeed, enslaved and formerly enslaved women needed all the spiritual power they could muster if they were to survive the physical traumas of slavery and the emotional turmoil of reliving scenes of sexual terror for abolitionist audiences. Scores of formerly enslaved women provided firsthand testimonies of slave owners interfering in the sexual, reproductive, and "married" lives of slaves. Nancy Howard, an escaped Maryland slave, remembered calling on God's help to see her through enslavement. She described her life in slavery as "one of the blackest, the wickedest things that ever were in the world."[34]

By the 1830s, anti-slavery activists were becoming increasingly well organized. As white and black Americans joined abolitionist organizations, members found it impossible to ignore the way "compromise politics" in Washington, D.C., appeared to be perpetuating slavery's extension westward. The debate about slavery's westward expansion provided the political framework that abolitionists needed to focus the nation's attention on issues like the sexual exploitation of enslaved women, the violence of plantation discipline, and the cruelty of separating family members through sale. Abolitionists insisted that the territorial extension of slavery would perpetuate what they saw as a train of moral and physical evils. In this context, the disparate threads of anti-slavery discourse during the early republic began to coalesce around the narrative of slave breeding. As one abolitionist quipped, the extension of slavery provides "a new motive . . . to the slave-breeding States to stock the market with human cattle."[35]

Antebellum abolitionists linked western expansion to slave breeding by arguing that the upper South "raised" slaves for sale in the lower South and Southwest.[36] Abolitionists charged that the infertile soil in states such as Virginia and Maryland, which allegedly made large plantations based on agricultural production unprofitable, encouraged the breeding and sale of vast quantities of slaves into the lower South. One anti-slavery writer explained that "the northern slave States, whose soil the system exhausted, have acquired a new interest in [slavery], by humbling themselves to the condition of slave-breeding and slave-trading communities."[37] Accusations of this nature crystallized in abolitionist discourse over the course of the antebellum era. Theodore Parker, for example, labeled Maryland, Virginia, Kentucky, Tennessee, and Missouri as "the *slave-breeding* States."[38] And an anonymous author writing in the *Christian*

*Spectator* decried the "brutal system of slave-breeding, supported by every device of cruelty and oppression, and resulting in a degradation of body and soul at which all civilized nations cry out with horror."[39]

In the South, pamphleteers and newspaper editors characterized slave-breeding allegations as evidence of sensationalized abolitionist propaganda designed to destroy southern civilization. Southerners with a direct socioeconomic interest in slavery and the internal slave trade insisted that abolitionist attempts to link the westward expansion of slavery to slave breeding was both scandalous and baseless. Indeed, pro-slavery politicians and propagandists insisted that allusions to the sexual exploitation of the enslaved were a distraction in the debate about slavery's extension and the North's hostility toward the South's politics and way of life. The real issue, pro-slavery politicians argued, was simple: slavery must extend into the West or die. As pro-slavery ideologues saw things, the issue of slavery's western extension was about the future economic viability of the South and the expansion of that region's noble form of civilization—nothing more, nothing less.[40]

Pro-slavery pamphleteers and newspaper editors believed that the best defense against the scurrilous accusations of abolitionists lay in highlighting how slavery constituted a positive good. Southern slavery, the argument went, was an institution in keeping with the "republican" ideals and humanitarian impulses embedded in American society.[41] Southern paternalism therefore emphasized the obligations the master felt for his "family." The master's white wife and children, in addition to his slaves, were part of a plantation "family" that the master felt obligated to protect and nurture. Southern paternalism also involved reciprocal responsibilities. Slaves reportedly felt a deep attachment to their white master and mistress, expressed in a determination to fulfill their duties as laborers. In return for faithful service, plantation owners encouraged their slaves to marry and form families.[42] Thus, southern slavery was portrayed as a socioeconomic system that was mutually beneficial to masters and slaves.

Abolitionists responded to such arguments by turning pro-slavery arguments against the South. For example, the accusation that the upper South "raised" slaves for sale in the lower South received what its exponents claimed was academic credibility following the publication of Thomas Roderick Dew's report on debate in the Virginia legislature during 1831 and 1832. Dew, a professor of "political law" at the College of William and Mary in Virginia and a pro-slavery advocate, claimed that "from all the information we can obtain, we have no hesitation in saying that upwards of six thousand [slaves] are yearly exported [from Virginia] to other states . . . [and] are a source of wealth to Virginia."[43] Economic gain from the sexual exploitation and suffering of other human beings was the worst kind of sin in the minds of abolitionists. Dew's report, abolitionists insisted, provided the "empirical" evidence needed to support accusations of slave breeding against the upper South.[44]

The leveling of slave-breeding allegations against slave owners and slave traders provided abolitionists with a rhetorical device to critique the politics of territorial expansion and the unethical conduct of slaveholding and slave-trading interests in American social and economic life. During the 1830s, sentimental and sensational rhetoric thus combined with the hard-bitten political discourse of sectionalism to make for an explosive antebellum debate over slavery's extension westward. For example, Elizabeth Margaret Chandler, the Quaker poet, appealed to the nation's conscience when she asserted that the internal slave trade "is a guilt and an infamy for which our country has no excuse."[45] Sentiments of this nature made their way into the rough-and-tumble world of state and federal politics. Slave breeding became an important component of political debate in the battle to shape the discourse about American territorial expansion. The abolitionist Theodore Dwight Weld, like so many abolitionists, drew on Dew's analysis of the Virginia legislature's proceedings to both condemn Virginia lawmakers and oppose the extension of slavery into the West. Weld argued that Virginia's effort to legally expel free blacks from the state was failing because of slave-breeding practices. The emigration of free blacks and freed slaves, Weld claimed, failed to check the growth of Virginia's black population "because it furnishes every inducement to the master to attend to the negroes, to ENCOURAGE BREEDING, and to cause the *greatest number possible to be raised.*"[46]

Weld was far from a lone abolitionist voice in making such accusations. William Ellery Channing, one of the nation's leading Unitarian preachers and a staunch abolitionist, warned that the American republic's extension into the West could play into the hands of slave-owning and slave-trading interests. Channing's concerns were a product of the powder keg that was sectional politics in antebellum America. Politicians from frontier states and territories, such as Thomas Hart Benton, faced public opposition from their pro-slavery constituents after they appeared to support abolitionist arguments.[47] Southern and pro-slavery Americans thus grew increasingly sensitive to attacks on slavery because they feared the "vassalage of the abolitionists" and territorial restrictions being placed on their way of life. The jurist and pro-slavery writer William

Figure 1. "United States Slave Trade, 1830." An example of abolitionist propaganda that insinuates a link between the internal slave trade and the federal government's implicit approval of that trade. Courtesy of the Library of Congress, Washington, D.C., LC-USZ62-89701.

Harper responded to this rising abolitionist tide by arguing that the failure to extend slavery westward would retard the advance of civilization in the "plains and forests of the West."[48] In stark contrast, abolitionists viewed the extension of slavery as "a wrong done to humanity."[49] Commenting on the heated debate over the admission of Texas into the Union, Channing cautioned that the acquisition of new western territories would provide potential new markets for slave breeders. "By annexing Texas," Channing argued, "we shall not only create it [demand for slave breeding] where it does not exist, but breathe new life into it."[50] Like Henry Ward Beecher, Channing may have been zealous in his anti-slavery preaching, but his keen intellect allowed him to see the question of slavery's extension for what he believed it was: an issue that struck at the moral core and meaning of the republic's founding and westward expansion.

The memory of what the republic's Founding Fathers said, and did not say, about slavery was reshaped in this volatile political climate. Citing the opinion of the chancellor of New York State, the editors of the *Anti-Slavery Record* asserted that slavery, and legal efforts to return freed slaves to a state of bondage, was contrary to what "the patriots of the revolution who framed the Constitution of the United States, and had incorporated into the Declaration of Independence" had intended.[51] The founders, however, rarely spoke explicitly about "slavery." While many agonized over the question of slavery in a republic devoted to the principles of legal equality, in the end the Founding Fathers left the question of slavery for future generations to resolve. In their own time, the founders struck compromises that included the abolition of the international slave trade to the United States by 1808, a decision that nineteenth-century abolitionists saw as stimulus to slave-breeding interests within the republic.[52]

Memory and politics proved a powerful cocktail for abolitionists as they condemned the "slave breeding South" and launched rhetorical attacks on lawmakers in Washington for not immediately abolishing slavery and the internal slave trade. One writer, arguing with typical Garrisonian bluntness, condemned the federal government for being "deeply involved in the guilt of violating the most sacred rights of liberty. Washington is the very focus of the slave-breeding trade."[53] Such views were both sensational and sentimental in nature; but they were becoming more common in abolitionist discourse during the 1830s. Both black and white abolitionists therefore seized on slave breeding as an evocative rhetorical device to elicit support for their bourgeois moral position, a position that linked liberal concerns about the sanctity of the marriage contract with republican anxiety about the common good of all Americans.[54]

### Slave-Breeding Discourse in the 1840s and 1850s

By the 1840s, the nation had established a tradition of lurching from one unsatisfactory compromise on slavery to the next. As tempers flared and sectional debate became increasingly cantankerous, abolitionists expressed displeasure over what they saw as Congress's ineffectual treatment of slavery and slave-breeding interests. Indeed, more-radical abolitionist voices were quick to point out that the ban on the importation of slaves into the United States after 1808, combined with pro-southern compromises on slavery, meant that slave-breeding interests had all the inducement necessary to expand their business westward.

Joshua Reed Giddings, a militant abolitionist politician from Ohio, articulated these sentiments when he stood before the U.S. Congress in 1843 and railed against "slave-growers." Just one year after Congress censured him for his strident abolitionist views, Giddings was breathing rhetorical fire when he declared that "corruption has marked every stage of its [the Constitution's] progress, and baseness has characterized those who have aided in carrying it forward. The whole was managed by slave-breeders and slave traders, aided by 'Northern men with Southern principles.'"[55]

An indication of just how persuasive abolitionist accusations of slave breeding were becoming in antebellum discourse can be seen in the writings of Ezra

Champion Seaman. Born in upstate New York in 1805, Seaman wrote extensively on American politics and the law.[56] Although he was by no means a radical, when he turned his attention to the inhuman practice of slave breeding in 1846 his prose became blunt in its accusatory tone. "The northern slave states," he argued, "have obtained the name of tobacco and slave breeding states and the southern slave states, the name of cotton growing states."[57] Seaman accused slave owners in Virginia, Maryland, Kentucky, and other upper South states of breeding and selling slaves to supply the ever-increasing labor demand of the cotton-growing states. In the wake of the international trade in slaves being abolished, Seaman charged that "slave breeding has been one of the principal resources for northern slave states during the last thirty years" and a reliable provider of slave labor for planters determined to extend slavery into the West.[58]

Former U.S. president John Quincy Adams offered an equally impassioned criticism of what he believed was the determination of the pro-slavery lobby to extend slavery westward, thereby perpetuating slave-breeding practices. Speaking before his Massachusetts constituency on the issue of Texas and slavery's extension, Adams referred to the "slave breeding passion for [territorial] annexation." He carefully described for his audience the political line that divided "the slave-breeding conspiracy against the freedom of the North," a binary division that, according to Adams, explained the tenor of compromise politics on territorial expansion. Of the "slave-breeding conspiracy," Adams left his audience in little doubt of the South's intent: "to obtain a nursery of slave holding States, to breakdown forever the ascendant power of the free States, and to fortify, beyond all possibility of reversal, the institution of slavery."[59]

By the 1840s, slave-breeding discourse had become shorthand for abolitionist claims about the South's moral bankruptcy. Maria W. Steward, an African American abolitionist, emphasized this position in her anti-slavery writings. Stewart, who was born in Connecticut in 1803 and orphaned at age five, emphasized the "wretched and degraded situation" foisted on enslaved women by the practitioners of slave-breeding schemes.[60] She added a religious note to her moral condemnation of the slave South, claiming that Christianity, in contrast to slavery, "is pure; it is ever new; it is ever beautiful; it is all that is worth living for; it is worth dying for."[61] Guided by Christian principles, Stewart argued that enslaved mothers struggled to endure the physical pain of sexual exploitation and the psychological trauma of "rape."[62] Believing they had God on their side, enslaved women steeled themselves to be mothers who, against all odds, strove to "create in the minds of your little girls and boys a thirst of knowledge, the love of virtue, the abhorrence of vice, and the cultivation of a pure heart."[63]

The testimonies of former slaves became especially important to abolitionist discourse during the 1850s. This was arguably the most turbulent decade in American political history. During these years, abolitionists and their political allies rallied against compromise politics, labeling it a complete failure that simply played into the hands of the pro-slavery lobby and slave-breeding interests. Anti-slavery politicians and abolitionists thus stepped up the rhetorical attack on slavery in the decade before the Civil War. For instance, abolitionists viewed the Compromise of 1850 and the Kansas-Nebraska Act of 1854 (which overturned the Missouri Compromise) as examples of Congress's apparent willingness to ensure the continuation of slavery and the extension of slave-breeding practices.[64] Abolitionist claims about slave-breeding practices therefore increased in intensity at the same time criticism for the inadequacies of compromise politics also increased. The African American Ohioan Charles H. Langston typified abolitionist frustrations when he criticized the Fugitive Slave Act (1850). Langston complained that "I know that the courts of this country, . . . the laws of this country, that the governmental machinery of this country, are so constituted as to oppress and outrage colored men, men of my complexion. I cannot then, of course, expect, judging from the past history of the country, any mercy from the laws, from the Constitution, or from the courts of the country."[65] George Barrell Cheever was similarly condemnatory. Cheever criticized compromise politics and added that "our Declaration of Independence, hitherto the hugest colossal maul, under God's word, that the angel of freedom himself could swing against the thrones of tyranny, and beat upon the heads of the ferocious and cunning despots of humanity, is no better than a feather dipped in olive-oil." He added that the political representatives of the slave breeders and slave traders "take the doctrines of popular sovereignty, and convert them into a network of usurpation and of tyranny, more subtle, more knotted, more implacable, and in league with the power put at their command, constituting a despotism more hopeless because the vaunted principles of your democracy have been perverted into its support, than all the nimrods, or Napoleons, or even the houses of Hapsburg in Austria sublimity of oppression, ever intended."[66]

Cheever's unvarnished criticism of the American political and legal system's pro-slavery sympathies was not an isolated screed against the expansionist tendencies of the slave South. James F. W. Johnston, for example, joined Cheever and other prominent abolitionists in condemning compromise politics and the American legal system as proxies for slave-breeding interests in the South. "It cannot be doubted," Johnston informed an international audience in the *London Quarterly Review*, "that a fresh and most potent stimulus will be given to this [slave] breeding and traffic of blacks, and stronger enthusiasm nourished for those 'domestic institutions' by which slavery is established and made legal."[67] His words reverberated with the increasingly caustic abolitionist condemnation of compromise politics during the 1850s, combining criticism for the practices that led to the physical and moral debasement of the enslaved with disgust for the state and federal politicians and the legal authorities responsible for codifying the brutality against and exploitation of enslaved human beings.[68]

In the 1850s, abolitionists reiterated accusations that the upper South was a slave-breeding region—or the "new slave breeding Guinea," as one abolitionist uncompromisingly put it—for the lower South and West.[69] These practices, abolitionists charged, corrupted the morals of the republic's inhabitants and destroyed black families. Marshall Hall, for instance, argued that "the 'breeding' of the human species is carried on just as that of cattle is carried on." He added, "the proceeding begins with irreligion and immorality; it proceeds to the eventual separation of parent and child."[70]

Hall's remarks reflect how abolitionists had by the 1850s settled on a slave-breeding discourse that emphasized the corruption of sexual morals, the debasement of human life, and the dissolution of family bonds. Abolitionists linked these factors with the economics of slavery and anti-slavery fears about the westward extension of slavery.[71] Like many of his abolitionist contemporaries, Hall claimed that only the immediate abolition of slavery could end such depravity. "The very idea of breeding," he reported, "will become extinct by emancipation." More importantly, he shared the abolitionist belief that emancipation would ensure that the "parents will pass into the South, and their children will remain with them, in or near the home in which they are born. The immorality of slave-breeding, and the cruelty of the separation of parent and child, will be extirpated together."[72]

Similar anxieties animated black abolitionists who maintained that the extension of slavery contradicted the republic's founding promise.[73] Frederick Douglass provided readers with one of the most pointed examples of southern hypocrisy when he criticized the unnatural state of sexual and marital relations in the slave South. Douglass argued in his 1857 memoir, *My Bondage and My Freedom*, that "the middle states [upper South] of the Union . . . are called the slave-breeding states." He cautioned readers that "although it is harrowing to your feelings, it is necessary that the facts of the case should be stated. We have in the United States slave-breeding states." Douglass claimed that slave owners in states such as Maryland and Virginia were engaged in the un-Christian, immoral, and exploitative practice of using black reproductive sexuality for commercial gain. He insisted that in the slave-breeding states of Maryland and Virginia, "men, women, and children are reared for the market, just as horses, sheep, and swine are raised for the market." Douglass's likening of the exploitative nature of human reproduction to the breeding of animals for commercial gain was reinforced by his blunt conclusion: "Slave-rearing is there looked upon as a legitimate trade; the law sanctions it, public opinion upholds it, the church does not condemn it."[74] In Douglass's representation of slave breeding, any moral sense of right and wrong had been lost in southern society.

Slave breeding provided Douglass and other black abolitionists with a powerful rhetorical shorthand with which to condemn slavery and demand its immediate abolition. Indeed, black abolitionists went to great lengths to highlight how the sexual and reproductive exploitation of human chattel was something greater than an abstract question about the ideals of the Union or debate over the terms of western expansion. For former slaves, sexual exploitation, slave auctions, and the breakup of families were all examples of the master's manipulation of black reproductive and family life—the insidious components of slave-breeding practices that would spread into the American Southwest and West if slavery's extension was not halted and the institution immediately abolished. The plantation "household" was therefore a site of political and personal power for whites, and the inspiration for black political protest and writing.[75]

Douglass's abolitionist rhetoric wove sensational claims about slave breeding into anti-slavery political protest.[76] He confronted readers of *My Bondage and My Freedom* with the moral implications of "my poor mother, [who] like many other slave-women had *many children*, but NO FAMILY!"[77] On other occasions, Douglass emphasized how slave owners, overseers, and traders "do what they will with them [enslaved women]—to dispose of their persons in any way they see fit. And so entirely are they at the disposal of their masters," Douglass added, "that if they raise their hands against them, they may be put to death for daring to resist their infernal aggression."[78]

Sexual exploitation, violence, and the threat of death all featured in black abolitionists' narratives of slave breeding. Thus slave-breeding discourse was not simply a narrative about economic exploitation; according to black abolitionists, slave-breeding practices shaped life for the enslaved and included white slave owners, overseers, and traders. The former slave Moses Roper emphasized the role that white slave traders played in slave-breeding practices. "The traders," Moses insisted, "will often sleep with the best looking female slaves among them, and they will often have many children in the year, which are said to be slaveholder's children, by which means, through his villainy, he will make an immense profit in this intercourse, by selling the babe with its mother. They often keep an immense stock of slaves on hand."[79] Moses' apparent conflation of slave traders with slave masters is revealing. According to Moses, slave traders and masters were as one, bound together in an immoral form of commerce that breached all Christian ethics, debased mother and child, and shattered families.[80] The impact of slave-breeding practices, Moses implied, lived on well after an enslaved woman was sexually exploited or a child torn from its parents and sold away.

It was one thing for black abolitionist men to level such accusations against portions of the South, but such allegations acquired a heightened level of immediacy when presented by black women. Sarah Forten, a black female abolitionist who was born free, observed in one of her poems that slave breeding was an affront to the common humanity of white and black Americans:

We are thy sisters,—God has truly said,
That of one blood, the nations he has made.
O, Christian woman, in a Christian land,
Canst thou unblushing read this great command?
Suffer the wrongs which wring our inmost heart,
To draw one throb of pity on thy part!
Our "skins may differ," but from thee we claim
A sister's privilege, in a sister's name.[81]

Perhaps the most famous black female voice to both condemn and expose the physical and emotional suffering endured by enslaved women was Harriet Jacobs. Born into slavery in 1813, Jacobs escaped her enslavement on the Underground Railroad and became an active abolitionist. Her writings targeted the sentimental feelings of white readers. Significantly, Jacobs described such horrific violence and sexual exploitation of slave women that readers should not weep; rather, they should become angry, rise from their armchairs, and support the abolitionist cause.[82] For example, she wrote of slavery:

> No pen can give an adequate description of the all-pervading corruption produced by slavery. The slave girl is reared in an atmosphere of licentiousness and fear. The lash and the foul talk of her master and his sons are her teachers. When she is fourteen or fifteen, her owner, or his sons, or the overseer, or perhaps all of them, begin to bribe her with presents. If these fail to accomplish their purpose, she is whipped or starved into submission to their will. She may have had religious principles inculcated by some pious mother or grandmother, or some good mistress; she may have a lover, whose good opinion and peace of mind are dear to her heart; or the profligate men who have power over her may be exceedingly odious to her. But resistance is hopeless.[83]

Like the writings of Frederick Douglass and the other black abolitionists, Jacobs's narrative combined disparate narrative threads—moral commentary, religious assertions, loyal family members, and a sense of "hopeless" victimhood—into a didactic narrative designed to condemn sexually exploitative practices and call for the immediate abolition of slavery in the United States.[84] In so doing, Jacobs presented her white audience with a test to see if they had the stomach to reflect on the moral importance of the imagery she presented, and the backbone to stand up and fight to end slavery.[85]

In one of the most famous anti-slavery memoirs of the antebellum era, Jacobs presented just such a test for white readers. *Incidents in the Life of a Slave Girl* (1861) was originally completed in 1858, but the bankruptcy of two prospective publishers delayed its publication. Jacobs's life story is well known, but her decision to write this book was inspired by her unflinching determination to end slavery and all of its abuses. She wrote that her childhood was a happy one, or as happy as a childhood in bondage could be. Her parents, however, bore the marks of slavery's exploitative nature on their skins, both being "a light shade of brownish yellow."[86] Indeed, Jacobs's childhood happiness soon gave way to years of anxiety because of the sexual harassment she experienced at the hands of "Dr. Flint," the fictional name that Jacobs gave to the father of a white child who legally owned her. The story of Jacobs's being forced to navigate the unwanted advances of Dr. Flint, her love affair with a free colored man, and her drawn-out escape from bondage are typically emphasized in summaries of her life. Of greater utility to our discussion is the manner in which Jacobs's memoir fits into the rhetoric of slave breeding that emerged as a central part of black abolitionist discourse by the 1850s.

Jacobs's memoir is a model example of how black abolitionists acquired knowledge of slavery and conveyed that knowledge in the form of a memoir with an overtly abolitionist moral. Jacobs combined personal experiences with oral histories passed down to her by family members to paint a dire picture of slavery. Reflecting on the objectification of human sexuality that had become a common part of slave-breeding discourse, Jacobs posited that the enslaved were "God-breathing machines" who were treated little better than "the horses they tend."[87] According to Jacobs, Dr. Flint used tactics common to trainers who worked to break a horse to its will. Once Jacobs reached puberty, Flint planted "unclean images" in her mind and attempted to seduce her with a combination of "stormy" overtures and "gentleness."[88] And just as black abolitionists before her connected the seemingly contradictory narratives of life and death with slave-breeding discourse, so did Jacobs note that the threat of death always hung over the sexual exploitation and reproductive manipulation inflicted on enslaved women by white men. After resisting one of Flint's unwanted sexual advances, Jacobs was met with just such a threat: "I have half a mind to kill you on the spot," Flint thundered.[89]

To the historian of economics and demography, the threat of death makes little rational sense if the slave owner truly wants to increase the quantity of slaves at his or her disposal. To former slaves like Harriet Jacobs, it made absolute sense; slavery, after all, was about power. In addressing the grossly unequal power dynamics between masters and enslaved women, Jacobs linked the structural forces of slavery to the limits of the individual slave's will. "Women are considered of no value," Jacobs asserted, "unless they continually increase their owner's stock. They are put on a par with animals."[90] In the very next sentence, Jacobs claims that masters are just as likely to shoot a slave woman in the head for any number of arbitrary reasons. Slave breeding, then, was not simply about demographics and profits; it was, according to black abolitionists, a set of interlocking practices that demeaned black people and left the life of the enslaved hanging by a thread.

Jacobs's memoir embodied the ways in which black abolitionist writers and orators appealed to the sentimental imagination of their readers and audiences in an effort to win support for the immediate—and, if necessary, violent—abolition of slavery. Unlike white abolitionists, however, many black abolitionists had witnessed or experienced the physical and psychological cruelties of

Figure 2. "White and Black Slaves from New Orleans," c. 1863. Both black and white abolitionists argued that evidence that white men took an active role in slave breeding could be seen in the skin tones of southern slaves. While slaves often resembled their master, Harriet Jacobs and other black abolitionists observed that few white men ever dared to openly acknowledge their paternity of such children. Courtesy of the Library of Congress, Washington, D.C., LC-DIG-ppmsca-11244.

enslavement. When memories of these experiences were conveyed to whites, the sentimentalism associated with abolitionist rhetoric about marriage, family, and raising children received a jarring dose of reality.[91] For the former slaves who remembered slavery as a chain of sexual exploitation, forced marriage breakups, family separation, and infant mortality, the experience of southern slavery was one of sexual and racial manipulation; it was, black abolitionists insisted, a reality defined by slave-breeding practices.[92]

Black abolitionists like Frederick Douglass and Harriet Jacobs thus gave an African American perspective to the abolition of slavery.[93] Other black leaders, such as Robert Purvis, emphasized the significance of sexual practices to America's past and future. Purvis highlighted the hypocrisy of white America's racial and sexual ideals when he insisted that slavery should be abolished and the right to vote extended to black men because it would act "as a shield against the strange species of benevolence which seeks legislative aid to banish us [back to Africa]—and we are told that our white fellow citizens cannot submit to an *intermixture of the races!*"[94]

Purvis's reference to "white fellow citizens" being averse to the "*intermixture of the races*" was more than a parting shot at white Americans who wanted to remove free blacks from the American republic and colonize them in Africa. His words constituted an explicit attack on white men who sexually exploited enslaved women and engaged in slave-breeding practices. In black abolitionist discourse, then, sexual and racial hypocrisy were the lifeblood of the slave South.[95] Black abolitionists maintained a sustained rhetorical attack on white slave owners, overseers, and slave traders who exploited enslaved women, interfered with slave marriages, and separated members of slave families through sale. The only solution to such immorality, Douglass argued, was the immediate abolition of slavery and real, practical reform, because "we are men, worthy men, good citizens, good Christians, and ought to be treated as such."[96] In a similar vein, Martin Delany, the African American abolitionist and black nationalist, thundered that "the United States, untrue to her trust and unfaithful to her professed principles of republican equality, has also pursued a policy of political degradation to a large portion of her native born countrymen, and that class is the Colored People."[97] Thus, in 1863, with the tide of the Civil War turning in the North's favor, the former slave Elizabeth Delany wrote: "Slavery! cursed slavery! what crimes has it invoked! and, oh! what retribution has a righteous God visited upon these traders in human flesh!"[98] Slavery's end was near, but its most brutal aspects would live on in the memories and family histories of future generations of black Americans.

## Conclusion

The trade in "human flesh" horrified both black and white abolitionists. For many, references to slave-breeding practices sharpened rhetorical attacks on slavery and their demands for immediate abolition. The bodies and souls of those enslaved people who were forced to participate in such practices thus became the narrative focal points from which abolitionist discourse attempted to highlight the irreligion of the slave South and its unscrupulous drive for territorial expansion. Sensational as slave-breeding discourse might have been, it nonetheless demonstrated how coerced reproductive sexuality played a critical role in framing an anti-slavery discourse that linked sexual violence to slavery and territorial expansion. The antebellum Union had reached a fragile point in its young history, and *"the propagation of slaves as articles of merchandize,"* as one white abolitionist put it, would only erode the religious and moral foundations of the republic if left unchecked.[99] In these ways, the sexual imagery associated with abolitionist accusations of slave breeding demands that historians take this rhetoric seriously in order to develop a deeper historical understanding of the social, cultural, and political ideas that moved men and women to oppose or defend slavery.

Embedded within the slave-breeding discourse of white abolitionists was the implicit assumption that they were fighting to save both the nation and the slave. For a number of African American leaders, such ideas struck them as condescending and overly paternalistic. While black abolitionists generally viewed white abolitionists as principled allies in the fight against slavery, they were not prepared to play the role of "humble, grateful slave" for white abolitionists. Nor, for that matter, were they satisfied with simply exposing the immorality of slave breeding in the hope of cleansing an expanding nation's collective conscience through a campaign of "moral suasion."[100] Slave-breeding discourse was not simply a narrative device for black abolitionists; it involved what many asserted were representations of real experiences and memories of life in slavery. For black abolitionists, these memories constituted a history in which masters and slave traders assumed the role of earthly gods and determined the fate—the life and death—of enslaved millions. Far from simply an exercise in Christian morality and partisan political debate, the slave-breeding discourse that black abolitionists developed prior to the outbreak of the Civil War constituted the material from which to forge a collective historical consciousness that would steel its adherents in the fight to end slavery immediately—and with blood, if necessary.[101] "We are one people," Frederick Douglass proclaimed of enslaved and free African Americans in 1848, "one in general complexion, one in common degradation."[102] With these sentiments echoing in the minds of African Americans, thousands of its menfolk picked up arms during the Civil War not to simply make the ideals of the republic a reality but to fight for the more immediate and personal goal of toppling the slave-breeding South so that they and their descendants could live in freedom and in peace. And once the Civil War was fought and won, and slavery abolished, black Americans dreamed, as President Lincoln hoped, that they would now live in "the era of good feeling."[103]

# 2

## Slavery, the Lost Cause, and African American History

The American Civil War (1861–65) was a bloody watershed in American history. More than six hundred thousand Americans sacrificed their lives, southern cities and towns were destroyed, and the nation was forced, as President Lincoln put it in his Gettysburg Address in 1863, to forge "a new birth of freedom."[1] Indeed, Lincoln, like many Americans, was looking ahead to a future without internecine warfare long before the Civil War concluded. But in looking ahead to this peaceful and prosperous future, Americans had to come to terms with their past. In particular, all Americans, black and white, pondered what the collective national history with slavery would mean to a future that, in theory, would rest on the principles of union, democracy, and the emancipation of all enslaved people.

As the war ground to its conclusion in April 1865, white southerners became particularly active in memorializing what they believed had been the righteous cause of the South. Southerners such as Edward A. Pollard, the editor of the *Richmond Examiner*, contributed influential memoirs and popular histories of the Old South and the Civil War in the service of explaining the South's history. Pollard is worthy of attention because he typified the white South's attempts to frame how Americans remembered slavery, the war, and the birth of a postbellum white identity. Pollard, in other words, joined scores of white southerners in debating what became known as the "Lost Cause" of southern history. In his 1866 book *The Lost Cause*, Pollard introduced readers to the idea that a failure of statesmanship and "Sectional Animosity" caused the South to secede in defense of states' rights, resulting in the Civil War.[2] Southern reviewers were initially critical of the book's thesis. One reviewer, for example, accused Pollard of presenting historical misrepresentations that prompted a plea for "reliable Histories of 'the Lost Cause.'"[3] Thus began a debate over the meaning of slavery in the decades after the Civil War, a debate that continued (some would argue, still continues) well into the twentieth century.[4]

Historians such as David Blight, Bruce Baker, and Tera Hunter have analyzed the legacy of slavery and the different meanings attached to the Civil War during the late nineteenth and early twentieth centuries. This was an era in American history defined by the Reconstruction of the South (1865–77), the economic growth of the "New South," of racial violence, the rise of Jim Crow segregation, and increasing flows of immigrants to the United States from Europe and Asia. In this context, the mythology of the Lost Cause emerged as the dominant narrative in American popular and scholarly discourse. David Blight defines the Lost Cause as a "public memory" characterized by images of "the fallen soldier, [and] a righteous political cause defeated only by superior industrial might."[5] Slavery, much less the enslaved, figured peripherally in the historical saga that was the Old South and the Lost Cause of the Confederacy.[6] Typically, one former Confederate reflected on the passing of the slave South and the Confederacy by stating, "One can't help regretting whatever it was that produced George Washington, and a crowd of other men like him."[7]

Lost Cause mythology constituted a culturally constructed framework for remembering the past and, more importantly, forgetting the unseemly aspects of southern history. If violent and sexually explicit imagery appeared in Lost Cause mythology, it was usually to deny that practices like slave breeding ever existed. However, the sexual coercion and violence associated with slave-breeding practices was remembered. Such memories lived on in the oral histories and memoirs of former abolitionists, amateur historians, and black Americans. As we will see, where professional historians asserted that if sexual impropriety and excessive violence existed during slavery, it was at the instigation of formerly enslaved black Americans, amateur historians, former abolitionists, and African Americans constructed very different images of the slave South. Increasingly, if one wanted to avoid the racism that blighted professional historical narratives at the turn of the century, it was essential to turn to African American perspectives on slavery and to the oral traditions and writings of black America.

Black Americans, and those white authors who braved the opprobrium of fellow white citizens and a large swathe of the historical profession, drew from disparate threads of memory and imagination to insert historical narratives about slave breeding into America's collective past. Narratives that focused on sexual exploitation and racial violence used slave breeding as a rhetorical device to either emphasize the brutality of slavery or, depending on one's perspective, to deny the severity of slavery's vicissitudes. In the late nineteenth century the significance of slave breeding was very much a topic of popular and scholarly conversation. However, the dawning of a new century brought with it a more objective, empirical, and "scientific" approach to professional history writing. This produced a narrowing of understanding about the past. Professional historians drew sweeping conclusions on the basis of economic data sets, legal and political sources, and demographic data. The result was a picture of slavery as a benign system of coerced labor, the plantation merely a "school" for the enslaved, and the Civil War a noble battle fought (by white men) over political principles. This was not only a sanitized version of America's racial past; it was grotesquely misleading. Black Americans recognized the flaws in this version of American history was misleading; nothing reminded them of that deception more forcefully than narratives about slave breeding.

## White Memories of Slavery and Slave Breeding

Just three days after the famous Battle of Gettysburg, Charles Sumner, the abolitionist politician who denounced "the harlot, slavery" in 1856 and earned a beating at the end of Preston Brooks's cane for his troubles, wrote an anxious letter to John Curwen, an English Congregational minister and staunch abolitionist.[8] In his letter, dated July 6, 1863, Sumner urged Curwen to maintain pressure on England's Members of Parliament for a declaration of support for President Lincoln and the Union. Sumner insisted that a failure to do otherwise would see the Members of Parliament run the risk of "sanction[ing] the idea of a slave-breeding, slave-trading government to flaunt in the face of civilization."[9]

To the relief of Sumner and abolitionists throughout the North, the battles of Vicksburg and Gettysburg in 1863 swung the fortunes of the war in the Union's favor and hastened the decline of the Confederacy. However, changes in the course of the war produced new anxieties. Questions about "what to do with the Negro" increasingly occupied the minds of abolitionists and lawmakers during the uncertain years of 1864, 1865, and 1866.[10] During this tumultuous period, memories of sexual exploitation, reproductive manipulation, and the separation of slave families were expressed in a variety of sources and literary genres. In the autobiographical publications of former abolitionists, narratives about slave breeding justified past political activism. In the speeches, published essays, and memoirs of former slaves and black abolitionists, slave breeding dramatically highlighted the righteousness of ending slavery but also emphasized how raw and painful recollections of slavery were to them. Government bureaucrats also wrote about the legacy of slave breeding in their reports. Federal officials sent by President Lincoln to assess the state of the war-ravaged South reported that former slaves, or "freedmen" as they were known at the time, informed them about the absence of "chastity" on the antebellum plantation. Reports of enslaved women being severely whipped "for not coming to the quarters of the overseer or master for the purposes of prostitution" were dutifully recorded.[11] The commissioner of agriculture, reporting on Virginia in 1865, asserted that Virginians profited from the sale of tobacco, flour, and slaves. The "capital invested in slave breeding," the commissioner concluded, "has been a source of profit to the owner, while it has been worse than wasted to society at large."[12]

As the uncertain reconstruction of the Union began, memories of slave breeding circulated through different levels of American culture and society. A growing number of memoirist and abolitionist authors of popular history placed these memories in the public domain following the publication of their writings. In 1866, Horace Greeley typified the tone of abolitionist recollections. Greeley wrote of slavery's horrors, emphasizing the plight of "slave-girls [who] were not only daily sold on the auction blocks of New Orleans, and constantly advertised in her journals, as very nearly white, well-educated, and possessed of the rarest personal attractions." These girls and women, Greeley and fellow abolitionists reflected, were the products of slave-breeding practices in the antebellum South. Greeley proved uncompromising in his recollections of the trade in human flesh. Keeping the image of exploited slave girls and women at the forefront of American collective memory, Greeley re-published one of his antebellum speeches in which he claimed that "slave-breeding for gain, deliberately purposed and systematically pursued, appears to be among the latest devices and illustrations of human depravity."[13]

The effort to shape the public's memory of slavery developed rapidly in the 1870s. Popular magazines such as Scribner's Monthly ran stories that echoed abolitionist claims about slaves being bred in the upper South for sale in the lower South.[14] The pages of the New Englander and Yale Review added to this store of collective remembrance in a review of the intense political debates that unfolded over territorial expansion in the 1840s and 1850s. The Review reminded readers of how "slave-breeding and slave-trading interests" demanded "new territory to be peopled with slaves."[15] And lest Americans forget that the link between slavery, slave breeding, and territorial expansion had been as much a moral question as a problem of politics and economy, the British Quaker abolitionist John Ashworth provided an unequivocal reminder from across the Atlantic. In an 1875 biography of Ashworth, Andrew Calman reminded readers of how the British abolitionist had once intoned: "America! Perfidious and guilty America! Slave-buying, Slave-selling, Slave-breeding, and Slave-destroying America."[16]

Abolitionists, with the aid of sympathetic publishers and popular media, worked hard to justify their efforts to highlight the justness of their cause to end slavery and preserve their legacy.[17] They worked even harder to remind American readers of the moral lessons that came out of the crusade to abolish the slave system. For instance, the Congregational minister and abolitionist Parker Pillsbury did his bit to keep the image of the upper South as a slave-breeding nursery in the forefront of the public's collective memory. Pillsbury, remembering the activism of one of the great "Anti-Slavery Apostles," William Lloyd Garrison, described antebellum Baltimore as a "slave-breeding, slave-trading, and slave-holding city."[18] More damning were the "reminiscences" of William Ellery Channing. Channing, ever critical of the slave-breeding states, added his condemnation for the compromise politics of the prewar decades, particularly the Missouri Compromise, as little more than an inducement to slave-breeding interests.[19]

By the 1880s and 1890s, former abolitionists had helped to shape what they thought was a relatively coherent public narrative about slavery's horrors. In their writings, abolitionists emphasized three historical factors.[20] First, the assumption that the upper South bred slaves for sale in the lower South and the southwest echoed prewar accusations. Second, the belief that the abolition of the Atlantic slave trade to the United States in 1808 provided a stimulus to slave-breeding practices. And third, the conviction that compromise politics over territorial expansion (not sectional extremists on both sides, as Lost Cause mythologizers claimed) gave slave-breeding and slave-trading interests the pretext for manipulating slave reproduction.[21] These three accusations became narrative staples in the memoirs of former abolitionists and in the reproduction of their antebellum speeches.

A growing number of popular histories also highlighted these three factors in leveling charges of slave breeding against the slave South. Henry Wilson's revised *History of the Rise and Fall of the Slave Power in America* (1875) relied almost exclusively on political speeches and antebellum pamphlets for its source base. Wilson also drew on Dew's study of the Virginia legislature in 1831–32 to argue that "when it is remembered that this [Dew's analysis] was not spoken in the heat of debate by a political partisan, but written by a cultivated, scholarly man in the calm retirement of his study,—an educator, too, of young men in the venerable college of his State,—discoursing on slave-breeding and slave-selling as if they were mere matters of political economy, precisely as he would write of raising stock and improved breeds of animals . . . something of the moral tendency of the system he defends and advocates may be estimated."[22] Wilson saw Dew's "evidence" as the proof needed to assert that slave breeding, tragically, had been a *reality* in the antebellum South.

One of the most influential popular histories of the late nineteenth and early twentieth centuries was James Ford Rhodes's four-volume *History of the United States.* Rhodes, a prominent industrialist, avid historian, and conservative Democrat, published volume one of his history in 1892. He observed that American territorial expansion, beginning with Jefferson's 1803 purchase of the Louisiana Territory, had been pivotal in the South's drive for slavery's extension and the emergence of slave-breeding practices. In the antebellum South, Rhodes argued, "slavery is a blessing, and cotton is king." But for the "blessing" to continue, territorial expansion was an absolute necessity.[23] This led Rhodes to the conclusion that a synergy between territorial expansion, economic greed, and southern racism produced an overwhelming motivation for slave breeding. He concluded that had "it not been for the new cotton-planters' demand for negroes, which made slave-breeding a profitable industry for the border States, Maryland, Virginia, and Kentucky" would never have gone into the business of breeding human beings for profit.[24]

Rhodes based his dark conclusions on abolitionist literature, popular periodicals—such as *North American Review* and *De Bow's Review*—and the memoirs and published journals of former slaves and prominent southerners. He used these sources to portray slave breeding as an article of established historical fact and popular knowledge. True to his sources, and to Victorian sexual morality, Rhodes highlighted the disproportionate suffering inflicted on enslaved women because of slave-breeding practices. He argued that the "institution [of slavery] bore harder on the women than on the men. Slave-breeding formed an important part of plantation economy, being encouraged as was the breeding of animals."[25] Rhodes expressed indignation for those slave owners and traders who partook in the degradation of human life in the quest for economic gain—profits that Rhodes argued came in the form of cash returns from the sale of human beings and cotton crops. Rhodes reiterated this point when he claimed: "When it became known that they [enslaved women] were pregnant, their task was lightened, yet, if necessary, they were whipped when with child, and, in some cases, were put to work again as early as three weeks after confinement, although generally the time of rest allowed was one month."[26]

The image of slaves being coerced to reproduce children and engorge the profits of slave owners and slave traders was bad enough, but the idea that successive generations of slaves were reproduced like animals clearly horrified Rhodes. By the time he leveled his historical accusations against the slave South, however, professional historians had grown uneasy, even disbelieving, about the *reality* of slave-breeding practices.[27] But before these historians could analyze data sets and lift their pens to join Lost Cause mythologizers in crafting coherent narratives that erased slave breeding from collective historical memory, the popular recollections of abolitionists and histories of slave breeding by amateur historians like Rhodes served important historical and social scientific purposes. During the late nineteenth and early twentieth centuries, American popular and intellectual culture was punctuated by repeated references to "nature," "evolution," and human "fitness." These were the buzzwords in the rhetorical arsenal of social Darwinian and eugenic thinkers. In the context of remembering slave breeding, then, this "scientific" discourse highlighted how slavery fostered "unnatural" sexual relationships between male and female slaves and, more specifically, how white men engaged in "unnatural" acts of exploitation with enslaved women. In an "evolutionary" sense, former abolitionists and sympathetic historians portrayed these "illicit" plantation encounters as harmful to the moral fiber of the southern body politic and destructive to the progressive evolution—the "survival of the fittest"—of a white American civilization.[28]

As noted above, a new generation of professional historians entered this social and cultural context and drafted histories of slavery that continue to influence popular memories of slavery in the twenty-first century. Viewing themselves as "scientists" of historical analysis, professional historians turned to the empirical records and memories of former slave owners. These were sources scholars believed they could trust; they were, after all, bequeathed to posterity by some of the most respectable white men in the Old South. Turn-of-the-century historians never seriously questioned whether the family members of former slave owners or slave traders might have purged, or conveniently lost, unflattering evidence of sexual exploitation and violence before depositing plantation records in some of America's great university libraries. Safe in the knowledge that these archives contained the written "facts" about slavery's past, historians systematically dissected plantation records. Professional historians—an overwhelmingly white and male profession at the end of the nineteenth and beginning of the twentieth century—insisted that the sources they drew from to re-create the past were far more objective and trustworthy than the face-saving reminiscences of former abolitionists, the unreliable memories of former slaves, and the "propaganda" of the African American historian Carter G. Woodson and his Association for the Study of Negro Life and History.[29]

However, just to be sure that professional historians did not misinterpret the "facts" contained in the country's archival repositories, former slave owners added their voices to the public contest over the meaning of slavery and the Civil War. Former slave owners portrayed slavery as a benign institution. Writing in the *New England Magazine* in 1891, M. V. Moore, a former slave owner, expressed his determination to move beyond what he saw as the polemical tenor of abolitionist recollections. Moore insisted that he wanted to express a commonsense account of slavery.[30] He did so by recalling his own moral shock at being confronted with the sight of the slave auction block. He wrote, "I shall never forget my first impression of the horrors of slavery—my first knowledge of the existence of those horrors. It was a great event, not only in my history, but in the history of the neighborhood also—that "BIG SALE OF LIKELY NEGRO MEN AND WOMEN."[31] Moore's memory of slavery was not framed by the enforced labor, brutal punishments, unbalanced diets, or sexual exploitation of slaves; instead, he framed the slave traders and auctioneers as the immoral historical actors "who sold slaves and separated families."[32] In Moore's rendering, slave owners, like the slaves, were history's victims.

Moore was not alone in these claims. Robert Quarterman Mallard, for example, recalled that slave masters worked tirelessly to instill religion and morality in slaves. Slave owners did this, Mallard remembered, to prevent "open immorality."[33] To professional historians, such recollections made perfect sense. Late-nineteenth- and early-twentieth-century historians viewed this impressionistic evidence as supportive of more reliable evidence, such as economic and population data sets, plantation logbooks, and slave auction records.[34] What did these "facts" reveal? The conclusions that professional historians arrived at were strikingly different from those of former abolitionists and amateur historians.

The scholarship of William Archibald Dunning, a Columbia University historian, epitomized the tenor of professional history writing at the turn of the century. The "Dunning school" of historical interpretation gave scholarly credibility to sanitized histories of slavery—with kindly, paternal slave masters tending to the needs of their slaves—and to memories of Reconstruction as an era defined by white carpetbaggers and inept black politicians. Dunning characterized Reconstruction as a "travesty of civilized government." His criticism of Reconstruction governments expressed his own racial and aristocratic class biases, and with it a lament for the Old South that disappeared when the Union army defeated the South during the Civil War. According to Dunning, "the ambitious northern whites, inexperienced southern whites, and unintelligent blacks" engaged in corrupt or economically dubious forms of government spending. In fact, the abolition of slavery meant that state governments now had to administer justice and education and assist in the regulation of formerly enslaved families, tasks previously performed by the slave master. These new governmental tasks, Dunning contended, swelled state budget deficits and amounted to special privileges for blacks—"the chief beneficiaries of the new system"—that were unavailable to whites.[35] At the turn of the century, then, the Civil War had come to represent a bloody and tragic period in American history. In its place stood, momentarily, a corrupt and immoral regime headed by unscrupulous whites and feckless blacks.

### African American Memories of Slavery and Slave Breeding

From the closing years of the Civil War to the emergence of the Dunning school of historical interpretation, African Americans constructed their own oral histories, literary traditions, and scholarly interpretations about slavery's violence and sexual excesses. Indeed, the violent white resistance to Reconstruction politics in the South, the rise of Jim Crow segregation, and the racialization of lynching after the Civil War kept memories of the traumatic days of slavery burning brightly in the minds of millions of black Americans.[36]

The emotional pain of family separations and the memory of sexual exploitation was repeated in the narratives of the "Freedmen" during the final years of the Civil War and the initial years of freedom. Former female slaves never forgot the overwhelming feelings of despair and depression that descended on them after being separated from loved ones. Slave owners and slave traders had a variety of motives for selling and separating enslaved family members, but framing this separation around the trope of slave breeding highlighted feelings of powerlessness and despair and expressed the inhumanity that freedmen associated with slavery. Mattie Jackson remembered the emotional pain she experienced after being forcibly parted from her mother. Coupled with a brutal beating at the hands of a cruel white overseer, Jackson remembered losing her "appetite, and not being able to take enough food to sustain nature, I became so weak I had but little strength to work."[37]

These were deeply painful memories. But through the pain shone stories of resilient parents and strong families. Freedmen recalled, for instance, that parental role models instilled a strong sense of loyalty to family and an even stronger moral sense of right and wrong during slavery. Elizabeth Delany, writing in 1863 of "cursed slavery," expressed the link that many freedmen made between freedom and family solidarity. "When my father was sold South," she recalled, "my mother registered a solemn vow that her children should not continue in slavery all their lives, and she never spared an opportunity to impress upon us, that we must get our freedom whenever the chance offered."[38]

Like so many enslaved women, Jackson and Delany echoed abolitionist claims that slave owners and slave traders cruelly separated black families. Treated like cattle and violently plunged into a melancholy that only freedom and the reestablishment of family bonds could remedy, Jackson and Delany provided readers in 1860s America with a reminder of just how inhuman the manipulation of slave reproductive and family life was under slavery. Such narratives opened a window into the feelings "of sorrow, of misery and anguish" that the slaves had previously "hidden from their tormentors."[39] Now that slavery was no more, black Americans were determined to expose the horrors of slavery and actively contest the distortions of the Lost Cause and the racism of professional historical writing.

Two of the most enduring fictions to emerge in Lost Cause mythology were the trope of the chivalrous white southern male and the dutiful (and asexual) white woman. Looking back over their enslavement, former slaves struggled to recall such individuals. Instead, freedmen exposed the sexual hypocrisy that they believed was the cornerstone of southern culture prior to the Civil War. For example, Louisa Picquet's autobiography described her "fair complexion and rosy cheeks, . . . dark eyes, a flowing head of hair with no perceptible inclination to the curl, and every appearance, at first view, of an accomplished white lady."[40] For slaves who penned their life stories during the 1860s, men and women of Picquet's physical appearance embodied the enduring legacy of forced breeding practices. In the fourth edition of his memoir, *Twenty-Two Years a Slave* (1867), Austin Steward gave voice to this perspective. "The time has passed by when

African blood alone is enslaved," he wrote. "In Virginia as well as in some other slave States, there is as much European blood in the veins of the enslaved as there is African; and the increase is constantly in favor of the white population. This fact speaks volumes, and should remind the slave-breeding southerner of that fearful retribution which must sooner or later overtake him."[41]

Retribution, according to William Still, had commenced during the pre–Civil War decades when enslaved men, women, and children absconded from the slave plantation along the Underground Railroad. Still was an influential African American "conductor" of the Philadelphia Underground Railroad, shepherding hundreds of runaway slaves into freedom. During the 1870s, Still, like scores of former slaves and black abolitionists, published suspenseful tales of life on the Underground Railroad.[42] These narratives were replete with references to reproductive manipulation, violence, and family separations. In publishing the recollections of runaway slaves, Still made a significant contribution to an African American narrative of slavery that directly challenged Lost Cause hagiography.

"The slave auction block," Still reported in the 1872 edition of *The Underground Rail Road*, inspired slaves to risk life and limb and flee for freedom. The "horrors" of the auction block were often said to be the cruelest of the slave-breeding South's tools—trading in human flesh, exploiting human beings like cattle, and resulting in the "daily heart breaking separations" of enslaved family members.[43] The story of Mary Epps highlighted the emotional wrench caused by the auction block. Still recounted that Epps, "about forty-five years of age, dark complexion, round built, and intelligent," fled from enslavement in Petersburg, Virginia, in the mid-1850s. Virginia was reputed by abolitionists to be a notorious slave-breeding state, and the fact that Mary had given birth to fifteen children—"four of whom had been sold away from her; one was still held in slavery in Petersburg; the others were all dead"—meant that she had reached a point in her life when she could no longer endure the physical and psychological terror associated with the reproductive demands on her body. Moreover, Mary's fecundity was evidently a product of a sexually exploitative slave master. Mary's mistress suffered from intense feelings of jealousy and betrayal because of her husband's lusting after Mary. According to Still, Mary recalled that her mistress, "being of a jealous disposition, caused me to be hired out with a hard family, where I was much abused, frequently flogged, and stinted for food." If Mary was the object of the unwanted sexual advances of her master, which his wife clearly wanted stopped, her hiring-out led to physical abuse of inhuman proportions. But it was the "sale of one of her children," Still informed readers, that "so affected [Mary] with grief that she was thrown into violent convulsions, which caused the loss of her speech for one entire month."[44] Mary's only way out of this nightmare world was death or flight. With Still's help, she chose the latter.

In heartbreaking and chillingly graphic detail, the narratives of former slaves like Mary Epps were direct and unflinching challenges to Lost Cause mythology and professional historical accounts of slavery. Slaves were not, as white memoirists and professional historians insisted, happy. The enslaved were abused, exploited, and utterly manipulated.[45] But most slaves did not passively accept their physical exploitation and psychological degradation. For example, the former slave James Green recalled running away from "the yoke of Joshua Hitch." Hitch was allegedly a morally bankrupt individual and, according to Green's account, a lousy businessman. Forced to sell his four slaves—three of whom were women, two being sisters, and all considered Hitch's "wives"—Green ran away from this sordid environment, using the Underground Railroad to find his way to freedom.[46]

African American narratives of escape along the Underground Railroad connected memories of unspeakable exploitation with the quest for freedom. That so many slaves narrated escapes from the upper South—states notorious for their alleged involvement in slave-breeding schemes—served to highlight the yawning moral gulf between slavery and freedom, morality and immorality, in African American memories of enslavement. The postwar narratives of former slaves and black abolitionists thus spoke matter-of-factly of how "slave-breeding for the Southern market was extensively carried on in Virginia, Kentucky and other border states; slave-traders made frequent trips through this section; and their coming brought the consternation, distress and separation to many a slave family."[47]

Slave breeding and other coercive sexual practices produced a postwar African American population that was a kaleidoscope of colors, a diversity of tints and hues that was, in African American narratives, a mark of the less-than-noble slave South. While many former slaves internalized feelings of shame and found it difficult to talk about their memories of slavery, others attempted to give historical meaning to such recollections. Still other black Americans tried to put the terrors of slavery behind them by finding loved ones and legitimating

marriages that had no legal standing under slave law. Taken together, the si-
lences, narrative remembering, and actions of late-nineteenth- and early-
twentieth-century African Americans presented a version of slavery that challenged the emerging white historical consensus. Henry Clay Bruce said it best
when he wrote in his memoir that "immoral [white] men have, by force, in-
jected their blood into our veins, to such an extent, that we now represent all
colors, from pure black to pure white."[48]

For African Americans who shared Bruce's take on American history, the
idea that "we are what they [white slaveholders] made us" spoke volumes for
the enduring legacy of violent sexual exploitation in the antebellum South.[49]
Thus, while the presence of a physically diverse African American population
reminded blacks of the coercive power that white masters, overseers, and slave
traders once exercised over them, the narratives that these former slaves crafted
were meant to highlight to whites the immoral nature of slavery and the sexual
hypocrisy that was at the heart of most white historical narratives. No historical
trope emphasized this point more clearly than slave breeding.

By the 1880s and 1890s, then, a significant number of African Americans
published revealing portrayals of slave-breeding practices. These accounts included descriptions of slavery that were reminiscent of the sensational passages
found in the anti-slavery writings of black Americans before the Civil War.
For example, John P. Green's *Recollections* (1880) emphasized how hard it had
been "for the poor slaves to be bought and sold at auction, and separated from
their parents and children and husbands and wives, and it was awfully cruel
to whip them so."[50] Such narratives confronted readers with firsthand recollections of slave owners manipulating the reproductive lives of slaves through
interference in courtship, marriage, and reproduction and through the threat
of family separation on the auction block. African American men and women
published accounts about this manipulation, although a growing number of
black middle-class women turned increasingly to writings that fostered a "cult
of respectability" among young African Americans. Black men, however, remained as critical of slave breeding as they became of the sexual exploitation
and rape of black domestics after the Civil War. The former slave Friday Jones
recalled that his mother was "traded for a tract of land and sent to Alabama."
Jones was hired out as a young man and claimed that he developed no sense of
communal belonging. His religious faith steeled him against the cruelties of the
slave South, and so too did his longing for the intimate emotional and physical
connection that comes with marriage. When Jones fell in love with a woman

on a plantation whom his master did not own—and who gave birth to eleven children—Jones's owner threatened him with sale. But Jones persisted because "I had all the craves for a wife and children, and I feel today that God gave me that woman to take care of."[51] After winning his "bride," however, Jones recognized that he and his family were not safe from the coercive and manipulative practices of slave owners and slave traders. He recalled, "Whenever there were traders in the county, I never felt safe with my wife and children."[52]

Jones eventually did lose his family on the auction block. In 1856, two of his sons were sold. Shortly thereafter, he and his wife were sold to a new master, a man who promised never to separate them. "See what a lie man will tell," Jones angrily reported, because a "short time after that he sold my wife and youngest child for as much as he gave for the four."[53] In the minds of former slaves like Jones, this type of manipulation was the most demoralizing aspect of slavery. Jones recalled, "I became so uneasy and troubled I could not work."[54] His anxiety about the welfare of his wife and family endured during the final days of slavery, the Civil War, and into the postwar decades. Indeed, his memories of slavery's brutalizing qualities presaged an even more brutally racist world after slavery had been abolished. As Jones put it, "How often have mortals been whipped to death and no one near to help or pity them. How horrible for a man to stand and see his wife whipped and her wounds bathed in salt water, and not be able to protect her. To-day, some of our race are not doing much better."[55]

The exploitative ways in which enslaved men and women had their reproductive lives manipulated by slave owners and slave traders bounded off the pages of African American memoirs and reminiscences after the Civil War. While men like Friday Jones recalled the feelings of emasculation that came with their inability to protect enslaved women from sexual abuse or to prevent the separation of family members, formerly enslaved men did not lose sight of the fact that the psychological and physical toll of slave-breeding practices bore hardest on enslaved women. Allen Parker remembered witnessing the heartbreak of slave mothers in Louisville, Kentucky. Using an anti-slavery song to express the rawness of the emotions he witnessed, Parker wrote:

> Oh deep was the anguish of the slave mother's heart
> When called from her darling forever to part;
> So grieved that lone mother, that broken-hearted mother
> In sorrow and woe.
> The child was borne off to a far-distant clime

While the mother was left in anguish to pine;
But reason departed, and she sank broken-hearted
In sorrow and woe.[56]

Postbellum references to abolitionist songs, poems, and political literature added interpretive layers to the public manner in which African Americans remembered slavery. For example, the black nationalist Alexander Crummell emphasized the centrality of reproductive manipulation and violence against people of African descent in the American South. Crummell argued that the "negro contingent was one of the earliest contributions to the American population." Evidence of this contribution, Crummell contended, was found in the racially mixed populations in America's towns and cities. In Crummell's mind, such populations were the products of the "gross and violent intermingling" that occurred in the plantation South and should not be taken as an index for consensual sexual relations between white men and enslaved women. Attempting to reclaim the moral high ground for black masculinity in an age when black men had the vilest of aspersions cast on their sexuality, Crummell demanded that it was in fact the depravity and hypocrisy of white men that had produced mixed-race populations. "Intermixture of blood there has been," Crummell thundered, "not by amalgamation, which implies consent, but through the victimizing of the helpless black woman."[57]

Crummell was not the only black minister or African American intellectual to point out the immoral nature of the white South's history. Black ministers combined biblical commentary, history lessons, and moral lectures to emphasize how slavery and slave-breeding practices treated the "Negro" like an "animal."[58] Speaking in Columbia, South Carolina, in 1899, Rev. R. F. Hurley placed American history in a biblical context, arguing that "the relation of Master and Slave" was a corruption of the natural ordering of the universe as God had ordained it.[59] Drawing loosely on the social Darwinian rhetoric that had come to pervade American culture at the turn of the century, Hurley instructed that the creation of "a false aristocracy founded upon property in man" undermined the natural equality of humankind. To emphasize his point, Hurley used the metaphor of childhood, arguing that the coerced enslavement of Africans in North America spoiled the "innocence and helplessness" of the "African" and inhibited the moral development of all humanity in the United States.[60] Hurley argued that the unnaturalness of the master-slave relationship undermined the moral core of American society—marriage and stable family life. In particular, "courtship and marriage were conducted largely with reference to" the slave owner's lust for profit. This was the "awful wrong of human slavery." Hurley insisted that the slave owner's manipulation of "courtship and marriage" had far-reaching implications, throwing "its dark form across every phase of social life, blighting the pulpit and the pew, perverting the Gospel and the law, and transferring God's oldest institution (marriage) from its Heaven appointed foundation, love[,] to the hell-born consideration of Ownership in Man."[61]

But not all was lost. While the memory of past injustices should not be forgotten, Hurley suggested that his black congregants adopt a scientific approach to rectifying the ill effects of historical wrongs. Combining social Darwinian language with the rhetoric of "racial destiny," Hurley explicitly engaged with memories of slavery.[62] He argued that the "mere forgetting of sins committed will never place us beyond the awful consequences." This was a challenge to "our duty to counteract as far as possible the evil results of past mistakes." He explained that to correct the enduring effects of those wrongs, "we should, like the physician, study the cause of present conditions." The only way to conduct such analysis effectively, Hurley declared, was by lifting "the curtain from the face of the past, even when that past be dark and revolting in every aspect," and taking "hold of the roots of the awful contagion, which throws its threatening shadow across the path of posterity, blunting its powers of perception, stupefying its moral sense, [and] easing or weakening its consciousness of right."[63]

To a certain extent, a growing number of African American intellectuals, most of them men, did lift "the curtain from the face of the past" and confront the historical significance of slavery and reproductive manipulation in the slave South. The ways in which black scholars both drew from and shaped memories of slave breeding to explore larger issues pertaining to violence and sex will be explored in greater detail in the next chapter. For now it is worth noting that black scholars, educators, and social commentators knew that they had to tread a fine line between exposing the past for what millions of African Americans remembered—or imagined—it to be, on the one hand, and emphasizing a message of "uplift," the "cult of respectability," and "racial destiny," on the other.[64] The African American educator Kelly Miller focused his historical reflections on "the false notions of political economy" that resulted in trading human beings as though they were livestock.[65] Others, such as Benjamin W. Arnett, a bishop in the African Methodist Episcopal Church, recognized that the memories of slavery were too painful for many black Americans to relive. Speaking before the Afro-American League of Tennessee's Emancipation Day celebrations in 1894, Arnett urged his audience to look to the future, exclaiming: "We are not here to revive the unpleasant memories of the past, nor to rekindle the camp-fires which are possessions of the dead past; but we are here to crown the head of him [Lincoln] from the fullness of whose great heart the second declaration of independence sprung."[66]

In trying to peer into the future and lay out a roadmap for the destiny of the African American people, Arnett's speech was punctuated with subtle reminders of the legacies of slave-breeding practices. Arnett may have wanted the past to be "dead," but he knew that the effects of slavery endured. Like so many clerics, scholars, and community leaders, Arnett could not ignore the gradations of color that existed among African Americans.[67] Indeed, the sense of powerlessness that enslaved men recalled in being unable to protect wives and daughters from white male sexual exploitation during slavery was, during the late nineteenth and early twentieth centuries, seemingly replicated in the sexual abuse of African American women who worked in white homes as domestics and in the lynch mobs that targeted black men with the hangman's noose and the castrator's blade.[68]

Strikingly, the vast majority of the public statements made by black Americans about slave breeding during the late nineteenth and early twentieth centuries were made by men. The "cult of dissemblance" that Darlene Clark Hine identifies in African American women's public statements about sex and sexuality meant that black women exercised circumspection when it came to such matters, especially in the company of whites. This is not to suggest that black women did not discuss sexual matters. They did. Ida B. Wells, for example, refused to shy away from issues of sex—particularly interracial sex and rape—in her campaigns against lynching.[69] But the "cult of respectability" that dissemblance fostered among black women, especially middle-class black women, meant that they challenged racial and sexual stereotypes by teaching young black Americans the efficacy of cultivating a positive self-image, living good moral lives, and being attentive mothers.[70]

In other words, black women found alternative ways to publicly address the legacy of slave breeding in African American culture. Historian Michele Mitchell observes that black women such as Sylvia Bryant instructed young African Americans that they should endeavor to avoid "disorderly homes, immorality, and careless breeding" because such practices would not produce a "strong healthy race." If black women were forced to be the breeders of future generations of slaves before the Civil War, in the decades after they were determined to take control of their own households, moral education, and reproductive life in an effort to nurture the best qualities of "body and soul."[71]

## Conclusion

The society and economy of the antebellum slave South rested on both the production and reproduction of the slave population. Black Americans—and their white, mostly former abolitionist, allies—remembered this combination of production and reproduction in dark terms indeed. The reproductive manipulation of the slaves—particularly enslaved women—produced what many felt had been unnatural and ungodly relations between masters and slaves. The African American writer and civil rights activist Archibald Grimké made this point in typically colorful terms when he insisted that "slavery is a breeding bed, a sort of compost heap, where the best qualities of both races decay and become food for the worst. The brute appetites and passions of the two act and react on the moral nature of each race with demoralizing effects."[72]

From an African American perspective, placing such characterizations of slavery in popular culture demonstrated how coercion and dominance, not paternal reciprocity, as the historical narratives of white Americans so often claimed, characterized the *reality* of slave life. In other words, black and white abolitionists, former slaves, and an increasing class of African American intellectuals viewed the political economy of the slave South as a moral perversion of an otherwise free and democratic republic. They argued, as the African American writer Frances L. Hunter asserted, that "many people purchased Negro women because they were good breeders, making large fortunes by selling their children. This compulsory breeding naturally crushed the maternal instincts in Negro women."[73] African Americans recalled that in slavery the best and worst elements of the white population—from the aristocratic slaveholders down to the "white trash" slave traders and overseers—contributed to a system that violently manipulated the reproductive lives of the enslaved and tore families apart. In freedom, as Henry Clay Bruce observed in overly optimistic language, the "better class at the South will soon see the errors of their past conduct," while the "white trash" would be drawn to the mobs of "stake-burners and lynchers."[74] As we will see, Bruce's premonition became a tragic and bloody reality. He made only one error: in freedom, as in slavery, the best classes of southern whites united with the "white trash" to terrorize black Americans in body and soul. As black America's intelligentsia came to insist, slavery's violent and sexually exploitative legacy lived on both in African American memories and in daily interactions with the white world around them.

# 3

## Black History and Slave Breeding in the Early Twentieth Century

Early-twentieth-century African American scholars added their perspectives on slavery, and on slave breeding in particular, at a time when white Americans were in the midst of cultivating an extraordinarily distorted image of antebellum slavery. Margaret Mitchell's Pulitzer Prize–winning novel *Gone with the Wind* (1936), and its adaptation into an epic movie of the same title in 1939, embodied the sanitized version of slavery that dominated American popular history and memory prior to World War II. The image of the slave South portrayed in *Gone with the Wind* proved a neat cultural fit with the historical conceit of Lost Cause mythology, a conceit built on conveniently selective lapses in white memories of life in the antebellum South. Adding to the nation's historical amnesia were those self-righteous late-nineteenth- and early-twentieth-century historians who insisted that their data sets simply made it impossible to believe that slave breeding had been real or that slavery had been anything other than a "school" for the "Negro."

No historian did more to validate the benevolent imagery of the slave South than Ulrich Bonnell Phillips. Born in 1877, Phillips received his Ph.D. in history from Columbia University in 1902, having worked under the direction of William A. Dunning. Phillips went on to have a highly successful academic career. Building on his famous adviser's work, Phillips portrayed slavery as a benign labor system in which slaves worked for kindly, if at times stern, owners and overseers. In his most famous study, *American Negro Slavery* (1918), Phillips argued that "racial antipathy was [in the South] mitigated by the sympathetic tie of slavery which promoted an attitude of amiable patronage even toward the freedmen and their descendants."[1]

Phillips had read accounts about the more sinister side of slavery, but these dark tales he chalked up to abolitionist propaganda. Slave breeding was perhaps

the most lurid example of abolitionist propaganda to endure in American historical imagination, he believed. While Phillips admitted that overseers were
instructed to treat "breeding wenches" with a "kind and indulgent" manner,
no rational economic motive existed for slave breeding.[2] According to Phillips, "even if masters had stimulated breeding on occasion, that would have created but a partial and one-sided relationship between cost of production and
market price. To make the connection complete it would have been requisite
for them to check slave breeding when prices were low."[3] Phillips believed that
slave breeding had little historical significance.[4] He concluded *American Negro Slavery* by observing: "There were injustices [in southern slavery], oppression, brutality, and heartburning in the regime,—but where in the struggling
world are these absent? There were also gentleness, kind-hearted friendship
and mutual loyalty to a degree hard for him to believe who regards the system
with a theorist's eye and a partisan squint."[5] Phillips's history was apparently
free from theory-driven scholarship and the politically motivated histories that
black historians produced. He would no doubt have disapproved of W. E. B.
Du Bois's review of *American Negro Slavery*. Du Bois criticized Phillips's casual
dismissal of slave-breeding schemes, insisting, contrary to Phillips's assertions,
that American slavery as "an institution . . . was at best a mistake and at worst a
crime." Du Bois concluded, "the mere fact that [slavery] left to the world today
a heritage of ignorance, crime, lynching, lawlessness and economic injustice,
to be struggled with by this and succeeding generations, is a condemnation by
Mr. Phillips and unanswerable."[6] Such reviews spoke to the absence of human
feeling in empirical histories about slavery and its legacies, issues that did not
interest Phillips; he, after all, produced *history*, giving Americans "facts" about
the past. And the fact was, according to Phillips, that slave breeding had never
happened.

What, then, did happen? How could the increase in the "Negro" population
be explained, especially increases in the "mulatto" population? According to
Phillips and historians of his generation, such as Claude G. Bowers, the rise in
the African American (and mixed-race) population resulted from the sexual
immorality and promiscuity of black women. Bowers argued in 1929 that "a
whole race of [black] whores" had given birth to a new nation during the Civil
War and Reconstruction. Bowers drew on white eyewitness reports which
claimed that "negro girls for miles around are gathered to the camps [of Union
soldiers] and debauched."[7] Analysis of this type highlighted how historical
works on slavery overlapped with late-nineteenth- and early-twentieth-century

anxieties about the "racial destiny" of white America. Bowers voiced popularly held white male anxieties about the loss of racial control (and power) that white patriarchs had enjoyed during slavery.[8] These patriarchs had been noble men, driven by their patriarchal responsibilities to protect and care for their slaves. Freed from such protection and from the master's disciplinary restraints, former slaves, especially women, surrendered to their animalistic sexual nature and produced a new nation of unwanted "mulattos."[9]

This was the scholarly context in which African American academics worked to craft their own analyses of slavery. Unlike their white academic counterparts, early-twentieth-century black historians showed an acute awareness of the legacy of slavery in African American life and culture. In an era when the phrase "Negro problem" complemented Lost Cause mythology by focusing on black Americans as a sociological "problem" in American life, black intellectuals struggled to have their voices heard, much less their findings taken seriously, by the white intellectual establishment that dominated discussions of history and contemporary race relations. It was in this cauldron of racial hostility that black intellectualism—in particular, professional African American history writing—emerged.[10]

At the beginning of the twentieth century there existed two broad types of black historical writing. One category consisted of self-taught African American historians. These writers generally focused on the contributions that people of African descent had made over several millennia to the building of "civilization." From the construction of Egypt's pyramids to the building of America, the African race had been integral to the rise of "civilization." The other category of black historians was a small group of professionally trained scholars. Most were men who had received doctorates in history and were supportive of programs for racial "uplift." The histories that these scholars produced were not simply "contributionist" studies designed to "vindicate" the African American contribution to the building of the American republic; they were deeply analytical in nature and contributed to a broader professional discourse about the meaning of American history. For professional black historians, one could not seriously contribute to a scholarly understanding of American history without exploring the depths of slavery's inhumanity and analyzing its legacy.[11]

This chapter focuses on the professional class of black scholars and writers of history during the early twentieth century. Faced with a hostile academic culture, black intellectuals were nonetheless determined to present their own historical interpretations of slavery. For the most part, these studies resulted from the labors of African American men. African American women were virtually locked out of higher education, most confined to an education that men (both black and white) deemed appropriate to the "feminized" professions, such as nursing and social work. However, some black women did receive doctorates in history prior to World War II—Anna Julia Cooper from the University of Paris in 1925 and Marion Thompson Wright from Columbia University in 1940 being two prominent examples. Nonetheless, the dominant black voices in African American historical and scholarly writing prior to World War II were those of men.[12]

The following analysis focuses on three of the most influential of these voices—W. E. B. Du Bois, Carter G. Woodson, and E. Franklin Frazier. While there exist many fine biographies of these men, we still know relatively little about how these scholars incorporated the controversial topic of slave breeding into their analyses of slavery. This chapter therefore explores how Du Bois, Woodson, and Frazier combined empirical data with their analysis of the sensational claims of slave breeding issued by abolitionists and amateur historians during the nineteenth and early twentieth centuries, and how they set out to highlight what they felt were the inadequacies of the "mainstream" historical profession. The result was a very different perspective on slavery and its legacy.

### Evidence, History, and Meaning

All published works of history are the products of the author's selection and/or discarding of evidence, framing that evidence to fit a larger narrative, and then editing—often many times over—that piece of historical writing before it is published. This is as true today as it was in the four decades before World War II. No group of American intellectuals understood the selectivity of historical writing more acutely than black scholars. When it came to writing the history of slavery in the United States, many black academics felt there was too much excising and finessing of evidence going on among their white counterparts.

Writing in the *Journal of Negro History* in 1940, Herman Dreer attempted to expose the "objective" historian's evidentiary sleight of hand. In a sustained critique of the American historical profession and the textbooks scholars had produced for history teachers, Dreer was direct and forthright in his criticisms. He observed that white scholars presented the "Negro" to students as a "servant," and little else. Dreer complained that the "innocent teacher" would be mistaken for thinking that people of African descent played no role in ancient, medieval, and modern history if they relied on textbooks written by America's leading professional historians. For example, Dreer contended that A. E. McKinley and A. C. Howland's *World History in the Making* taught students nothing of the "demoralizing of the Negro by two hundred and fifty years of broken and immoral family life." Dreer added, "The innocent instructor teaches that the Negro as a slave picked cotton and had a good time singing and dancing. He says nothing of the brutal beatings and nauseating slave breeding. The innocent teacher conveys the impression that the Negro readily submitted to slavery."[13]

Dreer, like most other African American intellectuals, was unwilling to sit idly by as "prejudiced or cowardly" white historians misrepresented black history.[14] These historians also refused to allow the institutional and individual forms of oppression meted out to African American people for generations to remain uncontested. Black scholars expressed a variety of views on slavery and expressed differences of opinion over whether to cultivate a separatist identity or take a more integrationist approach to racial politics.[15] All agreed, however, that enslavement was a severe form of dehumanization that had an enduring impact on black people. Harvard University's first African American graduate, Richard T. Greener, spoke for many black Americans when he said of slavery's legacy among African Americans: "The Negro has no tears to shed over that 'wonderful school of slavery, under Providence,' so often quoted."[16]

What Greener was alluding to here was the idea that slavery had an enduring impact on the lives and historical memories of African Americans. Implicit was an understanding of America's past in which black Americans recognized the root cause of their socioeconomic marginalization and in which white racism distorted historical representations of slavery. White intellectuals framed such matters very differently, preferring to refer to the "plight" of African Americans as the "Negro problem." The "Negro problem" had become a fixture in American popular culture and scholarly discourse by the early twentieth century. It referred to the existence of a black population that occupied an economically impoverished, politically disenfranchised, and culturally marginalized status in American society.

In the minds of many white Americans, then, the abolition of the "school" of slavery created a problem in America—the "Negro problem." In 1891 the white politician and Pulitzer Prize–winning author William Cabell Bruce referred to the "Negro Problem" at length in his famous book of that title. Bruce emphasized the way in which whites, particularly southern whites, viewed the "Negro problem" as a political dilemma that stemmed from black Americans voting almost uniformly for the Republican Party. Bruce argued that this political uniformity—a product of the Republican Party's association with emancipation—antagonized white southerners and fueled the racialized nature of the "Negro problem."[17]

The politics of the "Negro problem" also affected a slew of social issues, such as "race prejudice, amalgamation [race mixing], education, violence including lynching, race riots and peonage."[18] These were all issues that could be tied, in one form or another, to slavery and its legacy. According to black scholars and civic leaders, the solution to the "Negro problem" would occur in developmental stages. Reflecting the era's evolutionary theories of race, African American spokespeople emphasized a variety of strategies, such as "industrial development," education, and enfranchisement. Few black leaders disputed the link between the "Negro problem" and slavery.[19] As H. T. Kealing argued, "The emancipated Negro struggles up to-day against many obstacles, the entailment of a brutal slavery."[20] Hubert Harrison, the radical black socialist leader from Harlem, New York, shared this view, arguing that the "caste system in America today is what we roughly refer to as the Race Problem, and it is thus seen that the Negro Problem is essentially an economic problem with its roots in slavery past and present."[21]

For white people, agreeing on a solution to America's "Negro problem" was far more difficult than acknowledging its roots in slavery. According to some white intellectuals and political leaders, the American republic did not have the constitutional infrastructure to deal with the legacy of slavery and the "Negro problem." This perspective overlooked the role of the federal government in allowing slavery to flourish after the ban of the international slave trade, and, ultimately, its role in abolishing slavery in the 1860s. One scholar wrote, "The Revolutionary forefathers, the makers of our Constitution, lived in a very simple world compared to this streamlined age of ours."[22]

The "Negro problem," then, was not something the federal government had any business trying to remedy. Indeed, the problems facing black Americans were often assumed to be of their own making, a product of laziness, jealousy of white accomplishments, and an unnecessarily morose view of the past. Historians such as Walter Lynwood Fleming complained that African American interpretations of slavery were defined by intense racial animosity toward whites and the constant "clank of chains and the cutting swish of the lash."[23]

Social scientists were adding their insights to this discussion. The sociologist Edward Reuter, for example, sought solutions to the "Negro problem," but did so by arguing that since the passing of the Thirteenth Amendment, a long and painful period of "blind fumbling for a new basis of racial accommodation" had unfolded, making "some sort of tolerable working relations between the races" seem like a pipe dream.[24] The Swedish social scientist Gunnar Myrdal synthesized late-nineteenth- and early-twentieth-century interpretations of this nature. His study of American race relations, *An American Dilemma* (1944), emphasized the failure of African American scholars to articulate a "solution" to the "Negro problem." Myrdal argued that "The formation of popular theories among Negroes concerning the Negro problem . . . does not result in articulate, systematized and stable opinions."[25] Black America was thus an intellectually disjointed and culturally vacuous place in which the brutalities of slavery were exaggerated and political solutions to the "Negro problem" absent.

There were, however, historical explanations for the "Negro problem." The Works Progress Administration narratives that scholars began consulting on a regular basis after World War II contained some of these explanations. Prior to World War II, though, African American historians and intellectuals recognized that they were working against an academic establishment that ignored, misrepresented, or downplayed what their research indicated was the enduring legacy of slavery. African American intellectuals dug far deeper than white academics in exploring the history and memory of sexual exploitation, racial violence, and family dislocation in black America.[26] In the process, they began to lay the intellectual foundations for what became the civil rights movement after World War II.

## Slavery and African American Scholarly Activism

In the halls of academe, black intellectuals explored those grimmer aspects of American history that white historians found absent in their data sets.[27] African American scholars emphasized the impact that sexual exploitation and racial violence during slavery continued to have on black life and culture in early-twentieth-century America. The ministers of America's black churches generally avoided issues like sexuality, violence, and even slavery. If they did speak about such issues it was indirectly, and often within a message of racial uplift. This was the "cult of respectability" that was so important to the social work and politics of black women, a politics that instructed black men and women on their "proper" roles as husbands, wives, and parents.[28] W. E. B. Du Bois certainly shared this interest in black uplift and efforts to counter racist perceptions of black Americans. He did not, however, turn away from issues of sexuality, violence, and the enduring legacy of slavery.

Du Bois was born in Great Barrington, Massachusetts, on February 23, 1868. He was a child of the African diaspora—his father, by some accounts, being born in San Domingo, "Hayti." Du Bois grew to manhood in an age characterized by the racial uncertainty and violence of post–Civil War America.[29] A gifted student, Du Bois found opportunities to succeed in life, earning a Ph.D. in history from Harvard University. His dissertation on the African slave trade was published in 1896 as *The Suppression of the African Slave-Trade*.[30]

Du Bois's analysis of the international slave trade was a serious challenge to white professional historians determined to focus on the "facts" of the slave South's political economy. Du Bois was interested in these issues, but he was also concerned with the causes and legacies of the North American slave population's dramatic growth after the international slave trade to the United States was abolished in 1808. Like Henry Clay Bruce, Benjamin Arnett, and myriad other African Americans who addressed the memory of slavery during the late nineteenth and early twentieth centuries, Du Bois wrestled with the historical and sociological implications of sexual exploitation and violence in slavery and freedom. In *Suppression*, though, Du Bois does not take up these issues—and the related issue of population increases among slaves in the American South after 1808—as systematically as he would in subsequent work. David Levering Lewis explains this by arguing that Du Bois failed to recognize that most slaves imported from Africa after 1808 found themselves in Brazil or Cuba. As Lewis explains, "slaveholders in the American South not only mainly grew their own labor force, they encouraged living conditions that kept their investments alive, generally healthy, and augmenting in value."[31]

Southern slaveholders, in other words, did not need the clandestine international trade in African slaves after 1808; they simply bred their own. Du Bois, the scholar and civil rights activist, was deeply troubled by the idea of slave populations being augmented through sexual manipulation.[32] He conceded in *Suppression* that after 1820 the extension of slavery into the American Southwest led to a dramatic increase in the internal slave trade. This connection between the territorial expansion of slavery and black reproduction led Du Bois to explain, "The increasing crop caused a new demand for slaves, and an inter-state slave-traffic arose between the Border and the Gulf States, which turned the former into slave-breeding districts, and bound them to the slave States by ties of strong economic interest."[33]

In an 1897 essay, "The Conservation of Race," Du Bois tackled the meaning of race and moved toward a more explicit analysis of reproductive manipulation in African American history.[34] He placed his analysis in the context of a growing African American literature that debated the meaning and significance of racial pride, "uplift," and the "racial destiny" of black people in the United States.[35] Focusing firmly on "our future development," Du Bois insisted that the racial destiny of African Americans was "*not* absorption by the white Americans."[36] He went on to insist that "it is our duty to conserve our physical powers, our intellectual endowments, our spiritual ideals."[37] The legacy of slavery—the shades of color and the unstable social lives it created—is implicit in this analysis. It is implicit because the overt message is a call to action, a call to black Americans to draw on their inner strength to combat the legacies of slavery.

Like his black contemporaries—such as Kelly Miller, who argued that "the Negroes in this country are a thoroughly mixed people"—Du Bois's "solutions" to what white Americans called the "Negro problem" did not shy away from the legacy of violence and sexual exploitation that punctuated black history since slavery.[38] In particular, Du Bois became ever more explicit about the enduring consequences of reproductive manipulation during slavery times. Writing in *The Negro American Family* (1908), he cited James C. Ballagh's *A History of Virginia* (1902) to question the profitability of slave breeding. He asserted that if such practices did in fact exist in the slave South, they were likely confined to "a certain class."[39] Interestingly, Du Bois had made similar observations about the intersection of race and class in *The Philadelphia Negro* (1899). During the first decade and a half of the twentieth century, Du Bois continued to see the confluence of race and class as crucial to understanding slavery's legacy in American life. In 1908 he posited that the "essential features of Negro slavery in America was"

No legal marriage.
No legal family.
No legal control over children.[40]

As abolitionists (both black and white) and former slaves insisted, these were the three central components of reproductive manipulation in the slave-breeding South.

Given that Du Bois presented such analysis in an era characterized by Lost Cause mythologizing and the scholarly rewriting of slavery's place in American history, his conclusions were stark. Indeed, there existed a moral undertone to

Du Bois writing on slavery, a metaphorical finger-pointing at those he viewed as responsible for slavery's legacy—the "Negro problem." White Americans, and the socioeconomic structures they put in place, were responsible for the ill effects of slavery's legacy. Drawing on Du Bois's work (and that of the Irish abolitionist Daniel O'Connoll), Charles Victor Roman, the black physician, said as much when, in 1916, he observed: "The breeding of slaves for sale is probably the most immoral and debasing practice ever known in the world."[41] There is no intellectual sophistry here, just a blunt, matter-of-fact statement designed to counter the sentimental distortions of Lost Cause propaganda. Benjamin Griffith Brawley, the dean of Morehouse College, provided a similarly unvarnished presentation of slavery. Drawing on the travel narratives of Frederick Law Olmstead and Professor Dew's pro-slavery argument, Brawley argued that the territorial extension of slavery resulted in a growing demand for slaves, a demand that could only be met through slave owners' and slave traders' adoption of slave-breeding practices. Brawley asserted:

> The legal abolition of the [international] slave-trade . . . coincided with the heavy demands imposed by the Louisiana Purchase and the development of the lower South. . . . The slave increased in value, and Virginia and Maryland became famous breeding places for the plantations of the far South, a woman who was an extraordinary breeder being advertised as such [Brawley cites an example from Dew's analysis]. . . . On remote plantations the operation of the system was most gross; and a woman separated from her husband was forced to accept a new mate.[42]

Brawley and Du Bois lived for a time in the same city—Atlanta—and read each other's work—Du Bois actually recommended Brawley's *Short History of the American Negro* to a German law student in the early twentieth century. The two men shared a harsh view of the internal workings of the slave South, a view that was out of step with that of the white historical establishment. In black America, Du Bois's unvarnished representations of slavery met with a receptive audience. As his work evolved, his critique of slavery and its legacy became even more pointed.

In fact, Du Bois found it difficult on occasion to hide his contempt for white historical writing. He lambasted U. B. Phillips's influential *American Negro Slavery*, for example, referring to it as "curiously incomplete and unfortunately biased."[43] For the best part of two decades, Du Bois had been trying to undermine such "biased" history writing. By the 1920s, his commitment to such endeavors was as unwavering as ever.

Building on his magisterial *The Souls of Black Folk* (1903)—a searing treatment of black culture, identity, and American race relations—Du Bois published one of the greatest scholarly essays of the early twentieth century—"The Damnation of Women." Du Bois's essay appeared in his book *Darkwater* (1920), in which he wrestled with the issues of slavery and segregation, sex and marriage, femininity and motherhood. The essay is most often remembered for the clarity of its feminist vision and Du Bois's exposure of American hypocrisy on the issue of womanhood. Americans, Du Bois observed, "worship both virgins and mothers and in the end despises the mother and despoils [*sic*] the virgins."[44] Such was the case, Du Bois contended, for black women. With the history of slavery looming large in his analysis, Du Bois described America's "darker sisters" as both the "daughters of sorrow" and the "primal black All-Mother of men."[45] From "dusky Cleopatras" to Sojourner Truth, Du Bois insisted that "despite her curious history, her slavery, polygamy, and toil, the spell of the African mother pervades her land."[46] African American women and black motherhood were forced to endure the "crushing weight of slavery,"[47] but their strength, Du Bois insisted, enabled them to endure the exploitation of the "swaggering masters." Their strength also helped to lay the "foundations of the great Negro church of today" and to struggle against economic and social adversity to keep black families together.[48] In his evocative and moving conclusion, Du Bois reiterated the awe in which he held black women and black mothers. "No other women on earth," he wrote, "could have emerged from the hell of force which once engulfed and still surrounds black women in America with half the modesty and womanliness that they retain."[49]

Feminist scholars have observed that Du Bois grounded his discussions of black sexuality—particularly black female sexuality—in slavery.[50] This is important, because black religious and political leaders attempted to combat sexual and racial stereotypes with sermons and speeches that echoed the tenets of the "cult of respectability." Black women, such as the professional historian Anna Julia Cooper, also elaborated on the ideal enshrined in the "cult of respectability." They did so not because of an aversion to discussing racism and sexism—though for a significant number of black women, a disinclination to publicly discuss such matters was an issue—but because they recognized that the "cult of true womanhood," an ideal used in white America to prescribe a woman's place as being in the home, did not fit the reality of most black women.[51] Cooper was as well qualified as any professional historian—black or white, male or female—to make such claims. She knew that the legacy of slavery continued to press on the daily lives of black women. In slavery, Cooper's grandmother recalled the shame of giving birth to a child conceived when her master raped her. In the early twentieth century, black women continued to encounter such violence in work environments, particularly those who worked as domestics.[52] Du Bois understood the gendered dimensions of slavery's legacy. It was why he felt compelled to celebrate the strength of black women and support them in espousing the "politics of respectability."[53]

The "politics of respectability" was the most public way in which African Americans responded to the legacy of slavery (or what whites termed the "Negro problem"). In the hands of black men, the "politics of respectability" involved a masculine determination to protect "black women from rape, physical abuse, and economic poverty."[54] While some African Americans, particularly black church ministers, tried not to place too much emphasis on sex and slavery, it was difficult to escape the link between the "politics of respectability" and slavery's memory. Du Bois's "politics of respectability" was also characterized by a protective masculine pose denied to men during slavery and, bitterly, with the emergence of those racially discriminatory laws, political practices, and social conventions associated with Jim Crow segregation after the 1890s.[55]

Perhaps this was why, in a 1928 essay, Du Bois made explicit the link between slavery and the supreme bugaboo of early-twentieth-century America: "miscegenation." The "intermingling of blood" that Du Bois identified as a fact of life "in the slave South" had left an enduring biological legacy in the American population. According to Du Bois, the "so-called American Negro is probably less than 25 per cent of pure African." And since most of the "intermingling of blood" took place during slavery (not during the Civil War and Reconstruction era, as white historians argued), the racially mixed nature of the American population was a living embodiment of the rape, violence, and sexual exploitation that black Americans associated with slavery. The "intermingling of blood" and the presence of the "mulatto" in American society reminded African Americans how they, or their ancestors, had once been exposed to vile "slave-breeding" schemes.[56]

By the 1930s, Du Bois understood that the legacy and memory of slavery continued to affect black men, women, and families in ways that white Americans could never fully comprehend.[57] Equipped with this understanding of slavery's ongoing impact on the lives of African Americans, Du Bois drew the attention of readers of *The Crisis* to the population growth of the "Negro" in the United States. In the February 1933 edition, Du Bois wrote that the "growth of the Negro population in the United States has been an astonishing phenomenon, especially when we remember that in 1790, when there were only three-fourths of a million Negroes in the country, it was the generally accepted fact that without a slave trade Negroes could not survive. What happened is that slaves without a slave trade became more valuable; with cotton culture their value rose still further, so that they were fed adequately and their breeding systematically encouraged."[58]

These were explosive charges. Du Bois, however, had already leveled these allegations against the slave South. Just three years before his editorial in *The Crisis*, Du Bois, ever the vigilant social scientist, used census data to show the consistent increases in the African American population following the close of the international slave trade.[59] According to Du Bois, "hypocritical America" may re-create a more sanitized version of its history, but the struggles of black women, the fragility of black families, and white America's obsession with miscegenation did not emerge sui generis after the Civil War; it had its origins in slavery and the exploitative practices that slave owners and slave traders implemented. In Du Bois's words, "These emancipated slaves were victims who had been bred deliberately in sloth, ignorance, poverty and crime. Their emancipation meant that they must either be killed off, gotten rid off by compulsory migration, or that they must be educated and trained."[60] Poverty, sexual exploitation, race prejudice, and violence all had their roots in slavery, according to Du Bois.[61] He insisted that the "Negro" intelligentsia had an important role to play in helping black Americans overcome the legacy of slavery. Black scholars, Du Bois maintained, must encourage economic uplift, political equality, and acculturation, which he defined as the elevation of African Americans from their "low cultural station."[62]

But as Du Bois observed in his masterwork, *Black Reconstruction in America* (1935), overcoming the legacy of slavery and engendering racial uplift would not be a simple task. *Black Reconstruction* was a direct challenge to the Dunning-Phillips school of historical interpretation. Meticulous in its scholarship, clear and uncompromising in its analysis, this book exposed the enduring legacy that slavery and slave breeding had on black Americans and their families. Du Bois reiterated his earlier claims about the upper South breeding slaves for the lower South. His analysis, though, went deeper than it had ever gone before

in exploring the historical significance of slave breeding. Highlighting the economic value that slave owners and traders placed on slave breeding, Du Bois
noted that while the African American population increased during slavery,
the sale of children shattered families, and, he observed, "a breeding woman is
worth from one-sixth to one-fourth more than one that does not breed."[63]

According to Du Bois, slave breeding violated enslaved women, forced slave
men to act as "studs," and destroyed families. The impact of slave breeding on
black America was "sexual chaos," the product of "economic motives."[64] Du
Bois elaborated on these assertions, arguing, "The deliberate breeding of a
strong, big field-hand stock could be carried out by selecting proper males, and
giving them the run of the likeliest females. This in many Border States became
a regular policy and fed the slave trade. Child-bearing was a profitable occupation, which received every possible encouragement, and there was not only
no bar to illegitimacy, but an actual premium put upon it. Indeed, the word
was impossible of meaning under the slave system."[65] Generations of African
Americans would go on to live with the memory and legacy of slave breeding.
According to Du Bois, the breeding and trade in black bodies occupied such a
central part of black history that it remained a fundamental narrative structure.
For white Americans, however, the "tradition" of breeding and selling slaves did
not merit serious attention. What mattered in white America's master narrative
was the history of great men and the study of their ideas and battles. Black men,
women, and children were merely "cogs" in this larger story. Du Bois's analysis
looked squarely into the teeth of America's racial history and outlined the cause
of the "Negro problem."

The African American historian Carter G. Woodson shared Du Bois's commitment to understanding the history of slavery and its legacies.[66] Where Du
Bois insightfully combined historical and social scientific methodologies to
analyze slavery's enduring impact on African Americans, Woodson focused on
the history of black America. Woodson, along with contemporaries such as
Lorenzo Johnston Greene, claimed that they were using "scientific method" to
reconstruct the history of black America. As Woodson, Greene, and other black
historians saw their work, such endeavors involved a "life-and-death struggle"
to prevent the memory of their African American descendants from slipping
into the mist of the past.[67]

Woodson's scholarship was brutally insightful and politically blunt in its attempt to keep the memory of black history alive in the collective consciousness

of the American people. Like Du Bois, Woodson excavated antebellum slavery's colonial antecedents and highlighted the trials, tribulations, and accomplishments of African American people in North America. He argued that northern and southern whites had imposed immense challenges on black Americans. "While we must feel ashamed," he wrote, "of the South for its lingering medievalism inflicted upon the section by chattel slavery," he argued that black Americans must also "hold the Mayflower descendants responsible for accelerating that backward step into darkness which still overshadows the land of cotton."[68]

Although Du Bois was at times critical of Woodson's limited analysis of African American women, Woodson's scholarship was scathing of the way black women were forced to endure a history of violent sexual exploitation in the United States.[69] From an early period in the English colonization of the northeastern portion of North America, Woodson argued that the sexual exploitation of women of African descent explained the origins of miscegenation in the United States. In 1918, he argued in a famous essay, "The Beginnings of the Miscegenation of the Whites and Blacks," that a combination of legal developments and feelings of shame meant that white men tried to cover up their sexual exploitation of—or in some cases, love affairs with—black women, lest they incur the sanction of the community and the wrath of their white wives. The political evisceration that Thomas Jefferson endured for his sexual affair with the slave Sally Hemings, and his efforts to save face, was the most famous example of why Woodson and other black historians placed limited trust in population statistics and the accounts of plantation owners when it came to matters of sexual coercion and miscegenation.[70] In fact, Woodson viewed the contradictory and inaccurate statistics that the proslavery propagandists of the nineteenth century drew from, and which professional historians continued to rely on, with a suspicion bordering on contempt.[71]

Woodson's skepticism about the narrow source base that white, predominantly male historians relied upon was evident in his famous *The Negro in Our History* (1922). This was a major contribution to the black history movement, not least because Woodson's analysis of slavery paid significant attention to the sexual exploitation of enslaved women. Woodson argued that because of the closing of the international slave trade, Virginia, Maryland, North Carolina, Kentucky, Tennessee, Missouri, and Delaware became slave-breeding states. In language that other black historians echoed, Woodson argued that "to supply the Southwest with slaves, . . . the domestic slave trade became an important business, and the older states which suffered from migration devoted themselves to slave breeding for this market."[72]

Woodson's emphasis, like that of the antebellum abolitionists before him and the former slaves who testified about slave breeding during the late 1930s, was on the commercial exploitation of slave reproduction. Economic and bodily exploitation thus bled into one another as Woodson portrayed a system in which slaves were reproduced and sold for profit. He continued this line of argument into the 1930s. Writing with Charles H. Wesley in 1935, Woodson again insisted that there was a regional dimension to the sexual and economic exploitation associated with slave-breeding practices. "To rehabilitate things" in the upper South, they asserted, "efforts were made to fertilize the worn out soil, and temporarily it apparently succeeded; but more relief came when the planters of these states resorted to slave-breeding and used their surplus slaves in railroad construction. The Lower South in the meantime was apparently in its golden age."[73] As the technology of the railroads (along with canals) connected the economic regions of the slave South, the breeding of enslaved bodies facilitated the South's economic growth and became its own "technology of power."[74]

The sexual exploitation of enslaved women for breeding purposes combined various elements of economic, medical, and disciplinary culture to produce discourses of health and pathology about the "Negro" in American society. These discourses endured long after slavery was abolished.[75] Woodson recognized this in his most famous work, *The Mis-Education of the Negro* (1933).[76] In this book, Woodson argued that popular prejudices shaped the analysis of historians of slavery and social scientists when addressing the "Negro problem." He contended that white historians were unexamined in their own racism, presenting "real history" from legal and economic sources that mistakenly portrayed slavery as a school in which the slave toiled happily in good health. White historians used similarly skewed sources to pathologize the emancipated slave as a politically corrupt and sexually deviant in character.[77] Woodson countered that such portrayals prompted some white scholars to identify black people as the cause of racial tension in America. These arguments were not only racist, but they were so ridiculously sensational that they inhibited many Americans from attempting to understand the legacy of slavery in the twentieth century. Thus, Woodson argued, segregation "is the most far-reaching development in the history of the Negro since the enslavement of the race." He concluded, "It has been made possible by our system of mis-educating innocent people who did not know what was happening. It is so subtle that men have participated in promoting it without knowing what they were doing."[78]

For Woodson, a cultural system based on the power of the white man over black Americans made historical events such as slave breeding and racial segregation possible. The significance of such a culture—a racist culture—cannot be underestimated in Woodson's analysis. Without it, slavery's successor, de jure segregation, the legal foundation upon which Jim Crow America was built, would not have been possible. The African American sociologist E. Franklin Frazier was all too aware of the link between slavery and segregation. Sharing many of the scholarly concerns and interests that Du Bois and Woodson had about the legacies of slavery, Frazier produced some of the most influential (and controversial) work on the black family in the 1920s, 1930s, and 1940s. His analysis of black life and history in the United States came under intense scrutiny during the latter half of the twentieth century when newer social and cultural histories of the black family emphasized the importance of "agency" among the enslaved.[79] However, in his day, Frazier's work was hailed as a "natural history of the Negro family, documented by concrete materials, [one that] marks the transition from a philosophy of the family as set forth by Westermarck, Muller-Lyer, and Briffault to a study of types of families, in this case within biosocial groups."[80] In other words, Frazier's contemporaries considered his scholarship groundbreaking.

Frazier's most enduring scholarly contribution was his argument that the "Negro" family in the United States was matriarchal. He contended that the matriarchal nature of the black family was a legacy of enslavement. "Generally speaking," Frazier asserted, "the mother remained throughout slavery the dominant and important figure in the slave family."[81] Frazier here spoke to the impact that sexual exploitation—including slave breeding—had on African American families during and after slavery. He was, in short, attempting to explain what he viewed as the fragility (and in some cases, malformation) of black families. Frazier therefore attempted to explain the dislocation and instability of black families from a structural perspective that emphasized the historical and sociological forces that worked against stable black family units. Focusing on the hypocrisy of the white master class during slavery, Frazier argued that "cohabitation of the men of the master race with women of the slave race occurred on every level and became so extensive that it nullified to some extent the monogamous mores."[82] These practices were part of the economic and cultural structures of the slave South that left black women at the head of un-stable single-parent families.

Frazier's provocative assessment of slavery's impact on marriage and sexual mores among African American people was guided by his belief in the *fact* of slave breeding.[83] He was, therefore, unequivocal on this issue and in relating it to the long-term consequences for African American families. "Apologists for slavery have often denied that Negro women were used for breeding pur-poses," Frazier wrote, but "the evidence is too clear to leave any doubt as to the existence of the practice." Referring to one of his primary sources, a newspaper advertisement from the March 10, 1796, *Charleston City Gazette*, Frazier de-scribed how the advertisement touted the value of "prime" slaves, "their present Owner, with great trouble and expence, selected them out of many for several years past. They were purchased for stock and breeding Negroes, and to any Planter who particularly wanted them for that purpose, they are a very choice and desirable gang."[84]

In *The Negro in the United States*, Frazier continued to maintain that slave breeding was a fact of life in the slave South. Originally published in 1949, and revised and reissued in 1957, the book argued that the increase in the slave popu-lation between the founding of the republic and the outbreak of the Civil War was a product of this practice. Echoing the arguments of Du Bois and Woodson on slave breeding, Frazier maintained that the "border states became in a sense the breeding ground for the slave system."[85] The existence of this "breeding ground" had enduring emotional and material consequences in the form of economic impoverishment, fragile family structures, and a historical counter-narrative that was considerably darker than the master narrative that American audiences were exposed to in Hollywood movies.

The evidence suggested to Frazier that white slave owners and overseers played an active part in increasing the exportable slave population in the "breeding ground" of the upper South. In the decade before the Civil War, Fra-zier argued, the "mulatto" population increased from 405,057 in 1850 to 588,363 by 1860.[86] Adding to the perception that slave owners tried to increase the slave population through natural increase were data that Frazier believed showed an increase in African American mortality in the two decades after the Civil War. While numerous factors could account for these statistics—from poverty to ad hoc methods of family planning[87]—the implication is that once slave owners no longer saw social and economic advantages in breeding slaves, every effort was made to ensure infant survival and life expectancy was reduced among the black populations of the South.[88]

## Conclusion

The intellectual work of Du Bois, Woodson, and Frazier attacked what most black scholars saw as the inadequacies of professional historical writing during the early twentieth century. White scholars had been blinded by the mythology of Lost Cause propaganda, employed narrow methodologies that essentially rearticulated the economic rationale of the slave owner and slave trader (and silenced the enslaved), and exposed their own racial chauvinism by referring simplistically to the "Negro problem" in post–Civil War America.

African American scholars would have none of this. They believed that the historical and sociological narratives deployed by white academics involved gross historical and sociological generalizations. African American scholars argued that the legacies of slavery were not solely of African Americans' making. For example, Anna Julia Cooper laid at the feet of the United States' Founding Fathers—men she referred to as "these jugglers with reason and conscience"— the burden of blame for breathing, if only inadvertently, life into slavery. The decisions these men made at the end of the eighteenth century had profound consequences for generations of enslaved people. Cooper insisted that because white slave owners and slave traders had America's legal structures and economic motives on their side, they began "begetting and breeding mongrels of their own flesh among these helpless creatures and pocketing the guilty increase, the price of their own blood in unholy dollars and cents."[89]

Motivated by an unquenchable thirst for wealth and power, the slave owners and slave traders in Cooper's analysis, as in that of Du Bois, Woodson, and Frazier, used violence and sexual exploitation to profit from black labor and reproduction. Such historical interpretations, which extended the sensational claims of nineteenth-century abolitionists into the twentieth, made for a stark contrast to the Lost Cause mythology and "objective" scholarship of white professional historians. But the work of these black intellectuals was not simply polemical; their research constituted a forceful scholarly articulation of what millions of black Americans recalled and spoke about in private.

In the decades prior to World War II, black scholars thus crafted their own interpretations of the role of slave breeding in African American history. At the same time, other segments of black America began presenting their own versions of this history. In the following chapter we will see how black writers and playwrights added to the interpretive layers of African American memory by exploring the violence and sexual exploitation associated with the memory of slave breeding. Their work, performed at community theaters, presented African American audiences with formalized re-creations of those memories of slave breeding that black scholars worked so hard to weave into their analyses, and that most white Americans seemed eager to forget.

# 4

## The Theater of Memory

"In dis world, black women ain't nothing but breeders, tuh have chilluns fuh de white folks tuh sell down river lak dey do horses and cows."[1] With these melancholic words, Mammy, a key actor in Randolph Edmonds's dialect drama *Breeders* (1930), exposed one of the deepest historical wounds in the collective memory of early-twentieth-century black Americans: the violent sexual exploitation of African American women during antebellum slavery. Edmonds used the trope of slave breeding to frame his protest against the racism and violence that white Americans directed against black people. This was an era, it is worth remembering, when social Darwinian and eugenic discourse filtered through American culture and informed the nation's racism, when black women who took jobs as domestics in white homes were vulnerable to sexual harassment and rape by white men, and when lynch mobs prematurely ended the lives of thousands of black Americans—most of whom were men.[2]

In the 1920s and 1930s, African American men and women refused to let American racism go unchecked. These decades witnessed an outpouring of creativity and scholarly inquiry among African American writers, intellectuals, and religious and civic leaders. We saw in the previous chapter how black scholars crafted their own narratives of the past that aimed to challenge the hegemonic white culture's understanding of American history. Beginning in the 1920s, during a period known as the Harlem Renaissance, African American writers and playwrights added their stories to a growing catalog of black historical memories. These writers resisted efforts to sanitize the significance of slavery in American history and protested the racism and sexism that affected early-twentieth-century black Americans. Drawing on a tradition of oral storytelling, folk culture, and intellectual influences as diverse as Marx, Freud, and Gandhi, black playwrights such as Randolph Edmonds wrote plays and musicals with both spiritual and material objectives in mind. They wrote to protest racial injustice, and to inspire—to redeem what they felt was the brutalized spirit of the African American people.[3]

In small, community-operated theaters, black Americans explored these themes during the decades prior to World War II. From the Krigwa Players in New York to the Howard Players in Washington, D.C., the Olympian Players in Pittsburgh, and scores of other theaters in black communities throughout the country, African American performers re-created the past in all its joy and sorrow and presented searing commentaries on contemporary race relations.[4] Local black theater companies performed Randolph Edmonds's plays, along with scores of other plays and musical dramas by black playwrights such as Mary P. Burrill. Burrill's anti-lynching play *Aftermath* (1919) was an example of the type of political protests being performed by black theater companies. *Aftermath* focused on the fury of a white lynch mob, Burrill's underlying message being her condemnation of the "burnin' an killin'" of black bodies.[5]

Black playwrights like Edmonds and Burrill refused to turn a blind eye to brutalities that white Americans had visited, and continued to visit, on African American people. Their protests joined those of black scholars and an increasingly vocal generation of black political protesters, such as Ida B. Wells, who campaigned against lynching and sought ways to protect black women from the threat of sexual assault in the workplace. This chapter explores the seemingly unconnected histories of slave breeding and lynching in the work of black playwrights, focusing in detail on the work of Edmonds and Burrill. The chapter begins with an overview of the racial context of early-twentieth-century America—the very real theater of southern lynching. In an effort to highlight the ways in which black playwrights of this period placed the history of lynching (or wrongful death) into a broader historical context, I demonstrate how the history of slave breeding (or the coercive creation of life) was connected to contemporary racial concerns in the theatrical imaginations of Burrill and Edmonds.[6] What follows therefore is a textual analysis of how Burrill and Edmonds crafted narratives with black audiences in mind. Like their contemporary black playwrights, they hoped that their work would eventually be performed for black theater audiences and help to cultivate a collective political response to American racism. Burrill and Edmonds epitomize how African American playwrights felt such political objectives could be achieved by exploring the emotional and historical connections between sex, slavery, and violence in American history.[7]

## Slavery in American Popular Culture

During the late nineteenth and early twentieth centuries, African Americans from different class, gendered, and educational backgrounds spoke or wrote about the connection between the reproduction of life and the destruction of human existence in black history. Slavery was often the starting point for narrative explorations of the interconnected themes of life and death in black culture. In slavery, black men and women were socially and legally non-beings; the "desire," to borrow from one of Langston Hughes's suggestive poems, for the love of a husband or wife, and the affection of a parent for their child (or children), rested on the power of the slave owner. Alternatively, the sanctity of an enslaved couple's love could so easily be breached by the desire—be it for sexual gratification or profit—of the white slave-owning and slave-trading classes. Profound feelings of fear and anxiety, anger and frustration thus punctuated black literary and dramatic explorations of history and memory during the early twentieth century.[8]

In contrast, white readers and theater audiences found comfort in renderings of the past that marginalized African American characters and depicted slaves as "easygoing and good natured." Such characterizations existed well into the twentieth century, with comic, watermelon-eating "Negroes" becoming a staple of popular culture. From *Belle Lamar: An Episode of the Civil War* (1874) to *His Trust* and *His Trust Fulfilled* (both 1911), the depiction of loyal and happy slaves on one hand and comedic and bumbling "Niggahs" on the other united northern and southern whites in the shared self-deception that was Lost Cause mythology.

For native-born white and immigrant audiences alike, the melodramatic capstone of America's historical retelling of slavery and the Reconstruction era came not on the stage but with D. W. Griffith's film *The Birth of a Nation* (1915).[9] Griffith described *The Birth of a Nation* as an "overwhelming compilation of authentic evidence and testimony."[10] *The Birth of a Nation* highlighted the cultural hegemony that white Americans maintained over the presentation of memories about slavery and the Reconstruction era. Indeed, the melodrama portrayed in *The Birth of a Nation* inspired President Woodrow Wilson, himself a professional historian, to speak on behalf of the nation when he famously quipped that Griffith's movie was "like writing history with lightning."[11] On the stage or silver screen, then, the white public's imagination was captured by a historical narrative that celebrated the rebirth of a nation from the ashes of internecine war and trivialized (or erased) scenes of black exploitation and suffering at the hands of their white forebears.

Black Americans were not moved to accept unexamined historical platitudes by such culturally constructed self-deception. Faced with romanticized theatrical and cinematic portrayals of slavery, and confronting the daily realities of lynching and de jure segregation, the NAACP's *Crisis* editorialized that while black Americans have a history they should not be ashamed of, they "will wait a long, long time for white men to write this history in all fairness for the consumption of the great white public."[12] Unwilling to wait passively for this day to come, turn-of-the-century black playwrights joined African American scholars in challenging a national culture that preferred historical amnesia on issues such as slavery and favored obfuscation on the racial dimensions of rape and lynching.

Black playwrights addressed what they saw as the narrative continuities between pre– and post–Civil War America. Early African American productions such as *The Creole* (1891), *The Octoroons* (1895), and *Oriental America* (1896) fused elements of minstrelsy and vaudeville entertainment into black theatrical reinterpretations of slavery and its historical legacy. Black playwrights thus gave renewed meaning to memories of enslavement in an era of terrifying racial violence. Lynching and the ever-present threat of rape among black female domestics were the emblems of white supremacist violence in Jim Crow America. They were, as black playwrights insisted with increased clarity, examples of white masculine attempts to reassert male dominance over an interracial society. From Klansmen, white working-class men, and the most respected patriarchs of the "New South," these perpetrators of lynching aimed to reinstitute a cultural code of conduct that approximated the disciplined social lines that had once defined community life under slavery.[13]

With slavery abolished, white men used the physical and psychological terror of lynching to restage white supremacy in a very public fashion.[14] In the process, the antebellum focus on black reproductive exploitation shifted. While white men continued to view black women as objects of sexual exploitation, their avowed aim became the protection of white womanhood from black male rapists.[15] The slave men who once sired black children now became the objects of lynching and castration, lest the descendants of these "young bucks" rape white women, "pollute" the white race, and produce children who blurred the lines of racial privilege beyond recognition. As psychologist John Dollard

Figure 3. NAACP anti-lynching campaign. An NAACP cartoon in which an anguished woman kneels next to the body of a lynched African American man. Imagery of this nature was part of the NAACP's anti-lynching campaign and highlighted the tragic toll lynching had on black families. Courtesy of the Library of Congress, LC-USZ62-122177.

famously observed in his 1937 study of Indianola, Mississippi, there was a "general (white) belief that the negro not only possessed a larger penis than men of other races, but is capable of maintaining it in a state of erection for a longer period than is possible for a male of any other race"—the very qualities that made the slave "buck" an ideal breeding machine.[16] In "freedom," however, these stereotypically racist qualities made black men unmitigated threats to white womanhood and white (male) supremacy.[17]

White America's obsession with black sexuality in the century after the Civil War—be it in the sexual harassment and rape of black women or the obsession with the black man's genitalia—was, in its projected outcomes, different. During slavery, the semi-naked and naked bodies of enslaved *laboring* women were the focus of white violence and exploitation for reproductive purposes. Enslaved women lived with the threat of sexual violence, the public auction of slave family members, and the fear that male loved ones would become victims of violence or permanently separated from them. As most early-twentieth-century African Americans saw things, these types of threats remained; they existed in the form of rape and lynching.[18]

In the collective historical consciousness of early-twentieth-century African Americans, an awareness of how black people had long constituted figures of the white public's exploitation, control, and scorn pervaded the theater of historical memories and anti-lynching activism. In her exposé of lynching, Ida B. Wells, one of the bravest and most vocal opponents of lynching, made the connection between slavery and freedom, the rape of black women and the lynching of African American men.[19] "During the slave regime," Wells argued, "the Southern white man owned the Negro body and soul. It was to his interest to dwarf the soul and preserve the body." Wells asserted that following the Civil War, emancipation gave birth to "a new system of intimidation . . . the Negro was not only whipped and scourged; he was killed."[20]

Wells, like other members of black communities throughout the United States, knew that there was a link between rape and lynching. She attempted to lift the veil of ignorance about this connection among white Americans, insisting that when a white man rapes a black woman, "nobody is lynched and no notice is taken." White Americans were, by Wells's reckoning, sexual and racial hypocrites, the "apologists for lynchers of the rapist of *white* women only."[21] It was the lynching of black men, however, that gained the most public attention during the early twentieth century. Examples abounded in the black press. Wells reported that in one case, a crowd of around ten thousand witnessed the burning of a lynching victim's legs and feet. She explained that after this sadistic immolation, "the hot irons—plenty of fresh ones being at hand—were rolled up and down Smith's [the victim's] stomach, back, and arms. Then the eyes were burned out and irons were thrust down his throat."[22] Sadism, torture, and castration became the signature features of the lynch mob's repertoire of torture.

While sadistic acts of branding and burning could be found in the slave South, the castration of black men after the Civil War carried with it a very explicit meaning. Lillian Smith, a prominent white Georgian and opponent of segregation, lamented that the castration of lynching victims was "born of a savage fury . . . and a stern resolve to strike a deeper terror into [those] whom the other method had failed to awe."[23] The terror and mutilation inflicted on so many lynching victims had both physical and psychological motivations. Castration took from its victim the capacity to reproduce and, if the victim survived, a critical physical component of black male identity.[24] And lest the black community failed to recognize the intent of such lynchings, local authorities often ordered family members to collect the remains of a loved one. This was the case for August Turner, the father of a lynching victim, who "was summoned to the park to remove his son's charred remains" in 1921.[25]

African American playwrights drew upon these terrifying tales to critique the rationales behind lynching. The accusation of the black male rapist, so often repeated to justify the lynching and mutilation of black men, was the object of both commentary and satire in productions such as Georgia Douglas Johnson's *A Sunday Morning in the South* (1925). African American women like Johnson wrote most of the anti-lynching plays during the early twentieth century. Their works were performed at "community-based, nonprofit venues that offered alternatives to a predominantly white, male, and New York City–centered theatre."[26] Johnson recognized that while the rape—or attempted rape—of a white woman was often cited as the catalyst for a lynching, blacks knew that whites generally lynched people for any number of arbitrary reasons and that the most likely victims of rape—black women—rarely figured in public debates about sexual abuse.[27]

The black women who wrote lynching plays understood the implications behind the long and explosive history of interracial sex in the United States. Some playwrights, such as Myrtle Smith Livingston, recognized the sexually charged anger that white lynch mobs directed against black men, irrespective of the baseless nature of charges of sexual impropriety. In *For Unborn Children*

(1926), Livingston presented a cautionary tale about the dangers of miscegenation. Intermarriage, Livingston has her characters explain, hurts the "Negro race." One of these characters, "Grandma Carlson," explains that "when a colored man marries a white woman, he hurts every member of the Negro race!" As we will see in the next chapter, some former slaves shared similar views. The painful history of sexual violence against black people inspired Livingston to urge African Americans to forget the past, to especially forget ideas about interracial marriage, and to move into a future characterized by a proud "Negro race."

This was no easy task, as Georgia Douglas Johnson's 1926 drama *Blue Blood* helped to explain. *Blue Blood*, first performed by New York's Krigwa Players, portrayed an African American couple who discover that they share the same white father. Using the narrative devices of miscegenation, incest, and color-conscious class pretensions in African American communities, *Blue Blood* reflected the difficulty of forgetting the violent and coercive history that often lay at the heart of racial identity, and black-white sexual relations.[28] Early-twentieth-century black Americans could not forget this history, because they were still living it.

## Black Playwrights and the Production of Historical Memory

Anti-lynching dramas belong to an era in which all Americans felt deep anxiety about the racial implications of interracial sex and sexuality. Historians and cultural studies scholars have also observed that the forces of "modernism" heightened these anxieties.[29] In the North, the "New South," and the West, a growing American preoccupation with consumerism, leisure, and a "new permissiveness" emerged. For white Americans, the forces of modernism evoked both optimism about the economic future of the republic and pessimism about the frailties of the United States' racial future. On the American stage and screen, images of bumbling, fried-chicken-eating "Sambos" reassured white audiences that blacks remained subordinate and distant from mainstream society. These same audiences were cautioned, however, not to let down their guard and open the door to "social equality" and its inevitable final act: "race suicide." By the 1910s and 1920s, D. W. Griffith's silent movie *The Musketeers of Pig Alley* (1912), the romantic comedy *The Flapper* (1920), and Rachel Crothers's play *Nice People* (1921) presented audiences with cautionary tales of immigrant gangsters and teenage girls overindulging in the consumeristic and interpersonal excesses of the "flapper."[30] Social commentaries from the likes of former president Theodore Roosevelt to the eugenicist Madison Grant warned that such material indulgences should not be enjoyed at the expense of the reproduction of a vibrant, intelligent, and pure white American race.[31] Set against this social and cultural background, it made perfect sense for white playwrights and movie producers to either marginalize or demonize black characters as the plot line demanded.[32]

African American playwrights and audiences were also influenced by eugenic discourse, but in ways that reflected a different historical subjectivity. For example, Myrtle Smith Livingston's anti-lynching play *For Unborn Children* (1926) structured its narrative around the idea of race pride and the author's conviction that interracial marriage hurt black communities more than it harmed whites.[33] Recent scholarship has also noted the popular uses of eugenic discourse among African Americans. The historian Michele Mitchell demonstrates how popular theories of eugenics influenced "black analyses of intragroup vitality."[34] The early-twentieth-century memories of former slaves, who insisted, as historian Marie Jenkins Schwartz has shown, that "slaveholders expected to appropriate and exploit the reproductive lives of enslaved women," resulted in African Americans incorporating the language of popular eugenics to emphasize the importance of sexual morality, the judicious selection of a marriage partner, and family cohesion.[35]

The emergence of black theater companies in the early twentieth century aimed to rectify the racist portrayal of African Americans on stage and screen. Black theater companies combined high- and lowbrow aesthetics, fusing "minstrel humor, modern dance, ragtime music, divergent styles, and burlesque, along with parodies of race, class, and gender."[36] The productions that these theater companies staged also reminded black actors and audiences that the legacies of slavery endured in the racial politics of the Jim Crow era. Black theater performers used parody, a performative style that provided audiences with a politicized theatrical statement that subtly encouraged resistance against white historical accounts of slavery and early-twentieth-century race relations.[37]

The past and the present, the comedic and the dramatic—all of these elements were fused together in the black theater. Musical productions such as *In Dahomey* (1902–5); *Abyssinia* (1906–7); and *Bandanna Land* (1907–9) combined comedy, satire, and historical reconstruction to present an African American interpretation of black history that stretched from early modern Africa to the Jim Crow South. In scores of nonprofit, community-based theater companies, African Americans staged productions that dealt with a diverse range of historically interconnected issues that included the Middle Passage, sexual exploitation during slavery, and rape and lynching in Jim Crow America. The scope of black theater and musical productions was as diverse as black social, cultural, and intellectual life itself.[38]

None of these theatrical re-creations would have been possible had it not been for the creativity of black playwrights. Mary P. Burrill's *Aftermath* (1919), for example, epitomized the thrust of this creative spirit. Born in Washington, D.C., in 1884, Burrill attended the M Street School (which became Dunbar High School). In 1929 she earned her Bachelor of Literary Interpretation degree from Emerson College, Boston. Burrill published only two of her plays, *Aftermath* and *They That Sit in Darkness* (both published in 1919). During her lifetime, Burrill's energies were channeled into her work as a teacher and director, both students and colleagues agreeing that she was an inspirational mentor.[39] Burrill's two published plays, however, highlight her strength of mind and political convictions born from the racial realities of black life in white supremacist America. *They That Sit in Darkness*, for example, was a pro-birth-control play that reflected Burrill's "anguish [for] African-American motherhood."[40]

*Aftermath* also addressed themes of black motherhood, in addition to tackling themes such as African American masculinity, family fragility, and nationalism. The opening scene, set in the "Thornton Cabin in South Carolina," depicts slavery in all but name. In this dreary postbellum setting, Mam Sue, "an old woman," and Millie, "a slender brown girl of sixteen," are engaged in domestic chores. The burning logs in the cabin's fireplace crackle and split apart, offering the audience a prophesied vision of events to come. Indeed, we learn that Mam Sue lost her husband to a lynch mob, his body desecrated on a savage pyre. "Ah see'd *evul* doin's," Mam Sue informs Millie of the night her husband, Millie's father, was lynched. The splitting log jolts Mam Sue's memory, and she informs Millie that she "tole yo' po' daddy to keep away f'om town de nex' day wid his cotton." On that tragic night, God spoke to Mam Sue through the cabin fire, just as "He" had just spoken to her. Millie, however, is unmoved by her mother's prophecy. According to Millie, "Da Lawd's done fu'got us po' cullud people."[41]

Amid this mother-daughter conversation, news of John's homecoming from the World War I battlefields of Europe reaches the cabin. John is Mam Sue's son and Millie's brother; he has no knowledge that his father died at the hands of a lynch mob. After expressing his joy to be home, John offers audiences an explanation for why he fought. He recalls that "lots of times . . . in the trenches when I wuz dog-tired, an' sick, an' achin' wid the cold I uster say: well, if we're sufferin' all this for the oppressed, like they tell us, then Mam Sue, an' dad, an Millie come in on that—they'll git some good ou'n it if I don't!"[42] John, having been trained to perform his duty and fight for democracy and freedom, presents a masculine version of Millie's suspicion about the futility of religion. While not shunning the "Lawd," John is quick to observe that "beyon' a certain point prayers ain't no good!" Burrill thus crafts a powerful scene in which a divide over the importance of religious faith and the utility of direct political and military protest was developing along distinct generational lines.

It was an emerging generation of young black men and women—both on stage and off—who refused to be intimidated by white supremacy and lynch mobs during the interwar period. John symbolizes this generation. Unwilling to hide his World War I pistols, John receives the news of his father's lynching—"They burnt him down by the big gum tree!"—inadvertently. His sister explains that he had gotten into a "row wid ole Mister . . . 'bout the price of cotton." For his impudence to a white man, John's father lost his life in the most brutal way imaginable. John, who was especially close to his father, is enraged by this news. He complains bitterly that while "I've been helpin' the w'ite man git his freedom . . . they're burnin' an killin' my folks here at home! To Hell with 'em." In the final dramatic scene, John declares: "I ain't skeered o' none of 'em! I've faced worse guns than any sneakin' hounds kin show me! To Hell with 'em!" In haste, John leaves the cabin and "disappears in the gathering darkness." The audience is left to ponder his fate.[43]

Like many other anti-lynching melodramas (such as Randolph Edmonds's *Bad Man*), Burrill's *Aftermath* did not confine itself to issues of black masculinity, family fragility, and nationalism in the interwar years; it both addressed and represented a rising generation of black Americans determined to seek redress for history's ills and to attack the core expression of early-twentieth-century racism: lynching. Thus, by the 1920s and 1930s African American playwrights had committed themselves to framing both history and contemporary racial issues in increasingly political terms. This effort received a jolt of creative energy from the writers, actors, and activists associated with the Harlem Renaissance. It is important not to overstate the historical significance of the Harlem Renaissance; indeed, during the height of the Harlem Renaissance African Americans owned and operated only 157 of the nation's 5,000 theaters. Nonetheless, in their commentaries on race and the legacy of slavery and in their critiques of rape and lynching, the work of black playwrights presented both profound and rare public expressions of how black Americans lived with the legacy of slavery.

One of the more politically oriented theatrical movements of the 1920s was the black little theater movement. This movement originated among Harlem Renaissance intellectual luminaries such as W. E. B. Du Bois, Alain Locke, Jessie Fauset, and James Weldon Johnson. In his 1922 essay "Steps toward the Negro Theatre," Locke explained the motivation for the formation of the movement. He claimed that its members were driven by a desire to stage productions that avoided excesses of commercialism in preference for a type of "race drama" that would eventually "become peculiarly the ward of our colleges, as new drama, as art-drama, and as folk-drama."[44] Locke and the black little theater movement thus felt driven to project the voices and experiences of ordinary black Americans by promoting "folk culture" in their writing and in theater houses.

Whether Locke and the black little theater movement successfully promoted African American folk culture is a matter of ongoing scholarly debate. What is more important is the voice that the movement attempted to give to ordinary black Americans. In productions such as Willis Richardson's *The Deacon's Awakening* (1920), Flourney Miller and Aubrey Lyles's *Shuffle Along* (1921), Zora Neale Hurston's *Color Struck* (1925), and Marita Odette Bonner's *The Purple Flower* (1928), we see on stage, and hear in the dialogue, the memory of slavery, the fear of lynching, and the often biting, sometimes funny, treatment of racial and sexual stereotypes.[45] From reflective portrayals of sexism and male chauvinism in *The Deacon's Awakening*, Hurston's exploration of color prejudice among African Americans in *Color Struck*, and Bonner's overt call for social and cultural revolution in *The Purple Flower*, black playwrights and the theater productions they helped to create during the 1920s refused to avoid the tensions between slavery and freedom.

One of the most prolific and influential African American playwrights to address the memory and legacy of slavery was Randolph Edmonds. Edmonds was professor of English and director of dramatics at Morgan College. Born on April 30, 1900, Edmonds came to be known as the "dean of black education theatre." He provided black actors with roles that explored the depths of African American humanity, connecting modern encounters with racism with the dark recesses of American slavery. Edmonds wrote the types of melodramas and comedies that Eulalie Spence called for in her 1928 essay, "A Criticism of the Negro Drama." Spence urged black playwrights to "portray the life of their people, their foibles, their sorrows, ambitions, and defeats; that these portrayals be told with tenderness and skill and a knowledge of the theatre and the technique of the times."[46]

Edmonds's work embodied both Spence's call and Locke's theatrical vision. Edmonds produced a rich archive of plays and prose that shed a sliver of light on the life, memories, and feelings of black Americans during the early twentieth century. By his own admission, however, Edmonds was slow to appreciate the power of black history in early-twentieth-century America. Reconciling himself to the importance of engaging with black America's history, he grew to appreciate the work of the African American historian Carter G. Woodson.[47] Addressing the complexities of African American history, Edmonds acknowledged the profound cultural and political purpose of his own work in an overtly racist society. In 1949 he made an unequivocally clear statement about why it was important for black playwrights and artists to contest the historical distortions in white popular culture:

All the multiplicity of books of whatever type from "Gone With the Wind" forward or backwards, runs to the same pattern. There is the Big House or Mansion with its courtly slave master (or owner after 1865) and his wife, a pure and majestic southern belle. There are the slaves' or workers' quarters of dilapidated cabins with varied types of Negro stereotypes. Among these are the full-bosomed mammy or cook, subservient plantation uncles, banjo and guitar playing minstrels or buffoons, loyal servants of the big house, half wits, elders, free and easy sensuous women, voodoo characters, thieves, rogues, and bad men. All of these speak a dialect that is sometimes humorous and at other times full of poetic beauty and truth. The whole is overlaid with the psychological element of superiority of the whites, and the rightness of the Negroes' place as hewers of wood and drawers of water.[48]

Edmonds's critique of the self-delusions and historical misrepresentations of mainstream (white) culture bespoke the ongoing legacy of racial slavery in twentieth-century America. Through repetition and a willful manipulation of black folk culture, white culture makers presented a history that not only looked back longingly on the days of slavery but strove to re-create it.

So how did Edmonds imagine that the theater might be used to produce a counternarrative to the racial stereotypes and historical misrepresentations in mainstream popular culture? He used, not coincidentally, "dialect dramas." Dialect dramas were often criticized for reinforcing racial stereotypes of "Negroes" as "profane, shiftless, and exotic."[49] Edmonds disagreed.[50] He defended dialect dramas as a medium through which the "sorrows, ambitions, and defeats" of black American life and history could be presented on the stage. Edmonds aimed to tap into the nobler qualities of black "folk" culture and to find and celebrate heroic black characters amid the racist and pejorative imagery that pervaded American mainstream culture during the early twentieth century.[51]

Dialect dramas allowed Edmonds to explore the central concern in African American folk culture: the struggle for existence, particularly among black working-class families. Here the fragile balance between the reproduction of life and the inevitability of death came into focus.[52] None of Edmonds's plays highlight this tension better than *Breeders* (1930), a deeply moving play that explores the fragility of life for the enslaved and the specter of slave breeding on the antebellum plantation. Carter Woodson found himself so taken by *Breeders* that he offered Edmonds his highest praise, referring to his work as "historical."[53] Throughout the Great Depression, African American theater companies presented Edmonds's slice of history to African American audiences across the country. From the Morgan Players in Baltimore, the Olympian Players in Pittsburgh, the Columbus Experimental Little Theater in Ohio, and the Players Guild at Dillard University in New Orleans, black theater companies staged productions of this historically wrenching and politically confrontational play.[54] In presenting Edmonds's *Breeders* on the stage, black performers brought to life those traumatic stories of slavery that the elderly spoke about in hushed terms, if they spoke about them at all.

*Breeders* opens inside a slave cabin, its "rough and old" walls and "dilapidated" furniture setting a bleak scene. Mammy, a slave mother, sits amid this bleakness, consumed with her thoughts, her anxieties, and her inner grief. Mammy is middle-aged and graying. She looks older than her years, prematurely aged by a life of reproductive and physical labor combined with psychological terror that Edmonds imagined was part of plantation life.

In the opening scene, we learn that Mammy's grief and anxiety is a product of both past and present abuses. She gave birth to at least three slaves and has lived with a deep sadness since the sudden death of her children. Indeed, Mammy's pain is, in Edmonds's rendering, reflective of the synergy between life and death in the mind's eye of the slave mother. Perhaps this is why Mammy is always praying, as she is in the bleak surroundings of Edmonds's opening scene. Here Mammy reflects sadly on the fate that befell two of her sons. We learn that Mammy's sons recently tried to escape from slavery. Captured by slave catchers as they strove to steal themselves to freedom, one of her sons was shot and killed, the other badly beaten and sold. Wiping tears from her eyes, Mammy recalls: "Dey both was good boys, dey didn't mean tuh harm nobody."[55]

Mammy's daughter, Ruth, offers her mother little comfort in this melancholic opening scene. Reflective of the terrorism of Jim Crow violence as much as the exploitative nature of slavery, Edmonds has Ruth convey the idea that whites view blacks as subhuman. "Yuh know how de white folks feel," Ruth informs her mother. "Slaves is jes slaves wid dem. Dey ain't s'posed tuh have no feeling." Edmonds thus begins to unravel the connection between life and death in his rendering of African American folk culture. Mammy has presumably been a "breeder" as well as a domestic slave for her master, yet the white people thought as little about killing her sons as they did in encouraging Mammy to bear them in the first place. Conscious of this, Ruth instructs her mother to stop crying because "Dey is better off daid. Every slave is better off daid."[56]

Edmonds's *Breeders* exhibits a profound sensitivity to the suffering of enslaved women. In the early twentieth century, black Americans remembered slave women like Mammy as the victims of the vilest and most terrifying abuses. And it is the exploited nature of Mammy, her ideally unfeeling yet productive (and reproductive) function on the plantation, that prompts her to take flight from her conversation with Ruth and tend to her bread-making duties for the next day's guest. Mammy suspects that the mystery guest is a "slave buyer," and she rushes to the Big House to tend to her duties, leaving no time to come to terms with the depth of her loss. Instead, she feels ensnared in a complex web of slaveholding power and enslaved powerlessness in which the nameless slave buyer will likely cause unspeakable pain for a mother the following morning. Mammy states "sadly," "Dey aint told me his name yit, but Ah'se sho dat some mammy'll be breakin' huh heart crying when he leaves 'cause huh chile done gone."[57]

But something much worse than the unnamed slave trader's lust for profit is about to befall Mammy and Ruth. David, a slave on the plantation, is in love with Ruth. Ruth is unaware of David's feelings, but when Mammy leaves to tend to her domestic duties in the Big House, David enters and dramatically declares his love. Reluctantly, Ruth returns David's feelings, but she confides that she has no intention of ever getting married and having children. The manipulative slave-breeding practices imposed by slave owners and slave traders convince Ruth that death would be preferable to the type of emotional pain she sees her mother endure on a daily basis. She explains: "Ah don't want tuh marry nobody an' have chilluns lak Mammy so dey could grow up an' be whupped tuh death, or sold down de river. Ah don't want tuh grief ma heart out lak Mammy."[58]

Edmonds highlights a depth of feeling and emotion among the female members of this enslaved family that is designed to emphasize the cruelly exploitative nature of southern slave-breeding practices. He does this abruptly and, as a result, with great theatrical power. A knock at the cabin door sees the plantation overseer enter. At his side is the slave Salem, a towering figure of a man. Salem is the plantation "stud," and, under orders from the plantation master, Salem is to take the fifteen-year-old Ruth as his "wife"—his tenth "wife" to be exact. Ruth, having just pronounced her love for David—who is now hiding to avoid the overseer's detection—wants nothing to do with Salem or her master's dehumanizing slave-breeding schemes. Salem, however, is a determined man; his sense of masculinity—ordinarily circumscribed by the disciplinary boundaries of the plantation regime—is emboldened by his role as the plantation "stud." Salem therefore insists that he will make Ruth like him, declaring of his ten wives: "Ah'se been able tuh make dem all satisfied. An' dey growed tuh lak me, too."[59]

Having heard enough of Salem's boasting, David springs from his hiding place and confronts the plantation "stud." But Salem is unmoved by David's professions of love for Ruth, mocking the much smaller David by referring to him as sexually impotent. Salem's words strike a bitter blow to David's masculine pride, and a vicious and violent struggle ensues, resulting in David's sudden and bloody death. Amid this scene of violence and grief, Salem remains true to his determination to make Ruth like him and, if necessary, use force to have sex with her that evening. Ruth, grief stricken and terrified all at once, turns to Mammy, who has reentered the cabin, and receives her mother's hard-bitten wisdom. "In dis world," Mammy instructs Ruth, "black women ain't nothing but breeders, tuh have chilluns fuh de white folks tuh sell down de river lak dey do horses and cows."[60]

Ruth, unable to bear the thought of falling prey to the slave-breeding system and all the grief she knows it will cause her, takes drastic action. In a moment of Shakespearean-like drama, Ruth reaches between her breasts, reveals a vile of poison, and declares: "Ah ain't gwine tuh be no breeder."[61] She quickly consumes the poison and is soon lying on the floor, awaiting death. As Ruth lies dying, Mammy prays the slave woman's lament: "Stop it soon, Lawd! Stop it soon an' let Yo' chilluns drink of de water of freedom, an' put on de garments of righteousness."[62] Ruth chose death as her path to righteousness; she refused to be violated by Salem, and resisted her master's orders that she bear children who would later be sold down the river for a profit. When life meant so much pain, death was the only freedom imaginable.

## Conclusion

Randolph Edmonds's *Breeders* was written to be more than entertainment for black audiences; it was written as history. Written and performed in an era of intense racism, sexism, and widespread poverty, Edmonds's folk drama was history from the bottom up, a history about working people forced to labor and reproduce in the vilest context imaginable. Indeed, it was one's historical imagination that Edmonds hoped to ignite in those who read *Breeders* or saw productions of it throughout the country. And having sparked this historical imagination into action, readers or audiences would feel inspired to take political action to right the wrongs of the past, wrongs that felt so very real and ongoing to millions of black Americans in the 1930s and 1940s.

For Edmonds, as for many other African American playwrights of his era, black drama was much more than simply entertainment. It was a rich and diverse medium through which African Americans could *learn* about their shared history. In slavery and in freedom, the memory and daily reality of rape, family separations, and lynching merged. For black Americans, historical interpretation was as much a social commentary as a political statement. Perhaps the black writers and playwrights of the 1920s and 1930s were right; maybe it was time to take a stand and fight, once again, for a new birth of freedom.

Mammy's haunting words in *Breeders*—"black women ain't nothing but breeders"—captured the sense of degradation and sexual exploitation that African Americans associated with slavery and freedom. Where "bucks" and "wenches" were objects of sexual exploitation during slavery, after slavery the violence used to objectify black Americans as "horses and cows" was redirected toward the brutal control and, at times, destruction of African American life.

Embedded within the narrative layers of black theatrical writing, then, was an inescapable dualism: the struggle for life and against premature death. The bookends of life—birth and death—that white Americans took for granted harbored historical and political meanings for African Americans that had been born in the "dark void" of slavery times and perpetuated in freedom by segregation laws, white male rapists of black domestics, and lynch mobs. While many blacks tried, it was hard to forget slavery; playwrights like Randolph Edmonds and Mary Burrill refused to ignore the images of slave women being sexually violated, children torn from families, and black bodies hanging from trees. For former slaves in early-twentieth-century America, such imagery was more than a defining part of a collective historical imagination; it was the life they had once lived, witnessed, and tried so hard to forget. In the depths of the Great Depression, these memories were awoken and relived in the mind thanks to the prodding of federal government employees. The narratives of former slaves that employees of the Works Project Administration collected would, in time, add new interpretive layers to the way slave breeding was (and is) remembered.

# 5

## The WPA Narratives and Slave Breeding

During the Great Depression, formerly enslaved African Americans shared their memories of southern slavery with interviewers from the Works Progress Administration (WPA). Between 1936 and 1938, more than two thousand former slaves from seventeen states narrated their recollections of slavery.[1] John Lomax, a key adviser on WPA writers' projects, noted that "the main purpose of these detailed and homely questions is to get the Negro interested in talking about the days of slavery."[2] Given this objective, is it possible to recover the former slaves' memory of even the darkest aspects of slavery, such as allegations of slave breeding? According to historian Paul Escott, it is. Escott details the different types of "breeding" recalled by former slaves: "Master directed pairings on his plantation"; "Master influenced pairings on his plantation"; "Master rewarded fertility or sold the barren"; "Master used a man to impregnate through visiting or polygamy"; "Master rented a man (or men) from another plantation"; and "Other methods."[3] Given the racial dynamic of many of the interviews—that is, white interviewer and elderly African American male or female—it is safe to assume that the underreporting of breeding practices was fairly common. For some former slaves, especially women, concealing such information was a means of protecting themselves, their family, and their community from the racial stereotypes directed at black Americans during the early twentieth century.[4] For others, narrating episodes of slave breeding was a powerful means through which to point an accusatory finger at the slave South and highlight the immoral economy white southerners violently imposed on generation after generation of African Americans.[5]

The WPA narratives provide a rare glimpse into how black Americans who experienced slavery narrated their memories or, equally powerful, wanted to forget slave life. Many of the narratives are reflective of the "oral tradition and life histories" that have long been a distinctive feature of African American culture and literature.[6] While caution must be exercised when using the narratives, just as care should be used when analyzing all historical records, the WPA narratives are no ordinary set of documents. They narrate America's darkest sin, slavery, in an age when the racial etiquette of the early twentieth century demanded that black people tell white folks what whites wanted to hear.[7] The former Texas slave Martin Jackson gave voice to this sentiment: "Lots of old slaves closes the door before they tell the truth about their days of slavery. When the door is open, they tell how kind their masters was and how rosy it all was."[8]

The context in which the narratives were collected has also led scholars to question the "biases" and the historical "truth" contained within them. B. A. Botkin observed this "problem" when he wrote about the "bias and fallibility of both informants and interviewers" involved in the WPA project.[9] Historians have grappled with these issues for decades. Since World War II, two general trends have emerged in the way American historians use the WPA narratives. First, historians extract quotations from the testimonies of former slaves to make a larger point about antebellum slavery. Used in this way, the WPA narratives play a supporting role to the written records bequeathed to posterity by white plantation owners, government officials, and Euro-American and European travelers to the South. A second cohort of historians, beginning in the 1970s, have drawn on the WPA narratives to emphasize the agency of the enslaved in narrating their own social and cultural life. These historians—who include George Rawick, John Blassingame, Herbert Gutman, and, more recently, Stephanie Camp—have produced valuable histories of slave culture that reveal the polyvalent forms of slave resistance and emphasize how the enslaved strove to cultivate romantic relationships and forge families in the slave South.[10] For example, Camp's provocative use of slave narratives builds on a generation of slavery scholarship. Camp attempts to demonstrate how the songs, dances, and social gatherings of the enslaved were "inflected by the spirit of resistance."[11] Her history is a story of slave agency; it is a tale of the enduring spirit of African American people in chains.[12]

Not all slaves regaled WPA interviewers with tales of "sociables."[13] As such, the WPA narratives contain another history that warrants telling. It is a history that speaks to the intellectual agency of former slaves in early-twentieth-century America. It is, to be sure, a darker history, but one that is powerful for the lessons—both historical and contemporary—that it sought to convey. For those former slaves who dared speak about sexual exploitation in the 1930s, there existed a defiant insistence that the narratives they presented were "de facts." The historical and cultural value of former slaves' recounting of this darker history has less to do with the historical profession's noble, if misguided, quest for the "facts" about the past and more to do with the didactic nature of the history that former slaves narrated.[14]

In relation to slave-breeding practices, then, there are three main points that former slaves typically emphasized. First, slaves insisted that slave owners, overseers, and slave traders selected particularly fecund men and women to breed slaves. They insisted that these men were known as plantation "studs" or "bucks," the women as "wenches." Second, they said that the forced breeding of slaves not only represented the commodification of slave sexuality but also created a set of dehumanizing social practices that separated the "breeding" slaves from the average field slave. Third, and most enduringly, the imposition of slave-breeding regimes on black men and women separated family members and caused unquantifiable amounts of grief that lasted well into the twentieth century.

This chapter explores the language used by former slaves to describe slave-breeding practices in the era of Jim Crow segregation and violence.[15] Not unlike early-twentieth-century black scholars, writers, and playwrights, those former slaves who participated in the WPA interviews defined slave breeding with the above factors in mind. They emphasized how slave breeding constituted a coercive set of practices that included the sexual exploitation of enslaved women, violence against black men, and emotional suffering following the sale and separation of enslaved family members. These themes—sexual exploitation, racial violence, and the struggle to maintain enduring family bonds—had particularly powerful discursive qualities for the WPA interviewees.

## "Studs," "Bucks," and "Wenches" in the WPA Narratives

According to former slaves, slave breeding relied on the existence of plantation "studs" or "bucks" and breeding "wenches." The language that some slaves used to represent coercive sexual acts was sensational, but it served an important narrative purpose: it reflected the moral depths that former slaves believed white men and women had stooped to in order to keep them enslaved. Julia Malone, for example, remembered that her mother was a breeding "wench." She claimed, "My mammy was a big woman."[16] Peter Brown insisted that slave masters "prized fast breeders." Brown stated that his mother "was a fast breeder," giving birth to "three sets of twins."[17] Steve Robertson, reminiscing about his father's sexual prowess, referring to the existence of plantation "bucks." Robertson testified that "de marster picks de buck fo' to sire de chilluns wid de womens dey wants, an' it am usually de mostest p'olific."[18] And Willie Blackwell informed his WPA interviewer that his father had been a plantation "stud." Blackwell remembered that "my pappy am de Blackwell stud, de kind of a big, strong, powe'ful nigger dat de plantation ownahs wants to breed dey slave stock up wid."[19] The imagery these former slaves evoked was of men and women whose bodily proportions, physical fitness, and reproductive capacity were used to support a program of human engineering in the plantation South. For example, one former slave remembered that slaves "were propagated by selected male negroes, who were kept for that purpose, the owners of this privileged negro, charged a fee of one out of every four of his offspring for his services."[20] Another former slave, Alice Wright, claimed that her father told her that "they put medicine in the water (cisterns) to make the young slaves have more children."[21] In other words, a number of former slaves depicted slave masters willfully selecting slaves that they believed would add to the *quantity* and *quality* of their slave stock. Such representations were a far cry from the immoral practices and squalid living conditions that antebellum opponents of slavery emphasized. In an age when popular racial discourse was inflected with the tenets of social Darwinism and eugenics, these recollections present the slave master as cruel and oppressive, a type of antebellum mad scientist, while the enslaved men and women represent the raw material from which "droves and droves of Niggers" were biologically engineered.[22]

To better understand why former slaves used words such as *stud*, *buck*, and *wench* to represent those exploited by slave-breeding practices, it is important to briefly survey the etymology of these words. The word *stud* was used in England as early as 1000 C.E. It innocuously denoted knobs or nailheads in a wooden structure. By the early modern period, "stud" was used to describe a horse bred for reproductive purposes. This usage made its way to the American colonies. However, it was not until 1803, when Rev. Manasseh Cutler wrote about "the famous white stud, an Arabian horse, called the Dey of Algiers, on the ground," that American literature of all genres became riddled with references to "studs."[23] Linguistic scholars contend that only during the late nineteenth century did the term *stud* connote a sexually active man—a "ladies man"—a term that African American men appropriated in the 1920s to tout the mythical proportions of their sexual potency. This latter point is of direct interest to the WPA narratives. It raises questions about whether former slaves imposed the racial and sexual language of the early twentieth century back onto antebellum

America. They may have. It is likely, however, that the stories of slave management and animal husbandry that appeared in the South's agricultural magazines during the antebellum era reached former slaves, if only by word of mouth, and left an indelible mark on their memories.[24]

If historical uncertainty clouds the use of the word *stud* in antebellum slavery, the word *buck* exhibits a similar ambiguity. Linguistic scholars generally agree that the word *buck* was in use during the Middle English period. Around 1100 C.E., the word *bucca*, meaning "male goat," appeared for the first time. By the 1600s, *bucking*, a derivative of the word *buck*, denoted sexual copulation, usually between a man and a farm animal.[25] In the American colonies, a "buck" was a male deer and a "buckskin" was used as a type of currency between European and Native American traders. Thus the word *buck* acquired a commercial connotation as the American colonies developed and eventually slid into a revolutionary war with England. Indeed, the era of revolution in the late eighteenth century appears to have ushered in a shift in the use of the term *buck*. The historian Richard Follett argues that the word *buck* "derived from its Revolutionary meaning of a 'dashing, young, virile man,' which by the nineteenth century denoted a 'self-proclaimed fascinator of women.'"[26] Add a liberal dose of nineteenth-century racial "science"—as the Scottish physician Alexander Munro did in 1825 when he testified that "generally speaking, the penis is larger in the Negro than in the European"—and the word *buck* defined—not entirely out of line with its etymology—the animalistic lust of the typical male "Negro" slave in the American South.[27]

The word *wench* also had its origins in the Middle English period. The original meaning of *wench* was relatively benign, referring to a girl or young woman.[28] However, by the fourteenth century, *wench* denoted a servant girl whose qualities included fickleness, unsteadiness, and loose morals. These characteristics became increasingly common in defining a prostitute during the early modern period and into the eighteenth century. The historian Mark Morton observes that "by the mid fourteenth century *wench* had developed a negative sense as it came to denote sexually active women; this negative connotation was sufficiently faint, though, that it often needed to be reinforced through the use of adjectives, as in *common wench*, *light wench* and *wanton wench*."[29] English settlers brought these gendered and sexualized definitions of *wench* to the New World. However, by the late eighteenth and early nineteenth centuries, the word *wench* needed only minor qualification in the racialized context of North America. Indeed, while the *Dictionary of American English* dates the first usage of the term *nigger wench* to 1837, white men, such as Lieutenant Colonel Thomas Staunton St. Clair, appear to have used the term prior to this date.[30] In 1834, St. Clair spoke plainly about "my two nigger wenches," the sexual implications of such statements being understood implicitly.[31]

African Americans recognized the racial and sexual meanings associated with words like *buck, stud,* and *wench.* Whether these terms had the sexual connotations in antebellum America that they had by the 1930s is open to debate; what is more important is that former slaves recognized that "calling a man [a] 'nigger buck and a woman a nigger winch [*sic*]'" conveyed a powerful message about how enslaved human beings were treated like animals—to be bred, raised, and sold in a debasing form of commodification.[32] These sexualized terms had become part of the United States' racist lexicon by the early twentieth century. Accordingly, the *Dictionary of American English* lists derivations of these terms such as *Nigger-boy, nigger-talk, nigger-wench,* and *nigger-job.*[33]

This sexually and racially charged language shaped the way former slaves recalled sex, "marriage," and family life. For example, Josephine Bacchus combined vague references to early-twentieth-century racial "science" and recollections of slave breeding. "You see," Bacchus matter-of-factly stated, "dey would have two or three women on de plantation dat was good breeders." Bacchus, who claimed to know little of her mother's life, emphasized the importance that slave owners placed on the rapidity of childbirth, claiming that "dey would have chillun pretty regular 'fore freedom come." The motive for such schemes, Bacchus suggested, was both social and economic. She claimed that "de white people sho been mighty proud to see dey niggers spreadin out in dem days, so dey tell me. Yes, mam, dey was glad to have a heap of colored people bout dem cause white folks wouldn' work den no more den dey can work dese days like de colored people can."[34]

Bacchus's representation of slave breeding was of a system in which black people were bred to work tirelessly for whites. Embedded in this narrative, and echoing Harriet Jacobs's nineteenth-century portrayal of slavery, is a didactic tale of how enslaved men, and especially women, had little choice, much less control, over their reproductive lives. Bacchus's reference to "'fore freedom come" also suggested that change over time was important to the way African American women remembered the imposed purpose of pregnancy and childbirth before the Civil War, with greater reproductive freedom for black women being implied for the postbellum era. While the post-slavery reality may have differed, it is important to note the gendered nature of representations of slave breeding. Powerful "bucks," or "studs," were remembered as enslaved models of masculine vigor, while women were prized for being prolific childbearers, human vessels who would increase the master's profit with each live birth. The perceived potency of "de buck" foregrounds a hypermasculine male slave, while the "p'otly womens" who exhibited a tendency to be "mostest p'olific" acquired a special status as breeding "wenches."

Some former slaves informed WPA interviewers that the perception of sexual potency afforded the plantation "stud" and "wench" a special status on the plantation. For enslaved men, being seen as especially potent accorded a masculine status predicated on one's perceived sexual abilities. According to the former slave Jacob Manson, the plantation "stud" was a prized possession on the master's plantation. "Generally," Manson insisted, "dey give one man four women an dat man better not have nuttin' to do wid de udder women an' de women better not have nuttin' to do wid udder men."[35] Harre Quarls, a former Missouri slave, remembered the hypermasculine status accorded some male slaves in the context of plantation polygamy. Following the abolition of slavery, Quarls was distressed when Freedmen's Bureau officials instructed him that the law recognized only one of his three wives. Quarls complained, "Boss say I had three wives. When Ise sot free, dey wouldn't let me live with but one."[36] For Quarls, the postwar policing of his sexuality and marriages was onerous. "Captain, that ain't right," Quarls protested. "I wants all three."[37]

Former slaves, men mostly, also described the hypermasculine qualities of male relatives by referencing their physical proportions. Zeno John, whose father was reportedly a plantation stud, insisted, "My daddy was much of a man, yes, sir."[38] Similarly, George Austin claimed that his "Pappy am used wid de diffe'nt womens on de place . . . him am such a fine big nigger."[39] Size, it seems, mattered on the plantation. Ida Blackshear Hutchinson, for insistence, remembered that her grandfather was "the Giant Breeder" who fathered fifty-six children.[40] Within the prescribed boundaries of southern slave society, these former slaves suggested, some men felt physically empowered by their role as the plantation "stud."

Feelings of hypermasculine empowerment came at a price. Former male slaves gave voice to a deep and enduring sense of lost love and emotional pain at the forced severance of family ties. Willie Blackwell's recollections were revealing in this respect. Blackwell remembered meeting a former slave who informed him that "he was sold away f'om his wife an' chilluns jus' cause his Master wanted a big man fo' de stud, lak he was." Far from reveling in tales of sexual conquest, Blackwell's friend expressed his desire to find his wife, his first love. As Blackwell remembered it, "He still loved dat woman."[41]

This sense of emotional loss among formerly enslaved men could at times manifest itself in a tendency to represent female slaves—the breeding "wenches" of the plantation—as powerless victims of slave-breeding practices. Alex Woods, for instance, claimed that "if a woman wus a good breeder, she sold high, sometime bringin' five thousand dollars. De man who wus doin' de buyin' would inspect dem. Dey would look in dere mouthes, and look 'em over just like buyin' hosses."[42] According to Henry Buttler, this approach to slave breeding was driven by a desire to reproduce physically improved chattel specimens. "The position taken by the master," Buttler explained to his WPA interviewer, "was not wholly due to a disregard for the Negro's feelings, nor a disregard for the sacred bonds of matrimony. The main factor involved was the desire on the part of the master to rear Negroes with perfect physiques."[43] As another former slave recalled, the motive of the master was simple: to "make de woman let de big man be with her so's dere would be big children, which dey could sell well."[44] Former male slaves remember the victimization of breeding "wenches" with deep regret. In these traumatic narratives, enslaved men could do little to protect mother, wife, or daughter from the slave-breeding designs of the master. Thus an underlying tone of masculine regret mixed with tales of sexual boasting, the focus eventually falling on the emotional pain caused by being unable to adequately protect "our" women from sexual exploitation.

When formerly enslaved women spoke about violence, sexual exploitation, and "breeding," they generally focused on the physical and emotional pain that they or their ancestors were forced to endure during slavery. For example, Hilliard Yellerday's master "had so many slaves he did not know all their names. His fortune was his slaves." As such, Yellerday claimed that a "slave girl was expected to have children as soon as she became a woman."[45] Martha Jackson recalled that her aunt delivered children for her master's profit, almost on a yearly basis. Jackson evoked images of the physical toll that regular pregnancy and childbirth must surely have taken. She also spoke about the emotional scars that such abuse (or, from the master's perspective, use) produced in her aunt. She stated that her aunt "was er breeder 'oman en brought in chillun ev'y twelve month' jes' lack a cow bringin' in a calf."[46] If Jackson's testimony is to be believed, her aunt must have birthed her children and not suckled them at the breast, thereby increasing the speed at which her body was once again ready for pregnancy and childbirth. Nothing in Jackson's testimony indicates the master's paternalistic care for her aunt's long-term physical well-being, much less her emotional health.

Other formerly enslaved women remembered the regularity of pregnancy and childbirth. Louise Oliphant recalled that her mother seemed to be pregnant every ten months. To encourage such fecundity, Oliphant claimed that her Virginia master "wanted his slaves to have plenty of chillun [and] never would make you do much work when you had a lot of chillun, and had them fast."[47] Amy Chapman, interviewed in Alabama, recalled that she gave birth to many children of unknown paternity. She declared that her master had "a lot of slaves" and that she "had plenty of chilluns but not as many as my mammy." None of these children, however, were raised by Chapman or her sexual partners. In fact, she recalled that "I ain't never had no special husban'. I even forgets who was de pappy of some of dese chilluns on mine."[48] Like so many other formerly enslaved women, these memories clearly weighed heavily on Chapman. She thus offered as a summation of slavery the following: "I kin tell you things about slavery times dat would make yo' blood bile, but dey's too terrible. I jus' tries to forget."[49]

There were indeed many horrific memories of sexual exploitation that enslaved women would have preferred to forget. Betty Powers, though, could not forget. She remembered being enslaved on a plantation with over two hundred other slaves.[50] Echoing male memories of sexually abused slave women, Powers recalled that "de overseer and white mens took 'vantage of de women like dey wants to. De women better not make no fuss 'bout sich. If she do, it am de whippin' for her."[51] While enslaved women were violently assaulted for resisting the sexual advances of white men, the children they bore from these unions were often recognized as financial investments requiring special attention. Powers recalled, "De babies had plenty of food, so dey grow up into strong, portly men and women."[52] Not all children, however, made it to adulthood. Laura Clark, for instance, was born in North Carolina but knew little of her parents, who had been sold when she was an infant. However, she did recall that her mother "was de mother of twenty-two chillun."[53] But with life came death. Clark had nine children, and she reflected that "I got chillun dead in Birmingham and Bessemer. De ain't a graveyard in dis here settlement 'roun' Prospect where I ain't got chillun buried."[54]

For former enslaved women, then, the sense of grief and sadness that accompanied memories of slave breeding was manifold. Sexual coercion, regular pregnancy and childbirth, and the sale or death of children burdened the recollections of former slave women. In emphasizing these aspects of slavery, these women echoed the accusations made by black female abolitionists in the nineteenth century and made sure that these darker aspects of American history were not forgotten. Eliza Washington spoke candidly about the emotions involved in such remembered histories. Washington, a former Arkansas slave, recalled that her mother—"a strong woman"—was born in North Carolina, while her father was from Tennessee. She explained that "the white folks separated my mother and father when I was a little baby in their arms."[55] The pain of family separations continued throughout Taylor's life as a slave. She recalled the songs and stories slaves would tell, such as "The speculator bought my wife and child [a]nd carried her clear away."[56] While historians have rightly emphasized the struggles of enslaved people to nurture some sense of family under slavery, it is important to remember the anxiety and fear of separation that often drove these efforts.[57] And when such efforts confronted the power of the slave owner, the result, as Taylor's recollections conveyed, was feelings of deep melancholy.

## The Commodification of Slave Reproduction

The melancholic tenor of former slaves' memories was highlighted when narrators recalled the sadness associated with the sale of family and loved ones. Former slaves often grafted onto memories of slave breeding the fear of being separated from a husband or wife and the terror of losing one's children. Historians such as Walter Johnson and Steven Deyle have insightfully analyzed the domestic slave trade and the commodification of slave bodies for the profit of slave-trading and slave-owning interests.[58] Similarly, recent economic histories of slave sales suggest that discounts were sometimes offered on the sale of entire slave families. While the sale and separation of enslaved family members was not necessarily part of "breeding" schemes, that former slaves used the rhetoric of slave breeding when referring to coercive reproduction or the threat of sale highlights how intensely they felt about these issues.[59] This section focuses on the ways in which former slaves represented "breeding"—especially the prizing of "fast breeders"[60]—as the most dehumanizing aspect of the domestic slave trade. Prior to the Civil War, narratives about slave breeding and slave sales sensationally attacked the idea that slavery was a "positive good"; after the war, Americans—from former abolitionists to African American intellectuals— debated whether violent sexual exploitation was significant to the historical representation of slavery and an understanding of the "Negro problem" in the

Figure 4. Slave cabins at "Hermitage," Savannah, Georgia, where slaves were allegedly raised for market. Courtesy of the Library of Congress, LC-USZ62-110813.

twentieth century. Former slaves were noticeably absent from these debates. The manner in which former slaves narrated their memories of slavery, "breeding," and the internal slave trade reminded many of the fear, terror, frustration, and anger they had felt as slaves in the antebellum South.

As former slaves remembered slavery in the late 1930s, they identified the commodification of black bodies as the single greatest threat to their efforts to nurture any type of stable family unit. The practices associated with the commodification of slave "breeding" began on the plantation around the time a young enslaved girl reached puberty.[61] For example, Henry Buttler recalled that his paternalistic master managed his slaves as he would farm animals. Buttler's master was seemingly oblivious to the possibility that two of his slaves could share an emotional attachment, much less feelings of love, an emotion most white Americans typically reserved for themselves.[62] According to Buttler, slave marriages were permitted only when they served the profit motive of his master. In Buttler's words, "The slaves were allowed to marry, but were compelled to first obtain permission from the master, and he would not consent unless he considered it a proper mating. . . . The main factor involved on the part of the master was the desire to rear Negroes with perfect physiques."[63]

A number of former slaves claimed that the desire of masters and slave traders to not only increase the quantity of slaves for sale but also improve the quality of the "stock" led to family members being scattered over vast distances. For instance, Tanner Spikes recalled, "My mammy had fifteen chilluns which wus on Doctor Fab Haywood's plantation here in Wake County. . . . My daddy 'longed ter a Mr. Wiggins in Pasquotank County."[64] Other former slaves recalled the geographical distance that different slave masters put between their parents. Rachel Adams's parents lived in what historians refer to as an "abroad marriage."[65] Adams explained that her parents lived on separate plantations. Adams recalled that her master was not prepared to part with her mother because she was a good breeder, giving birth to one boy and sixteen girls.[66] However, not all former slaves remembered masters allowing "married" couples to live on plantations operated by different slave owners. Sally Brown mixed vague references to early-twentieth-century "racial science" and alluded to animal husbandry to emphasize the oppressiveness of the master's control over "marriage." Brown recalled that masters "didn't mind slaves mating, but they wanted their niggers to marry only amongst them on their place. They didn't allow them to mate with other slaves from other places."[67] As former slaves recalled the "mating" of enslaved couples, the master class allowed a variety of domestic and conjugal arrangements if it meant increasing the master's stock of slaves.

Far from masters assenting to slave marriages out of a sense of benevolent paternalism, former slaves often remembered slave marriages and slave family formation as part of a scheme to increase the slave population and enhance the profits of slave owners and the dreaded slave traders. Jim Gillard, for example, one of eight children, had been sold for $350 when just three months old. He remembered the squalid conditions in which he and his siblings lived, stating, "our house wasn't nothin' to brag about. Dey was built wif hewn logs an' had slab floors, havin' two rooms an' a shed cook room."[68] Gillard's imagery is not of a salubrious stud farm, but of a plantation in which the slave owner did the bare minimum to provide for his slave "stock." Stating what he believed were his master's true intentions, Gillard insisted that slaves knew that "marriage" was a union born out of the master's power and drive for profit. "Marriage," in short, was remembered as a way to encourage reproduction among slaves. "My aunt married up at de big house an' dey jumped over de brum to marry," Gillard claimed. Recognizing that such marriages had no legal standing, he added, "atter slavery dey had to git married agin."[69]

For some former slaves, the absence of legal recognition for their antebellum marriages spoke to darker motives on the part of the slave owners. Carl Hall remembered that "marriage between negroes, before freedom, had no legal standing."[70] Thomas Hall was blunt in his assessment: "Getting married and having a family was a joke in the days of slavery, as the main thing in allowing any form of matrimony among the slaves was to raise more slaves in the same sense and for the same purpose as stock raisers raise horses and mules, that is, for work."[71]

Former slaves recalled in various detail the structures used by slave owners to foster slave breeding. Few offered as much detail as Rosa Starke. Starke, who was eighty-three years old when she was interviewed in Winnsboro, South Carolina, recalled that her master, Nick Peay, owned nineteen plantations and thousands of slaves. According to Starke, Peay owned so many slaves that "befo' de numerator git 'round, some more would be born or bought."[72] The Peay plantations were hives of capitalist activity and a site of human misery for the enslaved. But it was the misery of the enslaved that kept Peay's plantations profitable. According to Starke, Peay's slaves were divided into a social hierarchy that comprised six tiers. The first "classes 'mongst de slaves" were the "house servants." Below them were "de carriage drivers and de gardeners, de carpenters, de barber, and de stable men. Then come de nex' class de wheelwright, wagoners, blacksmiths and slave foremen," followed by "de cow men and de niggers dat have care of de dogs." Slaves in these classes, Starke remembered, all lived in "good houses." This was in contrast to the bottom two slave classes on the Peay plantations, which included "de cradlers of de wheat, de threshers, and de millers of de corn and de wheat, and de feeders of de cotton gin. De lowest class," according to Starke's tabulation, "was de common field niggers." By Starke's reckoning, the slaves were divided into "classes" according to their occupations. But the divisions of slaves according to employment also had a reproductive function. As Starke remembered it, "A house nigger man might swoop down and mate wid a field hand's good lookin' daughter, now and then, for pure love of her, but you never see a house gal lower herself by marryin' and matin' wid a common field-hand nigger."[73]

Starke's articulation of the "house nigger/field nigger" dynamic is common in African American folklore; what is of interest to our understanding of memories about slave breeding is how she suggested that female house servants used their status among fellow slaves to put themselves, and presumably their children, in a position that would lessen the brutalizing physical effects of slavery.[74] But this power, if we can call it that, was limited. For enslaved women forced to perform the role of breeding "wench" the memory of slave-breeding practices was equally horrific. Rose Williams, who insisted that her testimony "am de facts," claimed that her "master am awful cruel." Williams remembered, "He whups de cullud fo'ks, wo'ks dem hahd an' feeds dem poorly."[75] Williams's candid testimony was indicative of those narratives elicited from former slaves by African American interviewers. Indeed, the candor that perceptions of racial affinity fostered between former slaves and black interviewers was underlined when Williams offered her unprompted recollection of slave marriages. She informed her interviewer that at the age of seventeen, her master forced her to marry a fellow slave by the name of Rufus. As Williams remembered, "Ise don't lak dat cullud man 'cause he am a bully." Explaining her feelings toward Rufus, Williams claimed that she had no knowledge that her master had insisted on the marriage as a means of impregnating her and increasing the size of his slave population. When Rufus attempted to enter Williams's bed, she exclaimed in terror: "W'at yous mean, yous fool nigger, a-gittin' in my bunk." Williams insinuated that the violence and repeated episodes of rape following this incident left her unwilling to marry once slavery had been abolished.[76]

Williams's testimony highlights the violence and oppression that former slave women often associated with slave marriages and reproduction. At the level of master-slave relationships, Williams provided insight into the hegemonic power that her master held over her, demanding that she marry a man she barely knew. At the level of the slave "marriage" or "family" formation, Williams recalled the gendered nature of her oppression and how her black "husband" physically and sexually abused her. Rufus, who was also enslaved, attempted to exercise what little masculine power he had on the plantation by raping Williams. Echoing the 1861 narrative of Harriet Jacobs, Rose Williams insisted that slavery fostered unnatural marriage relations between enslaved men and women that ignored the emotions of the parties involved. For former slaves like Williams, such memories highlighted a brutal, but all too common, form of "breeding" during slavery.

Other former slaves, such as John Cole, linked the master's disregard for courtship and nurturing family networks among the enslaved to the debasement associated with the commodification of slave reproduction. "If a hand were noted for raising up strong black bucks, bucks that would never 'let the monkey get them' while in the high-noon hoeing," Cole claimed, "he would be sent out as a species of circuit-rider to the other plantations—to plantations where there was over-plus of 'worthless young nigger gals.'" On these other plantations, Cole insisted, the "black bucks" "would be 'married off' again—time and again." Cole's implicit recognition of how slave owners devalued courtship and marriage among slaves was matched by his own perception of "worthless young nigger gals" and a grudging acknowledgment of why such practices existed. "This was thrifty," Cole insisted, "and saved any actual purchase of new stock."[77] Indeed, when masters did encourage "large families," as one former slave recalled, profit was the motive.[78]

Former slaves regularly alleged that profiting from the sexual exploitation of other human beings was a feature of slavery. Charlotte Martin informed a WPA interviewer that her former master "found it very profitable to raise and sell slaves."[79] Like Cole, Martin recalled the gendered nature of slave commodification. Martin insisted that she had witnessed her master select "the strongest and best male and female slaves and mated them exclusively for breeding." She described a systematic form of reproduction, the slave master not only determining whom some slaves would have sexual intercourse with but asserting his power directly over female slaves—and indirectly over men—by playing an active role in the reproduction of the slave population. Where plantation mistresses often played matchmaker to enslaved couples, Martin insisted that "sometimes the master himself had sexual relations with his female slaves."[80] Another slave remembered similarly: "Marster had no chillun by white women. I ain't no man for tellin' and dat is de truth. At dat time it wus a hard job to find a marster dat didn't have women 'mong his slaves. Dat wus a gineral thing 'mong de slave owners."[81]

According to former slaves, slave-breeding practices involved sexual exploitation, marriages unrecognized by law, and often the sale of kith and kin. There was a crude logic to the narration of these memories that one former slave summed up simply: "Kill a nigger, breed another."[82] Former slaves narrated memories not simply of human beings being bred and sold like "cattle, horses, an' cows" but of slave owners and slave traders having the power to determine when life should be conceived, and, if necessary, ended.[83]

In the memories of former slaves, nothing embodied the immoral power of the slave owner and slave trader more than the auction block. The road to the auction block, where human chattel was inspected, bought, and sold, was fraught with physical terror and emotional uncertainty. Dave Harper, recalling his life as a slave in Missouri, claimed, "I've seen slaves go through Danville in droves like cattle. Dey was chained together and dey walked 'em to St. Louis to de nigger yard." This type of forced march was exhausting, and some slaves found it difficult to complete the journey. The punishment for being unable to keep pace with the slave coffle, Harper claimed, often caused mother and child to be separated. "One mother give out," he remembered seeing. "De man in charge made her give her baby away, she couldn't carry it no further. Someone near Danville raised the baby."[84] Marilda Pethy may well have been one example of an infant slave sold (or left behind) in such a manner. Pethy claimed she was six weeks old when she was sold. Forcibly estranged from her birth parents, Pethy remembered the awful sight of slaves being led to market. "I sure remembers dem days," she told her interviewer. "I seen people handcuffed together and drivin' 'long de Williamsburg road like cattle." Adding to the popular imagery of upper South states breeding slaves for sale in the lower South, Pethy noted that "they was bought to be took south." Lest the truthfulness of her testimony be questioned, Pethy emphasized that "I had two brothers and two sisters sold and we never did see dem no more."[85]

Former slaves' memories of slaves being led to the auction block, inspected, and bid upon were graphic reminders of how the commodification of human life was soul crushing to observe. Annie Bridges recalled, "Ma muthuh tole' me dat dey used ta sell de little childr'n away fum de breasts ob der muthuh's."[86] Fanny Berry, who insisted that "us colored women had to go through a plenty, I tell you," recalled such distressing scenes in Petersburg, Virginia. She remembered seeing "young gals" being "marched down to the train—baby, baby! I can recollect it," Berry claimed, "a terrible time too, it wuz." Berry was traumatized by "a great crying and carrying on amongst the slaves who had been sold. Two or three of dem gals had young babies taking with 'em. Poor little things. As soon as dey got on de train dis ol' new master had trained stopped an' made dem poor gal mothers take babies off and laid dem precious things on de groun' and left dem behind to live or die."[87]

The narration of such scenes highlighted the cruelty that former slaves often associated with "breeding" during slavery. Narratives about the commodification of slave family members were tied together by the economics of slave "raising" and selling, a process that the formerly enslaved felt began on the plantation and was perpetuated by the technology of turnpikes and rail lines and by the printing presses' production of advertisements for slave auctions. Berry observed how slave breeding intersected with such technologies, insisting matter-of-factly that "when babies were left dat way [at a train station] dey didn't b'longst to nobody an' some po' white man would take dem an raise dem up as his slaves and make 'em work on his plantation an' if he wanted to, would sell 'em."[88] While poor whites did not participate directly in this stage of the "breeding" process, the memories of former slaves like Berry suggest that whites of all socioeconomic statuses benefited from the commodification of black life.

In the absence of written or statistical evidence, it would be easy to dismiss such recollections. Certainly, as the years aged bodies and fragmented the memories of former slaves, a coherent narrative of one's personal history became difficult to articulate. But moments of intense trauma and stress tend to stay with the individual, even as the fog of old age descends. Take, for example, Jane Simpson. While Simpson was weakened by old age and illness, she insisted on telling her experience of slavery, even if it was presented "scatterin' like." Her narrative of the past was disjointed, but the trauma she expressed about witnessing people being sold like cattle left an indelible mark on her soul. Simpson thus used direct and simple language to state unequivocally that "I been sold six times in my life."[89]

Jane Simpson was not alone in sharing such memories. Israel Massie referred to slave owners, overseers, and slave traders as "dirty suckers."[90] His bitterness was born out of a moral disgust for the degradation imposed on African American people on the auction block. He explained, "While a slave standin' on de block, ol' auctioneer say, 'Strong nigger! Good color! Good worker! Who'll buy? $100, $100, $100, $200, etc.'" Massie's recollections suggest that slave auctioneers focused on the physical proportions of the male slave and his promised capacity for physical exertion. These qualities had implications for slave-breeding purposes, but it was not until enslaved women stood on the auction block that Massie highlights the link between the slave auction and breeding practices. He stated, "Ef hits a 'oman, say pretty much de same. . . . Dey say sometimes, 'Fine Wench, Good breeder,' and de like."[91] Massie could not avoid dredging up such dark memories, the trauma they appeared to embody in his memory being evidenced in the brevity with which he ended his discussion of the auction block.

Other former slaves recalled the auction block and sale in more vivid detail. J. F. Boone, a former Arkansas slave, recalled that a healthy breeding-age slave could fetch as much as five thousand dollars. Boone remembered that slave traders and auctioneers would "put up niggers on the block and auction them off. They auctioned off niggers accordin' to the breed of them. Like they auction dogs and horses. The better the breed, the more they'd pay."[92] Snovy Jackson took a blunter narrative approach to slave breeding and the auction block. Recalling slave life in Virginia, Jackson echoed the words of antebellum abolitionists, stating: "Virginia was a slave breedin' state, and niggers was sold off jes' like stock. Families all broke up and never seed one 'nother no mo.'"[93]

### Memory, History, and the Black Family

The language used in the 1930s to describe traumatic episodes of sex and violence in slavery was influenced explicitly and implicitly by the rhetoric associated with black Christianity, early-twentieth-century "racial science," the chauvinism of black nationalism, and the ongoing pursuit of stable, nurturing black family units. Michele Mitchell's insightful book *Righteous Propagation* (2004) makes similar points in the context of racial uplift, the "politics of respectability," and "racial destiny" among black Americans at the end of the nineteenth century and the beginning of the twentieth. According to Mitchell, advice manuals and conduct tracts married the language of sexual propriety and "racial science" with a self-help ethos that was pervasive in African American culture. Advice manuals emphasized, among other things, the importance of exercising restraint in both public and private behavior.[94] As Mitchell succinctly characterizes the message of this literature, "morality, thrift, and hard work were essential to black progress."[95]

Since the 1970s, historians of the slave family have emphasized just how proactive enslaved parents were in teaching their children lessons in personal morality, hard work, family loyalty, and, revealingly, how to deflect questions about paternity.[96] In this historical context, former slaves remembered the domestic slave trade as the critical structure that exploited black bodies and fragmented families. The former slave W. L. Bost said it best when he claimed, "If they put up a young nigger woman, the auctioneer cry out: 'Here's a young nigger wench, how much am I offered for her?' The poor thing stand on the box a-shivering and a-shaking nearly froze to death." Bost concluded, "When they sold, many poor mothers beg the speculators to sell them with their husbands, but the speculator only take what he want. So maybe the poor thing never see her husband again."[97] In other words, former slaves recalled just how important "marriage" was to them, and to their ancestors during slavery times.

Narratives that emphasized the importance of "marriage" were often reinforced by memories of religious conversation. Religious narratives invariably incorporated commentaries about the importance of sexual propriety and family support networks. Former slaves regularly claimed that God entered their lives shortly after a parent or loved one was sold away. According to former slaves, the separation of enslaved children from their parents was a sin committed by whites who lusted after wealth at any cost. In the narrative retelling of such unscrupulous money-making endeavors, former slaves refused to present themselves, or their family and friends, as willing participants in such sinful schemes. One former slave recalled that "God started on me when I was a little boy." Grieving for his mother, who had just been sold away, this particular slave insisted that God helped to deliver his soul from sin, thereby ameliorating the pain felt after the loss, by sale, of his mother.[98]

There existed no greater sin in the minds of former slaves than the sexual exploitation of black people and the separation of family members during slavery. To counter the emotional pain contained in such memories, former slaves differentiated their own morality from that of masters. The narrative of the religious conversation contained within it the antidote to the immorality foisted on African Americans by sexual violence and coercive breeding practices: the discovery of God's love through the love of a spouse and children. One slave, who remembered being sold as "so much property" at the age of fourteen, linked slave owners and slave traders to the "devil" and countered these evil forces by emphasizing the love that comes with prayer and the love of one's family. Accordingly, this former slave recalled, "All of my family were God-fearing, and I came up in an atmosphere charged with faith, hope, and the Holy Spirit. Outwardly we sung; inwardly we prayed."[99]

Treated like animals, raised and sold like livestock, African Americans felt that the interlocking social, economic, and cultural structures that made slave breeding and the internal slave trade possible contradicted by the word of God. At the same time, memories of sexual violence and family separation shaped late-nineteenth- and early-twentieth-century attitudes about the importance of sexual propriety and marriage in contemporary African American life. Interracial sex and interracial marriage were particularly frowned upon. Frances Batson, interviewed in Nashville, Tennessee, declared that "I don't b'lieve in white and black ma'iages. Mah sistah ma'ied a lite man. I wouldn' marry one ef hit turn me ter gold."[100] Julia King, interviewed in Toledo, Ohio, shared these views. She labeled slavery "a terrible system," adding: "I think slavery is the cause of mixing. If people want to choose somebody, it should be their own color. Many masters had children from their Negro slaves, but the slaves weren't able to help themselves."[101]

Memories of coercive interracial sex during slavery no doubt shaped the sexual attitudes of former slaves. These attitudes, articulated in an era when a diverse range of black leaders—from Booker T. Washington to Marcus Garvey and Josie Briggs Hall—counseled self-help, racial pride, and sexual modesty, were designed to place a degree of narrative space between the memory of sexual violence during slavery and the racial stereotypes that white Americans used to label blacks as sexually promiscuous.[102] According to many former slaves, it was the "system" of slavery and the white men and women who oversaw its immoral operations that were the true sinners of the flesh.

A sense of moral propriety and uncertainty about the paternity of some children prevented former slaves from divulging too much information about the sexual contact between enslaved women and white men. Such propriety was born of a collective memory of slavery's sexual excesses against enslaved women. It also reflected an awareness of early-twentieth-century anti-miscegenation attitudes and laws and an acknowledgment that white missionaries— and white Americans generally—associated African Americans with "immoral piety" in the years immediately after the Civil War.[103] Aware of these racial perceptions, black Americans learned that they needed to choose their words carefully, especially in the company of whites. This was particularly true of discussions about racial violence and sex. Caleb Craig, for instance, instructed his interviewer that "de older people was mighty careful of de words dey let slip dey lips."[104]

Rhetorical caution, combined with the use of religious language, helped former slaves craft moral commentaries about the importance of sexual propriety.[105] These narratives reinforced a general distaste among former slaves for interracial sex and interracial marriage. Choosing his words carefully, Frank Bell, interviewed in Vienna, Virginia, presented a moral tale on racial violence and slavery that was as much a commentary on early-twentieth-century racial and interracial sexual relations. Bell spoke cautiously about the origin of mixed-race people in Virginia, stating: "Well I ain't sayin' he [his master] did, an' I ain't sayin' he didn't; course dey was many a little white-skinned nigger baby dat growed up on ole Masrer's plantation but ain't nobody knowed for sartain if dey his'n not. Leastwise, I ain't knowed."[106] Bell's cautious approach to the issue of sexual coercion in slavery was justifiable. In Jim Crow America, black men were wise to avoid explicit discussions about sex, much less interracial sex, lest they risk falling victim to the lynch mob. As with so many other former slaves, Bell's awkward commentary about violence and sex framed broader social anxieties about racial identity and social change in America.

Beginning, as we have seen, with the Civil War and Reconstruction, the late nineteenth and early twentieth centuries brought social change to the United States on a seemingly unprecedented level. Former slaves expressed mixed feelings about the impact of these changes. John B. Elliott, a former slave who went on to become a minister in Columbia, South Carolina, expressed amazement at how well former slaves adapted to the immediate aftermath of slavery. Reflecting on this transformative era, he recalled, "When I think of the '60s–'70s period, I am surprised that recent slaves, suddenly placed in administrative positions of honor and trust, did as well as they did."[107] Others were less sure about the positive effects of the Civil War and Reconstruction era. Louis Lucas, who relied on "old age assistance" to sustain himself, recalled that the abolition of slavery changed black people. He felt that "there is a big difference between the young people now and what they used to be. The old folks ain't the same neither."[108]

While former slaves grappled with the significance of change over time, the narratives about religion, morality, and family were interwoven to produce an insistence that even amid the immorality of slavery and coercive breeding practices, black families strove to unite men and women, the young and the old, and to create nurturing home and extended-kin networks. These narratives downplayed, and often overlooked, the violence and dislocation that historian Clarence Walker identifies in slave families and "communities."[109] This selectivity of memory, however, served a didactic purpose. One former slave, for example, recalled that most slave parents tried to teach their children to be "mannerable."[110] Sylvania Durant recalled the lessons instilled in her by her father: "Honey, pa always say dat you couldn' expect no more from a child den you puts in dey raisin."[111] Corporal punishment was part of the "raisin" of slave children during slavery, just as overseers and masters used the lash to discipline adult slaves.

For example, former slaves recalled seeing enslaved parents give their children an "unmerciful thrashing" for breaching family codes of conduct.[112] Slave parents also counseled teenage children, especially girls, about courtship, love, and sex.[113] While slavery had a major impact on enslaved families, on the issue of family morality and the cultivation of a nurturing home environment, former slaves tried to connect black America's pre- and post-abolition commitment to strong family units. Even amid the violence and sexual exploitation that tinged narrative recollections of slavery, some former slaves emphasized the determination of parents to raise children according to the dominant moral standards of the day, standards of courtship, intimacy, and sexual conduct that white Americans applied only to themselves.[114] One former slave insisted that despite the restraints imposed on his parental authority, "I am one man that do love my children."[115] A former slave by the name of Mary Teel explained, "Pa made us go clean. He made me comb and wrop my hair every night. I had purty hair then."[116]

Nostalgic narratives of this nature romanticized the slave family as a refuge, a shining light of Christian values, cleanliness, and moral fortitude amid the brutal commodification of black reproduction. Some former slaves worried, however, that the moral lessons they took from family life during slavery were lost on a new generation of black Americans. For instance, more than a few former slaves expressed concern that religion had lost its meaning among black people. Eighty-five-year-old Prince Bee insisted that religion meant something during slavery, unlike post-slavery times when religion became full of "so many empty words."[117] Other former slaves suggested that "empty words" were the least of black America's problems. Dave Harper told his interviewer of a time when the Ku Klux Klan burst into his aunt's church during Sunday service and "beat de people over deir heads with pistols. De people went out de doors and windows."[118] Without religion, former slaves prophesied, young black people would walk through life without a moral compass. Pinkie Howard lectured her interviewer on how "young folks ain't got no manners these days."[119] Another former slave complained, "I don't know what I think about de young Negroes today. Dey is all shined up an goin' 'round. If dey can read and write dey ought to know de difference between right and wrong. I don't think they will amount to much. Some of 'em ain't got no sense."[120]

Concerns that black religion had become little more than empty words, that young African American people lacked "sense," and that white terrorist groups could disrupt church gatherings at will worried former slaves. They insisted that black parents must strive to teach their children to overcome both the historical legacy of slavery and the racial and sexual violence that swirled around black communities in Jim Crow America. A former slave known as Uncle Jackson insisted that his parents provided him with the best education a black man could have to meet these challenges. Jackson's upbringing made it possible, he argued, not only to survive slavery but also to successfully navigate through the brutal world that southern whites policed during the late nineteenth and early twentieth centuries. "You know," Jackson began, "they lays a heap o' stress on edication these days. But edication is one thing an' fireside trainin' is another. We had fireside trainin.'"[121] Other former slaves expressed similar sentiments. One former slave quipped in despair, "I sho' don't know what dis new generation of nigguhs comin' to."[122] And Henry Jenkins, who claimed he was "'structed early in 'ligion," insisted that "dere's not much to a boy, white or black, dat don't need a whuppin' sometimes on dey way up."[123]

In slavery, as in freedom, many African American parents reportedly gave their children a "whuppin'" to instill in them the importance of observing America's prevailing racial etiquette. In slavery, racial etiquette meant displaying unquestioned subservience to the wishes of the master, mistress, and overseer, be it sexual or otherwise. In what passed as freedom at the turn of the century, displays of subservience seemed even more important. Joseph Badget recalled how little things changed before and after the Civil War. Badget, who claimed his mother "had Indian in her," had a tendency to "fight," and "was the pet of the [white] people," spoke of how former slaves needed to be mindful of their subservient position in American society in the years immediately after the Civil War. "I used to say 'master' myself in dem days," Badget recalls. He insisted that deference to white people was a commonly accepted part of life in the late 1860s and early 1870s. He added, "I remember the time when I couldn't go nowhere without asking the 'white folks.' I wasn't a slave then but I couldn't go off without asking the white people."[124]

Violence loomed just as large, if not larger, in black life after the Civil War thanks to the rise of the Ku Klux Klan. The outbursts of violence and brutal punishments that once shadowed black people in slavery now lurked ominously in every corner of the South, day and night, in the form of the Klansmen. Where former slaves recalled avoiding the wrath of the plantation overseers or conforming to the demands of the slave master, during the late nineteenth and early twentieth centuries the Klan terrified black Americans into submissiveness. The former slave Boston Blackwell testified, "them Ku-Kluxers was terrible,—what they done to people. Oh, God, they was bad."[125] Another former slave recalled, "I sho did keep out of de way of dem Ku Kluxers. Folkses would see 'em comin' an holler out: 'De Ku Kluxers is ridin' tonight. Keep out of deir way, or dey sho kill you.'"[126]

Other former slaves recalled the constant threat that the Klan posed to the family home. For example, Marilda Pethy blended her memories of sexual exploitation and family separation during slavery with a commentary on the Klan: "De Ku Klux Klan come and run de colored people away from home. Many a colored woman came to mother's house in de middle of de night with clothes covered with ice and snow to de waist and carrying her baby in arms 'cause dey ran her away from home."[127]

The Klan's impact on black Americans varied as widely as had relations between the slave and slave master. Some former slaves, like Charles Dortch, insisted that "I don't remember much about the Ku Klux Klan. They never bothered me, and never bothered anyone connected with me."[128] Responses of this nature likely reflected the caution that elderly former slaves exercised when talking to white people about race and slavery during the era of Jim Crow segregation. Dortch was therefore not alone in hastily dismissing questions about the Klan. Melvin Smith, for example, emphasized how "the niggers is better off since freedom come." Asked about the Klan, he responded, "I don't know nothin' 'bout that. I hear somethin' 'bout it but I never b'lieved in it."[129] Similarly, some former slaves hastily disavowed any knowledge of the Klan, one declaring that the Klan never bothered his town, while another remembered avoiding the Klan by keeping "my mouf shut."[130]

Many more former slaves, however, testified to the terror associated with the Klan, insisting that "dey kept Niggers skeered plum to death."[131] Like the poor white trash who worked as overseers during slavery, Klan members brought violence into black family or community life for any number of arbitrary reasons.[132] One former slave spoke of the Klan's presence in almost mystical terms, claiming, "De Klu Klux Klan sprung right up out of de earth."[133] Carrie Bradley, whose "Pa was [a] stocky, Guinea man" and whose mother was "rawbony and tall," recalled the utter terror that invaded family life after the abolition of slavery.[134] Bradley remembered, "I was scared to death of the Ku Klux Klan. They come to our house one night and I took my little brother and we crawled under the house and got up in the fireplace." She continued, "They knocked about there a pretty good while.... I was 'fraider of the Ku Klux Klan den I ever been 'bout snakes."[135] Of slavery, former slaves recalled the emotional pain that was associated with the violent separation and sale of family members. After slavery, fears of family breakup remained, but the forces behind those fears were domestic terrorists, white men in sheets who would sooner rape and kill the inhabitants of an African American home, and then set that home on fire.

## Conclusion

The language former slaves used to construct personal narratives about slavery and slave breeding echoed the rhetoric of nineteenth-century abolitionists and confirmed allegations of slave breeding by amateur historians, black scholars, and African American playwrights during the late nineteenth and early twentieth centuries. The narrative synergy is striking. Despite their varying political, intellectual, and cultural objectives, the narrative and rhetorical representations of slave breeding between the 1830s and the 1930s emphasized the significance of sexual violence, racial violence, and family separations.[136]

Former slaves described these elements of slave breeding, sometimes candidly. Their firsthand narrations of breeding practices present an understanding of the past that was virtually absent from professional history writing during the early twentieth century.[137] Like early-twentieth-century black scholars and playwrights, former slaves narrated episodes of violence and/or coercive breeding practices that underscored what they felt was an immoral social and economic system. For former slaves, though, the narration of memories about slavery evinced a certain degree of continuity between the past and the present. Just as former slaves recalled the white slave trader, master, and overseer as sources of past terrorism, exploitation, and sexual abuse, so in the early twentieth century did they narrate tales of the reinvention of the slave system in the form of sharecropping, lynching, segregation, rape, and the separation of black family members.[138] In other words, the narratives that former slaves presented to WPA interviewers were not simply recollections of a long-forgotten past but were memories with lived meaning. As the sociologist Herbert Blumer once argued, "meanings [are] social products . . . that are formed in and through the defining activities of people as they interact."[139] For former slaves, the slave past was contextualized by, and bled into, the Jim Crow present.[140]

To former slaves, the memories of slave breeding were as real and vivid as the threat of Klan violence and local lynch mobs. These were the historical and sociological "facts" of black life in America, "facts" that professional historians and Lost Cause mythologizers denied. But as the African American historian

Lawrence Dunbar Reddick observed in 1937: "All facts are not included in any history; those which are selected do not select themselves. They are chosen and ordered by the historian with reference to some frame of ideas, purposes, [and] philosophy which he has in mind, more or less consciously."[141] Black scholars and playwrights knew this all too well. So too did former slaves.

Former slaves knew as well as any Harvard-trained African American historian that, more often than not, demographic and economic data sets obscured more than they revealed about slavery's brutalities. That former slaves felt empowered enough to actively narrate violent sexual abuses at a particularly violent time in America's history suggests that while they understood the links between the past and the present, they were not willing to passively accept Lost Cause mythologizing or the professional (white) historian's erasure of them from collective memory.

As the descendants of former slaves took up arms and fought for "freedom and liberty" during World War II, the historical assertiveness that simmered in early-twentieth-century black scholarship, drama, and the narratives of former slaves burst forth on the American political stage. The emergence of the modern civil rights movement changed America forever. But in bringing about social, legal, and political change, the leaders of the civil rights movement from the late 1940s to the end of the 1960s recognized just how important it was to contextualize their efforts within America's history with slavery. As we will see in the following chapter, the themes long associated with slave breeding—racial violence, rape, and family separation—were vitally important to the protest narratives of civil rights protest. For a young and increasingly well-educated generation of African Americans, it was time to learn from the lessons of their enslaved ancestors, stand up, start marching, and demand change.

# 6

---

# Sex, Violence, and
# the Quest for Civil Rights

In slavery and in freedom, the historian Danielle McGuire argues, "sexual and racial violence functioned as a tool of coercion, control, and harassment." African American women understood this basic fact of American history better than most. The constant threat of rape that followed black women in slavery, and the incidences of sexual violence, kidnapping, and sexual assault after slavery, ultimately inspired the civil rights movement. In the popular imagination, the civil rights movement began with the Montgomery Bus Boycott during 1955 and 1956; in actuality, the movement was the culmination of decades—actually, centuries—of interracial sexual violence that affected the lives of black women, men, and their families. The civil rights movement was the product of militant "race women" like Rosa Parks saying enough to the sexual and racial abuses experienced by black women and their families; they were determined to challenge white America to live up to the democratic ideals it proclaimed to be fighting for during World War II.[1] Black women like Parks—politically determined, race-proud, and intellectually brilliant—began a movement for African American civil rights in the 1940s.

For multiple generations of African American women since the Civil War, the "cult of dissemblance" had meant that stories of sexual violence were hushed, or kept strictly within close family circles. The objective of such circumspection, as Darlene Clark Hine observes, was to shield black women from the racial and sexual taunts of white America and to project a dignified countenance to the outside world.[2] But as we have seen in the previous chapters, maintaining hushed tones about such matters when in the company of whites was one thing, but actively forgetting such abuse was another. Indeed, early- and mid-twentieth-century black women and men did not forget, much less ignore, interracial sexual violence. In fact, they confronted it in very public ways—in scholarship, in fiction writing and plays, and in increasingly well organized and financed legal and political attacks on the racist and sexist foundations of American society. If slavery's lifeblood was a black woman's physical ability to reproduce children, the segregation of the United States after the war was based on sex—be it the sexual terrorism visited on black women in their places of employment or the lynching and castration of black men.[3]

During the years that former slaves provided WPA interviewers with their reminiscences about slavery and slave breeding, African Americans stood on the verge of both challenging and changing America's racial landscape. In an era defined by Jim Crow segregation, the sexual assault of black women, the terror of lynching, and the anxieties associated with an unprecedented economic depression, black Americans were on the move. This movement was literal, metaphorical, and political in nature. African Americans migrated out of the South in the tens of thousands, heading primarily to the North in search of employment and sanctuary from southern racism. Black workers, shunned by white labor unions, formed their own organizations and pursued better work conditions and pay.[4] A growing black middle class joined the Urban League and the National Association for the Advancement of Colored People (NAACP) and fought against segregation, interracial rape, and lynch mobs by bringing their cause into American courts and the halls of political power.[5] And Marcus Garvey's United Negro Improvement Association both inspired and divided black Americans on how best to oppose American racism and assert their pride in being the sons and daughters of African ancestors.[6]

In the decades prior to the second *Brown v. Board of Education* (1955) decision, which decreed an end to educational segregation "with all deliberate speed," and Rosa Parks's now-iconic—and mythologized—decision to sit defiantly in the white section of a Montgomery, Alabama, bus, African Americans engaged with the memory and legacy of racial violence and sexual assault in ways that shaped the rhetoric, politics, and protests of the civil rights movement during the 1950s and 1960s. This chapter considers how the public narration and politicization of these memories were woven into civil rights discourse between World War II and the concluding years of the 1960s. Prominent civil rights leaders, such as the most prominent of them all, Martin Luther King Jr., viewed slavery's most intimate abuses as part of the lived reality of black America's intellectual, cultural, and political history. In publicly addressing this history, black men, women, and children strove to force Americans to confront the darkest aspects of its past so that it might change the republic's future course.

## Sex, Slavery, and the Civil Rights Movement

At the end of World War II, the Social Science Institute at Fisk University declared that "one of the most important race relations jobs of the next ten years will be the full integration of minority group veterans into a post-war world."[7] During the next two decades, the members of African American institutions of higher learning, black churches, and grassroots political organizations took up the cause of "full integration" for World War II veterans and all African Americans. Mary McLeod Bethune exemplified the drive for "full integration" when she called on civil rights activists to come together and keep their "rendezvous with LIFE." This "rendezvous," Bethune believed, would result in African Americans "enjoy[ing] the rich fruits of democracy."[8] For the vast majority of black America's civic, religious, and intellectual leaders, the fight for legal equality was a way to attack the historical legacy of slavery and to challenge the nation to live up to its founding ideals.

Black churches throughout the South played a critical organizational role in addressing the historical legacy of slavery. While black intellectuals analyzed the historical and sociological significance of slavery, black churches provided a focal point for community organizing and political activism. According to E. Franklin Frazier, the "black church" had been an organizational hub in successfully destroying slavery, and it played a similarly prominent role once black America mobilized en masse to fight for racial justice after World War II.[9] For the people drawn to black churches, the memory of slavery punctuated the rhetoric of their leaders and inspired the activism of the civil rights movement. Charlayne Hunter Gault, for example, recalled: "We could see that past—the slavery, the segregation, the deprivation and denial—for what it was; a system designed to keep us in our place and convince us, somehow, that it was our fault, as well as our destiny."[10] It was time for the nation to confront its history and fulfill its promise of legal equality for all Americans.

The imagery popularly associated with the civil rights movement during the 1950s and 1960s is of charismatic leaders, black men and church ministers, leading teenagers, college students, and working-class people in protest against racial segregation. Leaders such as Martin Luther King Jr. helped to situate the civil rights movement in historical context and deserve their place in the pantheon of influential Americans. King understood that to change America's discriminatory laws and racist institutional practices, historical, Christian, and sociological narratives must inspire grassroots campaigns and high-profile state and national political battles.

These efforts took shape during the 1930s and 1940s, as black women activists attacked the sexual foundations of segregation—that is, interracial rape and lynching—and African American civic and labor organizations launched assaults on economic and educational discrimination. During World War II, for example, African American leaders A. Philip Randolph, Bayard Rustin, and A. J. Muste threatened to protest racial discrimination in war industries by marching on Washington in 1941. Most famously during this period, the *Pittsburgh Courier* began a campaign promoting the "Double V" campaign, the fight to end fascism abroad and destroy racial segregation at home. This spirit of resistance touched most segments of African American society. It especially inspired black soldiers returning from service in World War II to fight against Jim Crow segregation. The scene was set for what became known as the civil rights movement.

As the civil rights movement gathered momentum, black Americans never lost sight of the historical backdrop they operated against. The history of slavery and segregation, with the violence and sexual abuses they helped to perpetuate, inspired nonviolent direct action. Robert H. Walkup, a black Presbyterian pastor and civil rights leader, delivered a fiery sermon in 1962 in which he addressed the historical motives behind the civil rights movement. Walkup preached that "there was more to slavery than we remember. Slavery involved more than magnolias and the mint juleps. Indeed, there was more to slavery than the happy carefree people, more to slavery than the nice aspects of ol' mastah' and ol' missus' that we like to talk about." According to Walkup, slavery was both vile and violent. He thundered, "There were people being put through the wringer so severe that they cried out: 'NOBODY KNOWS THE TROUBLE I'VE SEEN! NOBODY KNOWS BUT JESUS'! There were people being put through the wringer so severe that they cried out for a chariot to swing low and take them away from it."[11]

Walkup was educated at the University of Mississippi and the Louisville Seminary. He served as a pastor in Mississippi, Texas, and Arkansas. In the 1950s and early 1960s, while a pastor at Mississippi State University, Walkup maintained that slavery was "SIN."[12] But it was more than this. In one short, explosive paragraph in his 1962 sermon, Walkup articulated his suspicion that while slavery was "SIN," it must surely have been more violent, exploitative, and unjust than they could all "remember." Slavery was about how black life and death were determined by the ungodly power of the slave master. The rhetorical combination of life and death in African American narratives of slavery was not new; what was significant in the context of the civil rights movement was the way Walkup's evocative imagery reminded his audience of the historical depth—and thus, significance—of the civil rights movement. Civil rights activists were both engaging with history and changing its course in the same narrative breath.

If a sermon about the "SIN" of slavery evoked deeply felt emotions about the past, then language that emphasized the sexual exploitation of the enslaved, especially women, provided a discursive opening for sweeping statements about interracial sexual violence, African American gender relations, and family formation. References to violence, sex, and slavery during the civil rights movement were woven into narratives about the historical injustices that the civil rights movement opposed. The discourses of history and politics, the past and the present, were thus being used to inspire activists for the campaign ahead. Justifying the use of nonviolent direct action in the struggle for racial justice, Bayard Rustin connected slavery with the cause of the civil rights movement. "Slavery was maintained by violence," he argued, "and after slavery segregation and racial oppression were maintained by violence, threatened and actual."[13] In Rustin's mind, no tactic exposed the contradiction between the United States' historical oppression of black people and the republic's professed ideals of freedom and equality better than nonviolent direct action.

Rustin was one of the civil rights movement's great thinkers and organizers. Rustin was born in West Chester, Pennsylvania, in 1912. From his grandmother he was introduced to the ideals of pacifism, a philosophy that shaped his future thinking and political activism. He spent much of the civil rights movement in the background—in the "shadows," as some historians put it—because of his membership in the Communist Party prior to World War II and his homosexuality. His influence over the tactics and rhetoric of the movement, however, is undeniable.[14] To Rustin, the memory of slavery represented a history of oppression that connected black Americans of the twentieth century to the slaves of the previous two centuries. Where the slave plantation once existed as a "prison without walls," Rustin asserted that the twentieth-century penal system took its place and had become a "forced-labor camp."[15] Rustin also saw historical connections between slavery, segregation, and war, arguing that "segregation in any part of the body politic is an act of slavery and an act of war."[16] According to Rustin, segregation was as oppressive as slavery and as violent as war. "For two centuries," he insisted, "black families had been denied human status in order to safeguard the property rights and breeding prerogatives of slave owners."[17] As Rustin saw things, the only solution to such deeply rooted racial injustices and sexual violence was civil disobedience.

And civil disobedience was exactly what the civil rights movement delivered. For the ministers and organizational leaders of the civil rights movement, nonviolent civil disobedience was the ideal antidote to generations of sexual exploitation, violence, and racialized poverty. Martin Luther King Jr. espoused nonviolent civil disobedience as a moral and political tactic for overcoming the legacy of slavery and the crippling effects of segregation. King, who was born on January 15, 1929, and educated at Morehouse College, Crozer Theological Seminary in Pennsylvania, and Boston University, served, as had his grandfather and father, as pastor at Ebenezer Baptist Church in Atlanta. King's leadership qualities, charisma, and inspiring oratory took him far beyond the pulpit at Ebenezer, however, thrusting him into the national media spotlight. King became the figurehead of the civil rights movement and, in the words of A. Philip Randolph, "the moral leader of our nation."[18]

King's intellectual development and his rise to national celebrity revealed the central role that slavery played in his understanding of African American history. In 1944, while a junior at Booker T. Washington High School in Atlanta, he won an essay contest with a paper which argued that "slavery has been a strange paradox in a nation founded on the principles that all men are created free and equal."[19] As an undergraduate and graduate student, King continued to develop his understanding of slavery in American history. He combined an increasingly sophisticated historical narrative with his maturing views about Christianity, views that emphasized the power of God, the message of love contained in the Bible, and the God-ordained (and, in King's mind, scientifically proven) unity of humankind.[20]

As he emerged as the most influential figure in the civil rights movement during the 1950s, King regularly delivered a speech that emphasized the importance of slavery in African American history. For example, on May 17, 1956, at the annual dinner of the NAACP's Legal Defense Fund, King spoke about the Atlantic slave trade and the emergence, during the nineteenth century, of a proslavery lobby in the United States. These proslavery advocates, King argued, made the mistake of interpreting the Bible literally, not symbolically. They articulated arguments in favor of "a great wrong": chattel slavery. King asserted that under slavery the "Negro mind and soul became enslaved." Even after slavery was abolished, and Jim Crow segregation ushered in a new historical phase of limited freedom for black Americans, a "negative peace" between black and white Americans held sway. King insisted that this "negative peace" was in need of some "positive" force for good so that Americans could finally transcend the legacy of slavery.[21] In King's mind, the civil rights movement was thus a Christian mission to right the wrongs of American history.[22]

King often spoke about African American history in ways that connected the violence and sexual exploitation experienced during slavery with segregation, interracial rape, and lynching after slavery was abolished.[23] In *Why We Can't Wait* (1962), King instructed readers that "in the days of slavery" the oppression of the "Negro" was "scientifically" mandated and enforced by "sheer physical force."[24] Reiterating Woodson's thesis in the *Mis-Education of the Negro*, King emphasized the enforced ignorance, social isolation, and physical punishments that enslaved men and women endured. But these were not the worst of slavery's brutalities. King invoked the arguments of Du Bois, Woodson, and Frazier and echoed the recollections of former slaves to claim: "Fathers and mothers were sold from their children and children were bargained away from their parents. Young girls were, in many cases, sold to become the breeders of fresh generations of slaves. The slaveholders of America had devised with almost scientific precision their system of keeping the Negro defenseless, emotionally and physically."[25] Increasingly during the late 1950s and into the 1960s, King's speeches and published work expanded on this line of analysis, emphasizing the way slaves had been bred and families unfeelingly torn apart. He regularly channeled Du Bois's arguments about black women and motherhood, shared Woodson's understanding about the importance of education, and developed his own critique of the black family. If, as King regularly argued, the "Negro" is "maladjusted," it was the violence and interracial rape associated with slave breeding and Jim Crow segregation, not the African American's racial "nature," that caused such "maladjustment."[26]

King thus viewed the Jim Crow system of segregation that followed slavery as an "anemic democracy." He argued that America's "anemic democracy" kept African American people "defenseless, emotionally and physically," and exposed "fresh generations" of black mothers, fathers, and their family members to the types of physical and psychological violence that their ancestors suffered in slavery.[27] Listing the components that black Americans so often linked to breeding schemes during slavery, King once stated that "through forced separation from our African culture, through slavery, poverty, and deprivation, many black men lost self-respect."[28] The civil rights movement was, in King's mind, a historic fight for social justice that touched individuals, families, and communities who lived with the memory of slavery and the reality of segregation. In a sense, the civil rights movement represented an attempt by black men and women to take back (and assert) the self-respect that had been stolen from their ancestors during the slave-breeding decades of nineteenth-century slavery. Black Americans—and their white allies—made such action possible.[29] "Freedom," King thundered in words that echoed the great black abolitionist Frederick Douglass, "is not free. It is always purchased with the high price of sacrifice and suffering."[30]

King's commentary on slavery and segregation, racism and sexual exploitation, highlighted the historical burdens that black Americans, especially black women, lived with. Interracial sex in America had long run a moral gamut— from "tragic love to brutal rape," as Danielle McGuire has observed.[31] King understood this, recognizing that when black women and men spoke about the "horrors of slavery" they were often referring to the violence and rape associated with "breeding" on the slave plantation. To make this point King used a narrative device that nineteenth-century abolitionists exploited in their struggle to end slavery. It was also a rhetorical tool used by black playwrights, scholars, and former slaves during the late nineteenth and early twentieth centuries. In King's rendering of American history, African American women were the literal and metaphorical representatives of the race, beaten and exploited, but defiant and determined to overcome the historical legacies of slavery and segregation. During slavery, black mothers and their children were sexually exploited, violently managed, and sold apart. During the height of the Montgomery Bus Boycott, black mothers and their children were still enduring indignities of a similar stripe, albeit ones specific to the age in which they lived.[32] As King reflected, "One Negro mother, with two small children in her arms, put them on the front seat while she opened her purse for her fare. The driver ordered her to take the children from the seat, and without giving her the chance to place the children elsewhere, lunged the vehicle forward, causing the small children to be thrown into the aisle of the bus."[33]

For prominent civil rights leaders like King, the fight for civil and voting rights was more than a struggle for legal and political equality; it was a mission to insist that the dignity of this mother and her two children be respected and to redeem the soul of a race and of the nation.[34] King believed that this redemption process, like American history, would unfold in stages. Enslavement, the first phase of black American history according to King, was followed by the second stage, emancipation. However, King cautioned that black history had not unfolded in an upward evolutionary trajectory. Segregation, for instance, undermined emancipation and was "at bottom nothing but slavery covered up with certain niceties of complexity." This was a "nagging injustice" that African Americans now rose up as one to fight against. King maintained that black Americans refused to be exploited in "a very inhuman fashion" as their ancestors in slavery and segregation had been exploited.[35]

King's combination of historically calibrated language and biblical allegories helped him to contextualize the civil rights movement's place in America's moral and political history.[36] This powerful rhetorical combination had a long tradition among black preachers of all Christian denominations. King used the symbolic power of the Bible's stories to focus movement participants on the goal of fulfilling the promise of the third stage of black America's history. In a reference to Exodus, for instance, King explained that "we are all familiar with the historical circumstances and the psychological conditions that gave many Negroes a sense of inferiority." From antebellum slavery to Jim Crow segregation—the latter being a "new form of slavery"—King urged black Americans to join him in championing the cause of legal equality and social justice.[37] As King was wont to emphasize, African Americans were part of a "world wide struggle" for freedom in which millions of the world's historically oppressed peoples of color were using nonviolent direct action to overcome the historical legacy of slavery, sexual exploitation, and socioeconomic discrimination.[38] In King's words, "The great challenge facing America at this hour is to bring into full realization the ideals and principles of this third period."[39]

King's rhetoric resonated with scores of civil rights leaders and activists. Overcoming the legacy of slavery and segregation was a moral issue. This was certainly the view of James Farmer, a young civil rights activist who shared with Rustin and King a commitment to pacifism. Speaking before members of the Student Nonviolent Coordinating Committee (SNCC) in 1960, Farmer emphasized the magnitude of the task confronting the civil rights movement. He did this by combining historical and biblical language. "The Christian favors the breaking down of racial barriers," Farmer intoned, "because the redeemed community of which he is already a citizen recognizes no barriers dividing humanity."[40] Not all African Americans believed that nonviolence was the best approach to achieving civil rights reform. Malcolm X, the charismatic black Muslim leader immortalized in Spike Lee's movie *Malcolm X* (1992), often used threats of violence in his attacks on the historical legacies of slavery. Malcolm observed that white men and women oversaw slavery's operations, perpetuated its legacies, and divided black families and communities.[41] In his autobiography he spoke about the hypocrisy of white America's sexual morality and the ways in which the sexual exploitation of black women fostered in African American communities a healthy disrespect for white America.[42] According to Malcolm, then, "SLAVERY, SUFFERING, & DEATH" were the defining features of black American history.[43]

Malcolm X is often remembered for rhetoric that inspired black Americans and frightened whites. His musing on the "ballot or the bullet" and his unapologetic insistence that black Americans must claim their "freedom by any means necessary" was language that divided Americans along racial and class lines.[44] The NAACP's Robert Williams, a militant civil rights leader, argued that racial violence had conditioned American society to undertake change when, and only when, it encountered force.[45] Williams contended that "our people have dreamed and prayed for a peaceful transition from slavery to first class citizenship and human dignity." This dream failed the slaves and their descendants. It was time, Williams instructed, to consider more forceful methods: "Hand grenades, bazookas, light mortars, rocket launchers, [and] machine guns."[46]

Proposing the use of machine guns and rocket launchers went against the grain of civil rights rhetoric; in fact, it undermined the moral tone that movement leaders tried to set and compromised the quest for the creation of a "beloved community" in place of a nation deformed by the "horrors of slavery" and segregation.[47] No group of civil rights activists understood this more clearly than African American women. Black women confronted prejudice on two fronts during the 1950s and 1960s. They endured male chauvinism—from black and white men—and racism. The combined force of male chauvinism and racism was not new to black women. As we have seen, African American women confronted chauvinism and racism in slavery and in what passed for freedom after the Civil War. Cynthia Griggs Fleming has commented on the qualities that black women cultivated over the centuries because of this history. She wrote: "Strength and self-reliance had been part of the black female role and persona for generations, stretching all the way back into slavery."[48] Joyce Ladner, an active member of SNCC, held similar views. Ladner recalled growing up with strong female role models. Her mother was a particular source of strength and inspiration: "Mother never heard of Harriet Tubman, Sojourner Truth; Mother was one of eleven children; Mother went through third grade. But Mother also inherited the tradition that a Sojourner Truth or a Harriet Tubman set before her."[49] As Ladner recalled of her mother, African American women lived American history. Because of intergenerational violence, sexual abuse, and racially structured economic systems that put enormous strain on black families, the legacy of slavery was not something that one necessarily read about in textbooks, but was part of everyday life.

One of the ways in which black women lived with the overlapping histories of racism and chauvinism was in the tensions between men and women over leadership during the civil rights movement.[50] Long marginalized from positions of leadership in black churches, institutions, and the intelligentsia, black women nonetheless joined with black men to fight for the overthrow of Jim Crow segregation. Kathleen Cleaver, who became one of the few African American women leaders in the Black Panther Party, recalled that "we, young women and young men who flocked to the front lines of the war against segregation, were contesting the remaining legacy of racial slavery. What we sought to eliminate," Cleaver elaborated, "were the legal, social, psychological, economic, and political limitations still being imposed on our human rights, and our rights as citizens."[51] Black women like Cleaver pursued these goals in a sometimes uneasy coalition with black men; they also campaigned for the overthrow of the last vestiges of "racial slavery" by forming their own social and political organizations. This latter point has prompted some scholars to argue that African American women have a history of their own.[52] However, such analysis understates the significant ways in which the histories of race, sex, and gender have intersected in the lives of black women. As one black feminist scholar has recently observed, "Racial solidarity and race liberation have been and remain a fundamental concern for black Americans. Historically and currently, slavery, segregation, and institutional as well as individual discrimination have been formative experiences in most blacks' socialization and political outlook."[53]

## Sex, Violence, and Family

Black women shouldered a great many of the burdens of sexual exploitation, marriage breakups, and family separations rooted in the slave-breeding schemes of antebellum slavery. For many of the African American women who played an active part in the civil rights movement, childhood history lessons about slavery and the early days of Jim Crow segregation were powerful influences in the desire to correct the wrongs of American history. Black women such as the beautician Vera Piggy; Ella Baker, who tied her political activism to the history of slavery; and Septima Clark, whose mother worked as a washerwoman and whose father had been a slave, all recalled the family stories about slavery that shaped their sense of racial justice (and understanding of injustice). Thus, black children were directly exposed to oral traditions and history lessons from family members and their predominantly female schoolteachers.[54]

There existed no magnolias and mint juleps in the history lessons of early-twentieth-century black schools. Instead, lessons that emphasized the ideals of "racial uplift" were mixed with narratives about slave owners and slave traders who exploited enslaved women and shattered black families to increase their profits.[55] One former student of the African American teacher and civil rights activist Septima Clark recalled how Clark balanced lessons "about the Revolutionary War, the Civil War, [and] how people made money during slavery" with lessons about "how strong our ancestors back in slavery were and what fine people they were."[56] Some African American parents felt so strongly about their children receiving this type of education that even if segregation had not prevented black children from enrolling in white institutions, they would still have sought out black female teachers. This was the case for Ruby Middleton Forsythe, who recalled that her parents refused to let their child receive discipline from a white teacher because that "was too much like slavery."[57] The legacy of slavery and the burdens this legacy carried with it weighed heavily on African American girls as they grew into teenagers, womanhood, and ultimately joined the civil rights movement.

Actively participating in the movement carried its own economic and cultural challenges for black women. One former activist articulated these challenges when she recalled that "[black] female leaders, many of whom were public school teachers, were constrained by family roles and more so by their jobs," where male supervisors looked disapprovingly at any political activity.[58] Within the civil rights movement, male leaders sometimes expressed disdain for black women who maneuvered themselves into positions of leadership. A former staff member of King's Southern Christian Leadership Conference recalled that male leaders, such as Ralph Abernathy, questioned the value of having women in the organization. According to this former staffer, black men "just thought that women were sex symbols and had no contributions to make."[59]

These chauvinistic views were at odds with the public persona that Abernathy and other male leaders cultivated during the civil rights movement. After all, African American men insisted, black men and women had suffered centuries of discrimination together. For instance, they struggled against enormous odds to maintain the bonds of family during and after slavery. In a 1964 speech Abernathy expressed his own views on slavery, instructing his audience: "Even when they [slaves] were sold down the river to the highest bidder, husbands separated from their wives, fathers from their sons, and mothers from their daughters, they could envision a reunion in a land just beyond the river where the wicked will cease from troubling and the weary will be at rest."[60] Despite slavery and practices that African Americans associated with breeding on southern plantations, black Americans remained focused on the emotional and material comfort that family had the potential to provide. The fight for political rights and legal equality was, according to Abernathy, tied to that history.

Less than a year after Abernathy made these remarks about the black family, Daniel Patrick Moynihan's *The Negro Family: The Case for National Action* (1965) was published.[61] Moynihan's analysis built on the insights of E. Franklin Frazier in the way he emphasized how women headed an overwhelming number of African American families. This was not a particularly original insight. What stirred so much controversy was Moynihan's characterization of female-headed families as victims of a "tangle of pathology." The "Moynihan Report," as this study came to be known, sparked intense debate within black America. Critics labeled the report racist, sexist, and classist. By suggesting that white middle-class ideals of family were "normal," African American critics, especially women, countered that the report's author had demonstrated a profound insensitivity to the historical conditions that African American families encountered. Critics argued that Moynihan's focus on the "systematic weakening of the black male" and his negative portrayal of the "matriarchal" black family fueled racist stereotypes. However, it is important to remember that Moynihan's report was true to his liberal politics and intellectual determination to understand the historical and sociological structures that produced socioeconomic dislocation in black families. Indeed, it was an endeavor that received the approval of civil rights leaders such as Martin Luther King Jr., A. Philip Randolph, Whitney Young, and Roy Wilkins.[62] For black women who had been at the forefront of the civil rights movement, the Moynihan Report went against their memories of strong, supportive mothers and loving homes.[63] There was no pathology here, but if pathology did exist it originated in slavery and was perpetuated by Jim Crow segregation.

The publication of the Moynihan Report coincided with the passage of the Civil Rights and Voting Rights Acts in 1964 and 1965. With these significant goals achieved, the leadership of the civil rights movement sought a renewed sense of purpose. Martin Luther King Jr. tried to provide this direction by emphasizing the need to address black poverty. Black nationalists, on the other hand, espoused variants on Marxist theory and chauvinistic nationalist ideologies. A younger generation of black men, such as Huey Newton, Eldridge Cleaver, and LeRoi Jones/Amiri Baraka played prominent roles in organizations perceived by the "mainstream" media as racially militant. Newton, Cleaver, Baraka, and the young black men who joined organizations such as the Black Panther Party or Ron Karenga's US seized on the Moynihan Report to voice an intense misogyny and accuse black women of being "unfeminine" and castrating their men and sons.[64] As historian Deborah Gray White has observed, black nationalists viewed the Moynihan Report as an example of the "unnaturally strong and emasculating" qualities of black women.[65]

By the early 1970s, the civil rights coalitions of the 1950s and 1960s had fragmented. Young black men such as Newton, Cleaver, Baraka, and Stokely Carmichael—who is credited with coining the phrase "black power" and infamously quipping that the "position" of women in SNCC "is prone"—used misogynistic language that was overtly masculine and violent in tone.[66] The discourse of nonviolence and legal integration that had defined the civil rights movement was replaced by a more jarring rhetoric that emphasized black men reclaiming their manhood. The gendered debate about black identity and the legacy of slavery on African American life received renewed expression in black literature and in "blaxploitation" and "slavesploitation" films of the 1970s. More immediately, the former leaders of the civil rights movement weighed in on the debate about gender roles in black America. For example, Fannie Lou Hamer's comments on this issue highlighted a set of values that younger African American feminists began to espouse in the late 1960s, 1970s, and 1980s. Hamer, who grew up listening to her grandmother tell stories about slavery, argued that men and women had certain roles to play in black life. She asserted, "I am a woman, strong as any woman my age and size normally, but I am no man." She continued, "I can think but I am still a woman and I am a mother, as are most women.

I can carry the message but the burdens of the nation and the world must be shouldered by men." Hamer thus wanted more black men to become politically active, and believed black women should support men in these efforts.[67]

Hamer's understanding of gender relations echoed the perspectives of African American feminists during the 1970s and 1980s. Black feminists such as Michelle Wallace and Audre Lorde garnered inspiration and energy for their feminism from the civil rights movement and the women's liberation movement and focused their theorizing on concepts such as black women's empowerment. Like Hamer, African American feminists understood the historical burdens that slavery and segregation had placed on black Americans, particularly women. The Moynihan Report reinforced, albeit in an unwittingly chauvinistic way, what most African Americans already knew about the legacy of slavery.

Black feminists took issue with the accusatory tenor of Moynihan's analysis and developed insights on gender politics that were different from those of the white feminists who led second-wave feminism. Rather than emphasizing issues such as the right to work—black women had always worked—African American feminists highlighted the importance of maintaining relationships with black men and continuing to cultivate strong family units.[68] White women took these relationships for granted because they had never endured the violence and sexual assault that was part and parcel of black American history. With the roots of interracial rape and sexual violence in the breeding schemes of antebellum slavery, black women remained at the vanguard of civil rights efforts and social activism during the 1970s and 1980s, just as they were when the modern civil rights movement gathered momentum during the 1940s.[69]

## Conclusion

If racial slavery could not exist in the United States after 1808 without the reproduction of the enslaved population, when freedom came white Americans could not live in the same country as African Americans without the strict policing of the sexual color line. Jim Crow segregation was at its core about sex. White men sought to prevent black men from forging sexual relationships with white women because such relationships would symbolize the loss of power and control over social norms and practices. Violent interracial sex between a white man and a black woman during the twentieth century—as it so often was during slavery—signaled to black Americans that the white man continued to reign supreme. For black Americans, particularly African American women, the civil rights movement was not simply a battle for legal and political equality; it was a personal battle that dated back to slavery and touched multiple generations of black families, and was an historical attack on the slave-breeding practices and sexual violence—rape and lynching—that perpetuated slavery's legacy.[70]

By the dawn of the 1970s, black Americans had for the best part of a century understood the political and economic meaning behind slave breeding and the violence of interracial sex that characterized the long era of Jim Crow segregation. This was not a happy history. It was a history defined by the sexual hypocrisy of white Americans. It was also a history that black Americans did not passively accept. The African American women who helped set the civil rights movement on its course demonstrated through their actions a determination to engage the legacies of slavery. In the lessons of the past lay insights into how to dismantle Jim Crow segregation and build a brighter future.

But as the 1960s entered its final years, black Americans peered into the future with uncertainty. Martin Luther King Jr. gave voice to these anxieties. In the year he was tragically assassinated, 1968, King published *Where Do We Go from Here? Chaos or Community?* King had written this book at a time when race riots were exploding in cities across America. A new wave of black radicalism had captured the media's attention. And black feminists strove to articulate a program of political action that would address social and economic concerns specific to their history as women of an oppressed race. It was in this context that King wrote *Where Do We Go from Here?* In one powerful sentence he summed up what black Americans had long thought: "A stage has been reached in which the reality of equality will require extensive adjustment in the way of life for some of the white majority."[71]

These were not words that a majority of white Americans wanted to hear in 1968. Indeed, when black and white abolitionists used similar language to attack the slave-breeding South in the 1850s and early 1860s, whites met the demands for change with hostility. So, too, in 1968 did white America recoil from further demands for racial change. Most white Americans were fed up with black protests and believed that the "race problem" had been resolved when President Lyndon Johnson signed the Civil Rights and Voting Rights Acts. It had not. King and a new generation of black leaders knew that the civil rights movement was just a beginning. They knew that they had not yet adequately addressed grinding poverty, sexual violence, racial discrimination, and family dislocation.

For African Americans, the legacy of the "horrors of slavery" endured. More work remained to be done.

White Americans, however, had stopped listening to black America's history lessons and political demands. In the 1970s, black writers, actors, and filmmakers would attempt to shock white America into listening once again. As we will see in the following chapter, the "blaxploitation," "slavesploitation," and "shockumentary" films of the 1970s built on several decades of fiction writing in which the impact of slave breeding on black life was explored in graphic detail. Sex, and specifically violent, exploitative sex, was at the core of these pop-culture renderings of slavery and the breeding practices that made the slave economy possible.

# 7

## Slave Breeding in Literature, Film, and New Media

The late 1960s and 1970s were uncertain times in the United States. A protracted and unpopular war in Vietnam, outbreaks of race riots in American cities, economic instability, and political scandals that reached all the way to the White House produced in the American people feelings of frustration, fear, and anxiety. Into this cauldron of American angst entered the Black Power activists and leaders of the women's liberation movement.[1] From feminist guerrilla street theater, Black Power activism, and mass protest against the Vietnam War, the late 1960s and 1970s was an era in which social activists "spoke truth to power" by using allusions to slavery and references to the "chains" that they believed remained around the necks of African Americans and women.[2] The assertive Black Power rhetoric of LeRoi Jones/Amiri Baraka captured the spirit of the time: "Up against the wall mother fucker this is a stick up! Or: Smash the window at night (these are magic actions) smash the windows daytime, anytime, together, let's smash the window drag the shit from in there."[3]

Jones, to use a phrase from the feminist movement at the time, deployed "consciousness-raising" rhetoric to inspire and shock Americans into addressing the historical dimensions of racial discrimination in late-twentieth-century America.[4] His were angry words that spoke for a generation of black Americans who came of age at the tail end of the civil rights movement. Politically active, intelligent, and influenced by socialism and anticolonial literature, young black men and women (in spite of their differences over gender politics) demanded an end to the racialized poverty that continued to prevail in the United States. They also demanded an end to the "lies" contained in standard historical narratives about slavery. As such, they attempted to carve out their own spaces on university campuses, campaigning for the creation of black studies and women's studies departments. Black and feminist critics charged that the narrative of

American history repeated in American high schools and college lecture halls did not explain why so many black families experienced grinding poverty generation after generation; why infant mortality was far higher among African Americans; why (and how) the American health care and education systems continued to discriminate against black Americans; why black men were far more likely to be imprisoned or shot by police officers; and why black women were disproportionately more likely to be raped, and even more unlikely to gain justice from the American legal system.[5]

These issues inspired "militant" Black Power activism and sparked race riots across the United States during the late 1960s and 1970s. It was this social milieu that gave American and international writers and filmmakers the inspiration to focus their creative energies on the historical origins of racial and gender inequality.[6] In the literature and cinema produced by and about black Americans in the wake of the civil rights movement, representations of sex and slavery figured prominently in African American literature and in "blaxploitation," "slavesploitation," and "shockumentary" (or "mondo") films. These literary and cinematic genres echoed the assertive tone of Black Power and women's liberation rhetoric, highlighting the enduring significance of sexual exploitation and racial violence in American history. Indeed, filmmakers, especially foreign filmmakers, confronted audiences with movies about the exploitative and brutal nature of American slavery. In contrast, American filmmakers struggled to move beyond "plantation genre" movies, films that depicted loyal and contented slaves. While American filmmakers slowly developed neo-abolitionist plotlines after the 1950s, Hollywood films tended to rely on uncritical portrayals of the African and African American quest for "freedom" in America, to emphasize the intrinsic fairness of the American legal system, and to focus on the bravery of white historical actors.[7]

This chapter moves beyond these simplistic portrayals of slavery and analyzes literary, film, and new media representations of the violent and sexually exploitative practices associated with slave breeding. To understand the significance of such violent and exploitative representations of slavery in American culture since the 1970s it is necessary to move back and forth in chronology. Historians, who prefer chronological narratives with a start and end point, might find this movement unsettling. But to appreciate the narrative layers involved in constructing cultural representations of slave breeding since the 1970s, this back-and-forth movement is necessary to underscore the sensational, sentimental, political, and historical connections that late-twentieth- and early-twenty-first-century writers, filmmakers, artists, new media aficionados, and ordinary Americans draw between slavery and its sexually exploitative and violent legacy.

The representations of slavery that are analyzed in this chapter are typically ignored or dismissed by scholars and critics. There are a variety of reasons for this. Film and literature scholars Trevor McCrisken and Andrew Pepper argue that filmmakers worry that if they "represent the slave plantation in its full, unremitting grimness you run the risk of alienating audiences—black and white—who are either unwilling or unable to deal with such images."[8] This concern—which, for filmmakers, is primarily a commercial anxiety—was conditioned by the romantic image of slavery that emerged out of Lost Cause mythology. Moreover, graphic descriptions of violence or visual portrayals of sexual exploitation tend to be jarring to readers and audiences, many of whom are left feeling complicit in the racism and sexism being portrayed. Nonetheless, it is important to take these challenging representations seriously. The present chapter does this by paying particular attention to Frank Yerby's *Foxes of Harrow* (1946) and Kyle Onstott's *Mandingo* (1957); "slavesploitation" films like *Mandingo* (1975) and "shockumentaries" such as *Addio Zio Tom* (Goodbye Uncle Tom) (1971); African American folklore; and the potential that new media technologies such as the Internet have for the way Americans represent and understand the violence and sexual exploitation associated with slave breeding.[9] These texts/sources are among the clearest examples of how popular narratives challenge us to move beyond empirical historical renderings of slavery or accounts that rely on bills of sale, economic statistics, and demographic data. As important as this information is in helping us re-create a sense of the past, analysis of "markets," "trade," and "demography" depersonalizes the experiences of exploited human beings and transforms slavery (and slave breeding, for that matter) into an abstract discussion of economic utility and theories of material rationality. Moreover, "empirical" studies of the question of slave breeding have little residual emotional impact on readers, save for the ability to list the occasional historical "fact." In stark contrast, the material analyzed in this chapter is striking for its vivid, uncompromising portrayals of slave-breeding practices. Like the work of black playwrights in the 1920s and 1930s, this material challenges readers and audiences to think long and hard about slave breeding and what slave life must have "really" been like.

## Postwar Representations of Sex and Slavery

The themes of sexual exploitation, slavery and family formation, and racial violence have figured prominently in literature produced by and about African Americans since the nineteenth century. As we saw in the previous chapters, black abolitionists, post–Civil War memoirists, early-twentieth-century playwrights, scholars, and civil rights leaders have written works that address the significance of black America's experiences in slavery. In the twentieth century, this vast and diverse body of work provided a counterbalance to historical narratives produced by white Americans in which slavery was portrayed as either a school or a benign institution. A generation of early-twentieth-century white American authors—such as William Faulkner, Erskine Caldwell, and Thomas Wolfe—also helped to draw the reading public's attention to a grimmer version of the South's history. The impact that these authors had on America's historical imagination can be gauged by the way historians sat up and took notice of their narratives. Clarence Gohdes, writing in the pages of the *William and Mary Quarterly* in 1936—a publication that remains the most esteemed scholarly journal for early American historians—alerted readers to the proliferation of fictionalized accounts of the South that "are leading the country in a way that they never have before."[10] To the historical guildsman this was (and is) a troubling development, not least because the stories that American readers were being exposed to were littered with examples of racial and class injustices. In mid-twentieth-century America such imagery was a radical departure from literature in which writers emphasized (and empathized with) the myth of the Lost Cause, described the "school" of slavery, "pontificated" about the chivalrous white men, and squabbled over the value of one economic data set or another.[11] This politeness and abstract debate, then as now, was a mirage that masked the South's culture of racism and gender inequality. For example, the prolific Erskine Caldwell exposed brutal and unseemly aspects of southern economic and social life in novels such as *Tobacco Road* (1932), *God's Little Acre* (1933), *Journeyman* (1935), and his novel about a lynch mob titled *Trouble in July* (1940). For his efforts, literary critics condemned Caldwell's novels for being littered with "grotesque exaggeration."[12]

As the civil rights movement began to gather momentum in the years after World War II, African American writers worried about telling stories that might seem exaggerated at the same time that they were committed to confronting the more "grotesque" aspects of southern history. Like the playwright

Randolph Edmonds, novelist Frank Yerby re-created life during slavery in his many novels. Yerby's *The Foxes of Harrow* (1946) is a story focused on slavery that doubled as a commentary about the legacy of slavery.[13]

Frank Yerby was born into the segregated world of Augusta, Georgia, in 1916. He received an M.A. in English from Fisk University and worked for a time as a teacher among black children in the South. After working in a Detroit factory during World War II, he settled in New York with his "light-skinned octoroon" wife and started a family. He also began a writing career, going on to become one of the most popular African American novelists of the twentieth century.[14] Yerby wrote elaborate costume dramas that re-created the slave South in both its splendor and its violent excesses—a style that filmmakers brought to cinemas in the 1970s. His novels were popular among readers and were commercially successful. Academics, however, ever suspicious of writers who enjoy commercial success, dismissed Yerby as the "prince of pulpsters." As one scholar observed, "university critics" seemed to think that "if ignored, he [Yerby], like television, might go away."[15] Neither Yerby nor his work went away.

Yerby's first attempt to grapple with slavery in American history was *The Foxes of Harrow*. This was one of the first great African American novels to be published after World War II. Set in antebellum New Orleans, Louisiana, a state where, inexplicably, no WPA narratives were collected from former slaves, Yerby presents the South as a place characterized by the arbitrary rule of white men. The novel's protagonist, Steven Fox, is an Irish-born "bastard" who speaks both English and French, though he refuses to speak French because "it is a bastard tongue." Fox earns his living as a gentleman sportsman. In the language of the nineteenth century, he is a "confidence man," someone who is well dressed and articulate, but a con man nonetheless. So adept is Fox at his craft that he eventually wins enough money playing cards in the saloons of New Orleans to purchase a plantation and the slaves needed to make it productive.[16]

After purchasing his plantation, called Harrow, Fox raises white eyebrows because he "worked in the fields like a negro."[17] However, he quickly wins over local Creoles and Anglo-American whites by constructing one of the grandest homes in New Orleans. It is from this grand mansion that Fox ingratiates himself to New Orleans society by hosting sumptuous dinner parties that become major social events. Fox also assimilates into New Orleans society for another reason: he becomes a regular at slave auctions, buying slaves and attempting to breed them on his plantation. This is the case with two slaves, Achille and La Belle Sauvage, whom Fox purchases with a view of making them "husband" and "wife."

Yerby depicts Achille as a strong, robust full-blooded African, Catholic by faith, and seemingly loyal to Fox. La Belle Sauvage, whom Yerby also portrays as a full-blooded African, is, in contrast to Achille, haughty. She refuses to see herself as a slave or to submit to Achille's sexual advances. Her haughtiness—she refers to Achille as "slave nigra!"—angers her "husband" and seemingly offends Achille's sense of masculinity. In a scene that is repeated in the memoirs and oral testimonies of former slaves, Achille endeavors to assert his manhood by raping Sauvage. "You are my woman," Achille insists, "I your man, me!" Sauvage has none of this, asserting that Achille is "no man" and that the men in her tribe "no make slave. Warrior him die, but him no make slave. Even woman no make slave—die first, killee self first. In my tribe never no slave." This, to Achille's ears, is absurd. "You slave, you!" Achille states. "What for you think no, girl? You slave just like me, you." As the tension between Achille and Sauvage grows, the climactic rape scene is terrifying as much for what is described as for what is not. Yerby narrates that Achille sweeps Sauvage into his arms as "she kicked out and tore the skin of his face into ribbons, but he shouldered his way into the cabin with her and kicked the door shut behind him."[18]

Yerby's narrative is silent on what went on behind that slave cabin door. It is this narrative silence, however, that makes this and ensuing scenes between Achille and Sauvage all the more powerful. Indeed, the drama that follows, when Sauvage gives birth to a baby boy, is tinged by the memory of the child's traumatic and violent conception. Sauvage's son, Yerby writes, displays "an inky, bluish blackness, large and sound of limb."[19] Fox is happy with the child—after all, he purchased Sauvage *for* Achille so that there would be "no little yellow *negrillons* on the place," a statement that is meant to highlight Fox's disdain for racial mixing, something eighteenth- and nineteenth-century Louisiana was famous for, and a practice that Fox himself ultimately succumbs to.[20] But Fox's pleasure with the "inky, bluish blackness" of the enslaved newborn soon turns to despair when he watches Sauvage flee the slave cabin with the child in her arms. She heads, to the horror of eyewitnesses, toward the levee of a nearby river. Achille pursues Sauvage, catching her and taking the child from her. He cannot, however, prevent Sauvage from taking her own life and watches helplessly as her body is buffeted in the fast-flowing river. This tragic sequence of events ultimately ends with Sauvage maintaining her own sense of dignity through death. She will no longer be a slave, but her child and her "husband," Achille, will forever remain Fox's prize slaves.[21]

Yerby's rendering of slavery in antebellum New Orleans was a far cry from the epic tales of grand plantations, kindly masters, and the happy slaves of white fiction.[22] His version of slavery was defined by unbridled white power and the ability of the master class to manipulate slave marriages and families at will—that is, to impose a system of slave breeding. Other black authors addressed similar themes in the decades after the publication of *The Foxes of Harrow*. Works of prose and poetry by Margaret Walker, George Schuyler, Dorothy West, and Gwendolyn Brooks, to name just a few, also focused on slavery and its enduring legacies. Of course, African American culture has never been monolithic, and not all black writers (and audiences) were willing to connect black life in twentieth-century America with slavery. Nonetheless, key themes that had dominated African American literature since the nineteenth century, such as the republic's promised ideals of freedom and equality and the lived history of its physical and psychological brutality against black Americans, continued to resonate.

Margaret Walker explored these themes in her various writings. In 1942 she began her literary career when she published a book of poetry entitled *For My People*. Like her acclaimed novel, *Jubilee* (1966), *For My People* highlighted Walker's awareness of the enduring legacy of slavery in black life:

> For my people everywhere singing their slave songs repeatedly: their dirges and their ditties and their blues and jubilees, praying their prayers nightly to an unknown god, bending their knees humbly to an unseen power.[23]

Well might black Americans pray to "an unknown god," to "an unseen power." In slavery, black people, especially women, labored in many different ways. In the fields, enslaved women helped to produce the crops that enriched the slave-owning families; within the confines of the dingy slave cabin, women gave birth to children who grew up knowing little other than the drudgery of slavery. For Walker, enslaved women suffered dreadfully during bondage. In her most famous work of fiction, *Jubilee*, Walker describes a system that was debasing to black motherhood, with young women existing only to "breed" and give birth to slave children as quickly as they could.[24]

From slavery times to the era of the civil rights and Black Power movements in the twentieth century, representations of strong black women—mothers, sisters, wives—punctuated an often terrifying history of sexual exploitation and racial violence. Mari Evans's book of poetry, *I Am a Black Woman* (1970), gave voice to the dignity and humanity of black womanhood amid centuries of inhumanity and abuse:

I
am a black woman
tall as a cypress
strong
beyond all definition still defying place
and time
and circumstance
   assailed
      impervious
               indestructible
Look
   on me and be
renewed[25]

Homage to black women and "activist motherhood" came in different forms from other African American writers.[26] Gwendolyn Brooks, for example, left us haunted by her moving poem "The Mother," a stirring piece of poetry that evokes images of the past and present, rape and the physical and emotional pain that accompanies sexual violence. Other black authors have added their voices in admiration for black womanhood and motherhood. Alice Walker, for instance, wrote with compassion and insight about black women surviving centuries of cruelty and oppression, and of navigating the fraught sexual politics of the civil rights and women's liberation movements in the twentieth century; and Maya Angelou has written prosaically about the dignity of black womanhood with the words "Phenomenal woman."[27]

Black women have written about their strength and dignity because they imagined that these qualities were needed to sustain their great-grandmothers, grandmothers, and mothers through the sexual exploitation that was common on the slave plantation, the violence of the Jim Crow era, and the civil disobedience campaigns of the modern civil rights movement. Not that strength and dignity are qualities in the late twentieth and early twenty-first centuries that should be taken for granted. Writers such as Michele Wallace, Alice Walker, and bell hooks continue to remind readers of the connection between violence and sex, race and gender discrimination, in the United States. Ironically, though, it was not a black writer who presented readers of late-twentieth-century fiction with the most shocking and vivid images of slavery's brutal excesses. It was a homosexual white male who lived in Sacramento, California.

The author in question was Kyle Elihu Onstott, a man who made his living writing dog-breeding manuals. Born in Illinois in 1887, Onstott grew up listening to "bizarre legends" about slave-breeding farms in Kentucky. One of these tales involved an antebellum slave owner by the name of John Hart Crenshaw. Pop culture historian Paul Talbot relates how Crenshaw's plantation, Hickory Hill, was reportedly a slave-breeding farm.[28] Local legend had it that the third floor of the Hickory Hill Big House contained a "breeding room." Knowledge of the Crenshaw plantation reached Onstott indirectly. Evidently, a former Crenshaw slave, Robert Wilson, played a significant role in circulating lurid tales of slave-breeding practices on the Crenshaw plantation. Wilson, who was reportedly a "stallion slave" during slavery, became a preacher after the Civil War. He used this position to sermonize about the evils of slavery and to explain how much he despised his duties as a "stallion slave." For Onstott, these childhood stories left an indelible mark on his historical and racial consciousness. In a 1959 interview he insisted that the rape of enslaved women and slave breeding "happened. . . . Many planters expected and demanded that each of their slave women produce for them one child every year."[29]

With childhood memories of horrific slave-era tales still swirling in his adult imagination, Onstott wrote and published his most famous novel, *Mandingo* (1957). *Mandingo* was the first in a long line of novels that became known as the Falconhurst series, a series that had a significant cultural impact on representations of slavery well into the 1970s. Onstott authored the first novel, *Mandingo*, while Lance Horner and Harry Whittington (who wrote under the pseudonym Ashley Carter) penned all subsequent entries in the series. *Mandingo* was well suited to an age characterized by civil rights activism and the rise of guerilla street theater and consciousness raising. In blunt, uncompromising language, Onstott portrayed the slave South as a site of "sex, sadism, and miscegenation."[30] If the "plantation genre" embodied best by *Gone with the Wind* had not already been undermined by civil rights activism, then the cultural impact of *Mandingo* and the Falconhurst series would in a few short decades do just that.[31]

*Mandingo* quickly became a global cultural phenomenon. In the United States the novel sold over five million copies by the mid-1970s and remained in print until the 1980s. Its international success was also phenomenal. Foreign-language versions were published in France, Italy, Norway, Denmark, and Japan.[32] In the course of researching this book, I have listened to Australians tell me about their first encounter with *Mandingo*; in Scotland, workers in the North Sea oil industry told me in their thick Scottish brogue about how they whiled away the hours reading *Mandingo* and the other titles in the Falconhurst series.

The cultural significance of such broad market appeal should not be underestimated. *Mandingo* has clearly played a major role in the way readers imagined slavery since its original publication. African American readers greeted *Mandingo* with mixed emotions. In general, though, readers expressed the sense that Onstott's rendering of slave breeding was true to the reality of the antebellum South. The most famous African American reader to register such acknowledgment was the novelist Richard Wright. Shortly before his death in 1960, Wright "discovered *Mandingo*, a remarkable book based on slave period documents." Wright said of *Mandingo*, "You must read that book to understand what happened to the great American dream." For Wright, Onstott's *Mandingo* clarified the connection between police brutality during the civil rights movement and interracial sexual violence that was commonplace in slavery. Wright reportedly stated: "I can find in my heart deep pity of the nigger-hating Georgia cops and those screaming women in front of the New Orleans schools because the whole experience of slavery and the half slavery which followed destroyed them as men; killed their souls; made them subhuman." Wright adds, "After all, you can't burn and castrate the sons of your own fathers and rape the brown daughters who are really your sisters gotten by your fathers on helpless black women without becoming mad, raging animals."[33]

Onstott's novel, like the civil rights movement that was gripping the United States, was shining a historical mirror onto white America's soul, and white Americans, according to Wright, did not like the reflection that was coming back at them. This emotional discomfort goes a long way to explaining why literary scholars and historians not only underestimate the cultural impact of fictionalized stories like *Mandingo* but reflect popular (white) prejudices by dismissing such novels as "titillating," "pulp," "racist," and the best examples of the "worst" fiction ever written.[34] There is more than a grain of truth to some of these criticisms. *Mandingo* does play on racial, gendered, and sexual stereotypes to give its plotline the cultural traction needed to engage readers who take stereotypes about black sexuality for granted. While Black Power leaders such as Stokely Carmichael and Eldridge Cleaver played on *Mandingo*-style imagery to emphasize the virility of black male sexuality, *Mandingo* also reinforced the racism that contributors to the civil rights movement worked against. Additionally, the novel is not a model of stylized prose. Immediately after its publication, reviewers dismissed *Mandingo* as a "trash novel" that was a "slimy mess." Indeed, by 1975 the *New York Times* began the tradition of sardonically awarding the worst novel of the year under the title "The Kyle Onstott Memorial Award."[35]

The overwhelmingly negative responses to *Mandingo* from critics and scholars had as much to do with the cultural and political contexts in which the novel was published as it did with literary snobbery. For white Americans sensitive about the legacy of slavery and issues like racial violence and interracial sex, *Mandingo* opened historical wounds that critics felt prevented black and white Americans from "getting over" the past. For black nationalists, Onstott's novel undermined the message of racial uplift and the Black Power mantra that "black is beautiful." According to black nationalist critics, *Mandingo* simply reinforced racist representations of African Americans as historical victims. However, there is another explanation for the visceral responses to *Mandingo*, an explanation that exposes the importance of Judeo-Christian moral traditions in the United States and the enduring significance of Enlightenment concepts of order and human improvement.

The issue here involved the intertwined narratives of sex and violence. *Mandingo*, like all narrative accounts of slave breeding, combined sex and violence in an effort to focus our attention on the "reality" of slavery's brutality. Brutality is not a theme that Lost Cause propagandists, professional historians, and Hollywood filmmakers emphasized during the nineteenth and much of the twentieth century. Thus, Onstott's descriptions of rape, homosexuality, sadistic violence, and slave breeding in antebellum America entered late-twentieth-century cultural discourse in a jarring—and, for many, unbelievable—fashion.[36] Remember, Cold War Americans were still grappling with Alfred Kinsey's analysis of sexual life in the United States and the growth of the civil rights movement in the 1950s. These cultural and social developments were disconcerting enough, but the specter of slave breeding in the antebellum South completely disordered neatly packaged historical narratives about paternalistic slave owners, happy slaves, and "Negroes" who were happily segregated from whites.

The introduction of coercive sex acts into pop culture narratives about slavery was therefore a radical challenge to representations of slavery. This type of imagery presented the economics and labor associated with slavery in a new light. In Cold War America, most Americans took for granted the idea that the agricultural societies of the antebellum South were peaceful, orderly places. The introduction of sexual violence into the historical imaginary shattered this narrative complacency. In mid-twentieth-century American culture, sexual intercourse, much less coercive sex acts, was linked to concepts of "shame," "dirt," "madness," and "disorder."[37] These were not the qualities that Americans associated with the slave South and the well-meaning patriarchs who governed the South with sobriety and moderation.[38] It seemed utterly improbable to most white Americans that morally scrupulous plantation patriarchs would ever— indeed, could ever—impose vile and intimate forms of exploitation upon an enslaved population they considered part of their "family." Black Americans had long challenged such myopic representations of slavery. They knew that white men had a long-held obsession with sexually exploiting black women, something the civil-rights-era journalists Robert Sherrill and Harry Ashmore noted when they referred to the "scrotum sociology" of the South.[39] Like Sherrill and Ashmore, Onstott knew that white men in the South would never admit to such practices, so he confronted Americans with its history of sexual hypocrisy and placed "scrotum sociology" into the imaginations of millions of Americans through his infamous novel.

*Mandingo* is, as critics charged, a racist story of sexual exploitation. But this was Onstott's point. Onstott wrote what we might call a neo-abolitionist novel that highlighted what black Americans already knew: the slave South was a site of physical and emotional brutality. It was also a racist society, immoral to its core. Onstott wanted to portray this racism and immorality. He did so by writing about the violence and sexual exploitation that antebellum abolitionists and multiple generations of black Americans associated with slave breeding. *Mandingo*, then, is the story of a slave-breeding farm in Alabama called Falconhurst. Warren Maxwell and his son, Hammond, run a "nigger farm," raising slaves, or as Warren Maxwell puts it, producing clean "stock" with "good blood." One of Onstott's central characters, a slave by the name of Mede, focuses our attention on the author's disdain for southern racism and slavery. Mede is a "Mandingo" slave, a slave from a tribe of Africans coveted by Maxwell because he believes they reproduce at a rapid rate. Historically, the Mandingo people worked trade routes between Mali and the coast of west Africa from Senegal to Ghana. The Mandingo spoke four distinct dialects, practiced Islam, and contributed to the spread of the Islamic faith in West Africa. Those Mandingos who were enslaved and transported to the New World worked on plantations in the Caribbean and Central and South America, and to a lesser extent, the Gulf Coast region of North America.[40]

In antebellum Alabama, slaves belonging to the Mandingo ethnic group were not as common as they were in other parts of the Americas. For Warren Maxwell, who we learn is "Mandingo mad," the relative scarcity of these enslaved Africans makes them all the more valuable. Maxwell believes that a "pure" line of Mandingo slaves, irrespective of how inbred they might become, will fetch a higher price at slave auctions. Therefore, Warren and his son transgress the Victorian morality that inspired antebellum abolitionists by securing Mede to be both a prizefighter and to serve as the plantation's prize "stud."[41]

At Falconhurst, Mede's job is very simple: to copulate with "nigger wenches" and reproduce "suckers" whom the Maxwells eventually sold at auction. One slave in particular, Big Pearl, is set aside for Mede. Big Pearl is also a Mandingo slave, "the very gem of Falconhurst."[42] Onstott narrates that Big Pearl succumbs to a sudden illness, prompting Warren Maxwell to call Doc Redfield, the "veterinarian." Doc Redfield examines Big Pearl and quickly dispels concerns about her health, declaring that she is "hipped, plumb hipped." Big Pearl has entered puberty, and according to "Doc Redfield," it is Hammond's *duty* to have sexual intercourse with her.[43] This, at first, is a task Hammond balks at. He complains that he is sick of the "musk" smell of slave women, but ultimately he agrees to do his "duty" and go through with the "bestial" task.[44] Onstott thus plays on the centuries-old link between sex and smell (or "funk") and the association of sex with "dirt" in Judeo-Christian cultures. Hammond, in spite of his protests, is attracted to "dirt."[45] He has long kept a "bed wench"—who is never more than fourteen or fifteen years old—and finds it difficult to become sexually aroused by a white woman. For instance, when Hammond marries Blanche, the white daughter of a plantation owner, we learn not only that Blanche is not the ideal of virginal white womanhood (she had sex with her brother when she was thirteen) but that Hammond finds himself "revolted" at the thought of sexual contact with his "wife's blond body." Blanche's sexuality intimidates Hammond Maxwell. Blanche, whose name means "to whiten," and "purity," has sexual desires that southern white women are not supposed to have. Such desires compromised the future purity of the white race in the South and undermined Hammond's masculinity because he felt unable to control Blanche sexually in the way he controlled enslaved women.[46]

So it is that Hammond Maxwell is able to convince himself that a sexual act initially considered "bestial" is in fact the duty of the master class. In having sexual intercourse with enslaved women, Onstott suggests that white patriarchs believed that they were taking objects of "dirt" and disorder and asserting control and order over them. They were also engaging in acts of bestiality given the construction of enslaved women as mere chattel and the sex act between a white man and black woman as "bestial." "Ham" thus performs his duty, taking Big Pearl's virginity from her and preparing her for Mede. Together, Big Pearl and Mede will reproduce a regular supply of "suckers" because, as the Maxwells were wont to emphasize, "It's the nigger crop whut pays."[47]

For Onstott, Warren and Hammond Maxwell embody the racism and moral bankruptcy of the slave-owning class in the antebellum South. Warren Maxwell is thus depicted as being driven by an absolute contempt for black life, seeing black bodies only as vehicles to the aggrandizement of his own wealth.[48] With this moral bankruptcy come risks, however. Mede and Big Pearl, we learn, are not only the products of incest, but siblings. The incest involved in keeping the Mandingo bloodline "pure" alarms Mede's seller to such a degree that he raises concerns about the reproduction of something quite "monstrous." But incest does not bother Warren Maxwell. He is determined to keep the Mandingo bloodline "pure," insisting that doing so will produce bigger, stronger slaves and therefore fetch a higher price at market.[49]

Big Pearl's eventual pregnancy is thus a cause for celebration at Falconhurst. But the celebratory atmosphere soon turns to tragedy. Hammond Maxwell's sex life is the driving force behind the upheaval. Hammond, preoccupied with training Mede for a prizefight and sexually repulsed by his wife, pays little attention to Blanche and spends each night with Ellen, his longtime mulatto "bed wench." Angered by her husband's rejection, Blanche acts on her feelings of sexual jealousy by summoning Ellen to her room. In a fit of drunken rage, she accuses Ellen of being a "whore" and her husband of loving "black meat, he ruther pleasure with a baboon." Blanche's revenge is not simply to abuse and taunt Ellen. In contradiction of gendered stereotypes about the asexual southern belle, Blanche's desire for revenge is carnal in nature. She turns to one of her personal house slaves and orders them to "Fetch me up here the bigges,' blackes' nigger buck we's got on that place. That Mede nigger. He the one. Go fetch him along here."[50]

Onstott uses the ensuing scene to demonstrate that Blanche, the representative of the plantation mistress, is a woman with sexual desires that not only burn brightly but cross racial lines. Spurned by her husband, Blanche sates her desire for revenge and sexual gratification by having sexual intercourse with Mede—her husband's prized stud. But Blanche's revenge is not simply to have sexual intercourse with Mede. Her vengeance plumbs the depths of sadomasochistic torture and psychological abuse. Blanche marks Mede's body by ordering him to submit to a crude and bloody ear piercing. After piercing Mede's ears, Blanche violently inserts a pair of ruby-red earrings that her husband gave her as a gift, the very same style of earrings, Blanche discovers, that Ellen also received.[51] If Blanche wants to compete with a "nigger buck" and a slave "whore" for her husband's attention, then she realizes she is going to do so by asserting her agency in the marriage by marking her husband's prized slave and challenging Hammond's patriarchal power to control the lives of other human beings as he pleases. Indeed, Hammond becomes all too aware of the challenge to his patriarchal authority when Blanche gives birth to a black baby; in response, her husband murders Mede in a cauldron of boiling water.

## Sex and Slavery in Late-Twentieth-Century Film

Onstott's *Mandingo* graphically portrayed the sexual exploitation and racial violence that he imagined was a reality of life in the slave South. In late-twentieth-century America, a society conditioned to imagine the antebellum South in romanticized ways, Onstott's version of slavery proved overwhelming in its shock value. Nonetheless, *Mandingo* was a "pulp" novel that eventually opened the floodgates to other writers and, ultimately, filmmakers, who felt the "real" history of slavery in the United States had not been told.

Before any reshaping of the popular narrative about slavery could take place, filmmakers faced significant cultural obstacles. We have seen how America's popular imagination was influenced by an overwhelming scholarly and popular literature that deemphasized sexual exploitation and violence in American slavery and emphasized the "noble" and familial qualities of the plantation South. Despite the efforts of African American writers and scholars, twentieth-century schoolchildren received a steady literary and cinematic diet of Lost Cause and "plantation genre" propaganda during the first decade of the Cold War. For example, in *The Plantation System in Southern Life* (1950), a documentary made by Coronet Instructional Films, a company that produced educational films for American high schools, students learned that exploring the South's history represented an opportunity for family "sight seeing" vacations.[52] *The Plantation System in Southern Life* thus presented students with a romanticized snapshot of slave life. The camera's focus, and the narrator's commentary, emphasized the importance of the plantation owner's mansion as the embodiment of an "aristocratic way of life" defined by "gentle manners, courtesy, and hospitality." Students also learn about the layout of the plantation, the types of agricultural products produced, and how the enslaved and enslaver interacted on the basis of "an unusual class system." The history of slavery was not a story defined by sexual exploitation and racial violence, but was the story of an orderly agricultural society. Next to nothing, then, is said about the life of the slaves, who did "almost all the work."[53] Indeed, racial and class harmony prevails in the South of the 1950s, just as it allegedly did during slavery.

The message of harmonious "class" relations between black and white Americans was projected, albeit for different purposes, in a spate of "problem films" throughout the 1940s, 1950s, and 1960s.[54] Films like *Imitation of Life* (1934 and 1959), *Lost Boundaries* (1949), *Japanese War Bride* (1952), and *Guess Who's Coming to Dinner* (1967) challenged audiences to grapple with the United States' interracial history. Unlike earlier films, such as *The Birth of a Nation* (1915) and *The Jazz Singer* (1927), which played on popular racism, "problem films" refused to demonize racialized characters or interracial couples. The didacticism of these films urged audiences to embrace "racial reconciliation."[55] Although "problem films" were often dismissed as "communist propaganda," they were not as revolutionary as contemporary film critics claimed. Indeed, "problem films" did not engage with sexual exploitation and racial violence during slavery, thereby leaving the historical origins of mixed-race Americans unexplained.[56]

But with neo-abolitionist plotlines developing in American cinematic representations of slavery during the 1950s and 1960s, filmmakers became inclined to portray slavery in darker terms.[57] Films such as *Band of Angels* (1951) and *Black Like Me* (1964), for instance, indicated that an oppressive racial and sexual history lay behind black America's experiences with racism during the nineteenth and twentieth centuries.[58] But no movie contained the types of graphic scenes described by Onstott in *Mandingo*—not, that is, until Onstott's novel was transformed into a motion picture.[59]

Two important factors made the adaptation of Onstott's novel into a movie possible. First was the 1968 introduction of the Motion Picture Association of America's ratings system. These ratings allowed the film adaptation of stories such as *Mandingo* to be released to mainstream cinemas. The second was the seriousness with which Italian reviewers and scholars treated the *Mandingo* novel. The Italians, unlike American reviewers and scholars, were unflinching in their engagement with the "sex, sadism, and miscegenation" that Onstott portrayed.[60] Perhaps it is unsurprising, then, that it was Italian filmmakers who purchased the rights to adapt *Mandingo* into a motion picture. The Italian producer Maleno Malenotti and movie mogul Dino De Laurentiis teamed up to make the movie version of *Mandingo*. Preparations began in 1968 and soon stalled, however, and it was not until 1970, after De Laurentiis moved to New York, that preparations resumed in earnest.[61]

De Laurentiis hired American Richard Fleischer to direct the film. Fleischer was well known in Hollywood, and after initially expressing reservations he was eager to make the film. Fleischer felt that an accurate account of slavery had not yet been presented to American cinema audiences. His motives for making the film echoed the activist sentiments swirling around American society in the 1970s. Fleischer said of his willingness to make the movie, "The whole slavery story has been lied about, covered up and romanticized so much that I thought it really had to stop."[62] These were sentiments shared by the entire cast and crew of *Mandingo*, which was distributed in the United States by Paramount Pictures. Shot mostly in Louisiana, the movie had a star-studded cast. The English actor James Mason played Warren Maxwell, a young Perry King played Hammond Maxwell, while English actress Susan George took the role of Blanche. George, like her co-stars, was initially hesitant about accepting a part in the film. Fearing the movie would be gratuitous sensationalism, George and her fellow actors overcame their initial reservations by reading up on the history of slavery. All agreed that slave breeding had occurred and that it was time to reveal what black Americans had endured for so long. It was also time, George felt, to undermine the sentimental imagery of *Gone with the Wind* and the popular romanticization of its lead character, Scarlett O'Hara (also played by a British actress, Vivien Leigh). George, reflecting on her role as Blanche in *Mandingo*, recognized at least one similarity between her character and Scarlett O'Hara. "After all," she quipped, "aren't they both bitches?"[63]

The African American actors in the film included the stunning Brenda Sykes as Ellen and the professional boxer Ken Norton as Mede. Norton was most famous for breaking Muhammad Ali's jaw on his way to defeating the boxing legend in a 1973 bout.[64] Norton was indeed well cast. Despite having no acting skills, his physical presence on screen embodied the type of virile black masculinity that caused white Americans such anxiety throughout the nineteenth and twentieth centuries. In his autobiography, Norton wrote about the significance of the film and his role in it:

*Mandingo* was a departure, as far as slave pictures go. It dared to illustrate the seedy, sexual side of black-white relations in the antebellum South. The movie was based on the enormously popular novel by Kyle Onstott. My part was that of the towering black slave named Mede whose taut muscles vibrate with power and sensuality. When I read the script, my first scene had me placed in the middle of a city square where I was to be sold. A potential owner, a white woman, wanted to "take a look under the hood," so to speak, and unzipped my fly to get a gander at my dander. She wasn't disappointed.

Norton was thus aware of how the movie version of *Mandingo* would not simply unsettle popularly accepted interpretations of the Old South but also challenge Americans to think about the legacy of racial and sexual violence during slavery. For black as well as white audiences, this proved to be a particularly uncomfortable experience, but it was an experience that the cast and crew of *Mandingo* felt American audiences needed to have. As Fleischer described the type of movie he wanted to make, "the image we should keep in mind [for Falconhurst, as for all slave plantations] was a beautiful wedding cake that's filled with maggots."[65]

Whether Fleischer's movie delivers an externally beautiful plantation is debatable. *Mandingo* is a film in which the camera is constantly moving, capturing the unkempt, run-down, and disorganized surrounds of Falconhurst. It is the antithesis of the Twelve Oaks plantation in *Gone with the Wind* and is thus designed to highlight the moral bankruptcy of the whites who exercise power over the region. As with all movie adaptations of novels, the filmmakers took liberties and departed from some of the more tangential storylines in Onstott's novel. In general, though, the novel's representation of sexual exploitation and racial violence remained in the movie version. According to Fleischer, his movie was "the first honest representation of slavery," and it spoke directly to slavery's enduring impact on American society. Fleischer insisted, "I'm not interested in making white people feel guilty about slavery but just to show what black people had to go through to arrive where they are today."[66]

Film critics labeled this "lusty antebellum drama" as "ludicrous," "a potpourri of racism," "Black comedy," and a "bestially vulgar film" and accused its makers of producing little more than an "animated comic book."[67] Black reviewers and audiences expressed a more mixed set of perspectives. Some expressed anger that black actors Brenda Sykes and Ken Norton lent "their efforts to a film" that was a "'rip off' of Black people's past."[68] Others quibbled

Figure 5. Poster for the movie release of *Mandingo.* In possession of author.

with comments made by the film's star, Ken Norton, that *Mandingo* portrayed fictional events. Writing from New York, Marcia Kilpatrick disagreed with Norton, claiming the boxer-actor need only "talk with enough of our old people" to realize "what Kyle Onstott originally wrote in fiction form was once a reality."[69] Indeed, the editors at *Jet* magazine described *Mandingo* as a "powerful movie drama . . . which portrays Black-white relations in the antebellum South as they probably were."[70] For all of the competing critiques of *Mandingo*, Fleischer's movie enjoyed considerable box-office success. According to the July 10, 1975, edition of *Jet* magazine, *Mandingo* grossed $2,433,010 during its first five weeks in cinemas, making it one of the most popular films of that summer.[71] By 1979 the film had earned $8.6 million, more than the $7.8 million earned by the blaxploitation film *Shaft*.[72]

## From Black Folklore to New Media Representations of Sex and Slavery

The didacticism of the film version of *Mandingo* presented what some viewers considered a type of historical realism. Based on the adjectives used by white reviewers to describe the film, most white Americans in the 1970s were unwilling or unable to engage with the film's themes. Since then, little has changed. Indeed, the "white backlash" to the civil rights and Black Power movements has become "mainstream" in American popular and political culture. The increasingly rightward drift of the Republican Party and the rise of vocal fringe groups such as the Tea Party tap into a popularly held belief that the 1960s and 1970s ushered in an era of "political correctness."[73] The sense of white grievance that such mantras evoke is historically misplaced and misinformed. Nonetheless, examples of such grievances abound. In November 2010, for instance, during celebrations for the 150th anniversary of the Civil War, the "commander-in-chief" of the Sons of Confederate Veterans, Michael Givens, spoke for many white southerners when he declared: "We in the South, who have been kicked around for an awful long time and are accused of being racist, we would just like the truth be known."[74] This image of the victimized white South dates back to the era of Reconstruction when, following the Civil War, white southerners complained about being under siege from Yankee soldiers, carpetbagger politicians, and inept blacks. It is disingenuous imagery to evoke, but it helps to explain the visceral way in which narratives of sexual exploitation and racial violence during slavery have been dismissed as mere sensationalism since the 1970s.

With cultural debates increasingly polarized in the United States, foreign filmmakers have for the past quarter century observed Americans struggle with questions about interracial sex and violence. They have endeavored to understand the origins of this struggle. Most prominently, Italian filmmakers produced "mondo" films, or "shockumentaries," during the 1970s to tackle the nineteenth-century antecedents of racial and sexual violence in America. One of the best-known "shockumentaries" was *Addio Zio Tom* (Goodbye Uncle Tom) (1971). Critics and film scholars have labeled *Addio Zio Tom* "transgressive," "excessive," and unnecessarily shocking. Gualtiero Jacopetti and Franco Prosperi, the makers of *Addio Zio Tom*, were not fazed by such critiques. They wanted to shock audiences, and the scenes of violence, sadism, physical degradation, rape, and slave breeding were meant to challenge audience sensibilities. It is questionable whether Jacopetti and Prosperi succeeded. They were correct in asserting that the slave South was a grotesquely exploitative society, but questions about how filmmakers effectively portray sexual exploitation and racial violence without alienating audiences remain problematic. As film scholar Mark Goodall observes, the "crude retelling of the sexual perversity of the American slave trade in *Addio Zio Tom* was too much for many audiences and critics in the early 1970s."[75]

Whether black audiences were as shocked as whites by *Addio Zio Tom* is questionable. This is because tales of racial violence and "sexual perversity" during and after slavery have long been a staple of African American storytelling and folklore. Black folklore operates at a public level of narration, but unlike movies it generally does not use the technologies of filmmaking to reach (and "shock") a mass audience. Since slavery times, black folklore has exhibited etiological qualities. Through myth and storytelling, narrators attempt to explain things as they are. For example, the devil in black folklore is often portrayed as a white southerner. Alternatively, humor is regularly invoked to highlight the absurdity of social situations created by whites with political power.[76]

Few elements of modern black folklore are as evocative and humorous as stories about sex and human genitalia. The historian Lawrence Levine observes that "no part of the traditional stereotype of the Negro was more commonly played with and joked about in black expressive culture than the element of sex."[77] Laughter and comedy can reveal much about a group's anxieties, attitudes, and aspirations. For black Americans, jokes about human genitalia and sexual intercourse serve all of these purposes. African American ministers, for example, have historically been among the most influential and publicly recognizable figures in black communities. Their position of power and authority has also been grist to the folklore mill for tales about sexual intercourse between a minister and female members of his congregation.[78] There's more than a grain of truth to tales of clerical lechery in American culture. Many will recall examples of white preachers, such as Jimmy Swaggart, as well as prominent black ministers like Martin Luther King Jr., experiencing intense public scrutiny for their sexual affairs. Alternatively, stories about "big black dicks" borrow from racial stereotypes to assert a masculine power that African American men might not necessarily possess in social and political life.[79]

Folkloric tales about sex have also played a prominent role in this informal library of social commentaries about slavery. Often, the chronology of slavery and Jim Crow segregation are brought together to symbolize the racial and gendered power dynamics that have existed between black and white Americans since the nineteenth century.[80] Stories about rape, the separation of enslaved families because of sale, and the lynching of a male family member evoke images of historical suffering. In such contexts, storytellers sometimes revert to comedy to mask great pain.[81] At other times, the narrators either emphasize the determination of the enslaved to resist sexual exploitation or use biting satire to highlight the absurdity of white racism and sexism.

Folklorist Daryl Cumber Dance has recorded an extensive range of African American folklore. One story, for example, combines narrative threads from the history of slavery, the Underground Railroad, and slave breeding. The story focuses on a male slave named John. John's master values him highly because he is the plantation stud. Thus, the unnamed master is unwilling to part with John. Dance records that John, on the other hand, is determined to gain his freedom: "During the days of slavery Ole Massa owned a very valuable slave named John. John decided, though, that slavery was not for him and he wanted his freedom. So there was a great underground movement, and John was able to get in on it, and through some friends he finally got to Philadelphia. Well, Ole Massa was certainly disturbed because John was one of his most valuable slaves. He was very strong and had so many children among the slaves; and this was very valuable because he was selling the slaves, you know, and he certainly didn't want to lose John."[82] Tales of this nature reflect how the memory of slave breeding lived on into the late twentieth century among African American people. There was no forgetting of interracial sexual exploitation during slavery in such tales. But while the commodification of slave sexuality was remembered, so too was the slave's resistance to such practices. In this case, "John" refuses to submit to his master's immoral will and draws on a network of unnamed friends to steal away to freedom in the North.[83]

Other folkloric tales are more crude but no less poignant. The "Fornication Contest" is one such tale. Folklorist collected various versions of this story during the 1960s and 1970s.[84] Dance recorded the following version in the 1970s:

> It was generally known that a Black nigger could outfuck a white man. But this particular white man did not believe it, and his friends didn't believe it.
>
> So they had a fucking contest: the Master fucking a white wench, and the nigger fucking a nigger wench. And the scorekeepers were keeping score.
>
> The white man fucked her twelve times and fell away—couldn't do no more. The nigger went right on fucking. When they got to twenty-four times, the scorekeepers got confused. One said it was twenty-four; the other said twenty-five. There was an argument.
>
> The nigger said, "No need to argue and fuss. I will start over again."[85]

Projected onto the movie screen, such narratives would undoubtedly shock and even anger audiences. But while these narratives exist at a public level, they are not screened in movie theaters and therefore do not leave cinema audiences feeling uncomfortably complicit in scenes of sexual excess. Such reactions, of course, miss the point of black folktales. Narratives of this nature circulate among black Americans, constituting a type of "race talk" in which the absurdity of white racial stereotypes, the history of interracial sex, rape, and violence, and an assertion of black masculine prowess combine to produce tales that are both pointed and humorous.

These types of folktales, and the imagery they convey, are increasingly finding their way into a wider public realm thanks to new media technologies. Since at least the 1980s, and certainly since the explosion of the Internet, the ways in which interracial sex and violence are associated with slave breeding have become more accessible. As a result, America's master historical narrative is more than ever a site of great intellectual and cultural contestation. Both individuals and groups use history to push political agendas, make artistic statements, or simply contribute to the din of Internet discussion in the blogosphere. However, it is important to note one significant caveat to these observations. Race continues to affect the earning capacity, and thus the purchasing power, of African Americans. This means that black people are far more likely than whites to access the Internet via mobile phones, devices that are generally cheaper than laptops or personal computers. Therefore, how black Americans engage with the Internet is affected by personal income, the ongoing legacy of racialized poverty and underemployment, and the limits of cellular phone technology. The result is less African American entrepreneurial activity on the Web (relative to white activity) and limits to the democratizing qualities of new media technologies.[86]

Nonetheless, there are many examples of how new media is being used to present the history of slavery in the United States. Some sites purport to be purely educational, such as the U.S. National Slavery Museum Web site, which is dedicated to garnering support for a national slavery museum in Washington, D.C.[87] This Web site is by no means shocking or confrontational. Rather, it attempts to strike a "neutral" tone in the way slavery is remembered. Other Web sites are provocative. For example, *We Are Respectable Negroes* is a blog dedicated to racial issues in twenty-first-century America. It mixes racial commentary with the wit and sardonic humor historically associated with African American folklore.[88] Blogs of this nature create communities of like-minded people who can post comments and contribute to the tenor of historical discussion. The blog *Racialicious*, for instance, revealed the plans of a Haitian couple who wanted to open an "amusement park" dedicated to slavery. Posted on January 6, 2008, the blogger detailed plans for the "park," which the would-be operators hoped to title "Memory Village."[89] Responses to this post ranged but were generally negative and expressed a concern that such endeavors trivialized the suffering endured by millions during slavery.

New media thus encounter many of the same representational difficulties experienced by novelists and filmmakers. Once the memory of historical trauma is translated to any medium that can be "consumed" by a "market," the specter of the "lurid," "sensational," and "money-grabbing" arises. One artist who has successfully negotiated the terrain of the artistic and commercial in recent decades is Kara Walker. Walker's work plays on the historical imagery of the "nigger wench." Like recent works of fiction by Dolen Perkins-Valdez, Walker's work strives to invert racist and sexist imagery and to highlight the humanity of enslaved women.[90] Her artwork, as Gwendolyn Du Bois Shaw so elegantly observes, presents the bodies of the enslaved "in erotic, satiric, and violent poses that were both attractive and repulsive."[91] Walker is, in short, a brave and brilliant artist. She re-creates shocking scenes of enslavement that are both violent and sexually explicit. Her imagery, however, is far from gratuitous;

instead, she forces us to grapple with the brutalities of slavery and inspires viewers to come to terms with human complexity in the slave South.

Walker conveys this complexity with antique silhouettes, an artistic style that in the early nineteenth century was the preserve of the white middle class. Walker wrenches this art form from white America's (largely forgotten) past to depict sex, violence, childbirth, defecation, and death in slavery. The shadowy nature of Walker's images, their life-size proportions, confront the viewer in a way cinema cannot. These are both public and personal encounters with historical imagery, encounters that do not leave one feeling voyeuristic but instead deeply moved to reexamine the content of our collective understanding of slavery in United States history.[92]

Walker's skilled use of the silhouette reflects the narrative complexity of America's history with slavery. At the level of the historical, her work reacquaints viewers with the faceless images of slaves that were common in nineteenth-century drawing and painting. During this earlier period, enslaved African Americans were not "people" worthy of having their emotions, feelings, and sufferings depicted in any detail. Walker recovers these expressionless silhouettes from the dustbin of artistic history. In the late twentieth and early twenty-first centuries, such imagery stirs our historical imaginations and challenges viewers to reflect on the emotions of the slaves depicted.

## Conclusion

Walker's work brings together many of the narrative elements that have traditionally been associated with black literature and filmmaking: interracial sex and violence, humor and poignancy. These are issues and emotions explored by Walker. And like many works of art, racial commentary, and politics in twenty-first-century America, Walker's work can be viewed on Internet sites as diverse as personal Web pages, blogs, and *YouTube*. What impact these new media forms will have on the master narrative of American history remains to be seen. What is clear, however, is that the sources used to interpret the past, as well as the media through which history is narrated, are more dynamic than ever.

The dominant narrative threads in slave-breeding discourses—rape, violence, and family breakup—have long been addressed by African American literature, film, folklore, and art. The legal scholar Sherrilyn A. Ifill has recently observed that the African American narration of U.S. history has traditionally revolved around traumatic stories about a mother's heartbreak over a child being sold away, the rape of a black girl, or the lynching of a son, brother, or husband. These tales of sexual violence are told in creative ways to circumvent "patterns of racial silencing and marginalization" in "mainstream" American culture.[93] Richard Pryor, the great African American comedian, quipped about these historical counternarratives: "Niggers just have a way of telling you stuff and not telling you stuff. Martians would have a difficult time with niggers. They be translating words, saying a whole lot of things underneath you, all around you . . . that's our comedy."[94]

Pryor emphasized how black Americans use humor, just as they have used spirituals, scholarship, fiction, plays, films, and works of art, to narrate a history characterized by violence, sexual exploitation, and injustice. This is a version of United States history that many white Americans find either shocking or unrecognizable. While the new media of the twenty-first century hold the potential for the articulation of historical narratives more commonly embedded in black culture, there is no guarantee that the "age of Obama" and "post-racialism" will usher in a new and more inclusive understanding of the significance of slavery and slave breeding in American history.

# Epilogue

Since the first publication of John Hope Franklin's *From Slavery to Freedom* (1947), this wildly successful college textbook has addressed the topic of slave breeding. In its first printing, Franklin focused on the economics of slave breeding, contending that "surplus" slaves were bred in the upper South and dumped on the slave market in the lower south at times of economic distress.[1] In subsequent editions, Franklin elaborated on this analysis. In the 1956 edition, he argued that slave owners protected themselves from a reduction in the supply of slaves following the 1808 ban on the international slave trade to the United States by adopting schemes for the "systematic breeding of slaves."[2] In editions written since then, especially since the 1990s, the tenor of the narrative about slave breeding has become pointed in the way it explores the sexual and racial hypocrisy of the slave South. Writing with Alfred A. Moss Jr. in the 2008 edition, Franklin argued that slave breeding "was one of the most approved methods of increasing agricultural capital. Traders were castigated by the slaveholding gentry as being inhuman, vicious, and extremely venal, but slave-breeding owners were far more common and much more highly esteemed in the community."[3]

For more than half a century, *From Slavery to Freedom* has constituted the official narrative of African American history for American college students. Within its storyline, John Hope Franklin positioned slave breeding as a matter-of-fact aspect of slavery's history in the United States. He did this at a time when the historical establishment dismissed slave breeding as a myth, or the product of sensational abolitionist propaganda and the unreliable oral histories of former slaves. Since Franklin's death in March 2009, professional historians have shown no indication that they are any closer to reaching consensus about slave breeding. Methodological divisions over how to reconstruct the history of slavery continue to produce intense, often passionate debates. Since the global financial crisis in 2008, these divisions have become more entrenched. Economic historians, marginalized in the 1980s and 1990s for their overly theoretical and technical analysis, feel that the time is ripe for their brand of history to make a comeback, as though putting the "economics" back into our understanding of the past would result in a "return of history."[4] Should this occur, there exists the potential for a new era of "list histories" in which the experiences, emotions, and ideas of human beings are lost beneath an avalanche of numbers, "rational choice theory," and "markets." The point to emphasize here is that although few social and cultural histories ignore the economics of the past, many economic histories overlook or dismiss the importance of the social and cultural dimensions of history. In relation to a deeper engagement with historical topics like slave breeding, a methodological turn back to economic history runs the risk of rearticulating the logic of the slave owners and slave traders and of parroting the scholarly dismissal of slave breeding that began when late-nineteenth- and early-twentieth-century historians revised amateur historical accounts of slave breeding.

Slavery, much less emotionally charged topics like slave breeding, remain open wounds in American history. The use of statistics and data sets enable scholars and the general public to talk about slavery. Indeed, framing discussions of slavery in purely economic or statistical terms makes it possible to suggest that life for the enslaved was not as bad as abolitionists, former slaves, and black intellectuals have claimed.

Having said that, America's elected officials have in recent decades tried to confront the historical wound that slavery has left in American history. They have done this in a variety of ways, most notably by considering the pros and cons of an apology for slavery. During the course of these debates, Presidents Bill Clinton and George W. Bush made what amounted to "near apologies" for slavery—Clinton strangely apologizing to Africans, but not African Americans, for slavery, while Bush acknowledged the link between slavery and "racial bigotry."[5] While the national debate about an apology for slavery has attracted a good deal of media attention, most white Americans remain opposed to an apology and oblivious to the racial and sexual abuses it unleashed on American society. In contrast, a majority of African Americans believe an apology for slavery constitutes an appropriate national statement about the significance of slavery in American history and contemporary life.[6] The wound that slavery left in American history and cultural life continues to divide.

Over the past two decades, slavery has remained a focal point in many discussions about racial and sexual violence. African American leaders acknowledge that an apology for slavery and its legacy would constitute a fitting token.

But tokenism doesn't go far enough. In the 1960s, Martin Luther King Jr. criticized racial "tokenism" and insisted that monetary compensation for slavery was warranted.[7] More recently, the president of the Southern Christian Leadership Conference, Dr. Joseph Lowery, warned in 1997: "The danger of an 'apology' for slavery is that it may become the benediction (end), instead of the opening hymn (means)! So if you are going to apologize, please print it on the back of a deed to my 40 acres and send it by way of my mule!"[8] The specter of reparations for slavery divides Americans.[9] A 2002 poll found that 79 percent of African Americans favored an apology for slavery (in comparison to 30 percent of whites) and 67 percent favored reparations (in comparison to only 4 percent of whites).[10] In what form African Americans should receive reparations remains unclear. What is significant about this debate, though, is the way black Americans continue to discuss an apology and reparations by combining history—change over time—with memory—or the articulation of similarities. Professional historians go to great lengths to differentiate between history and memory, but for most African Americans such distinctions are far too arbitrary to have any narrative meaning.[11] Millions of black Americans, in short, live with, and see, the legacies of slavery on a daily basis.[12]

Weaving descriptions of slave breeding into "remembered" histories of slavery forces individuals to grapple with the emotional dimensions of the past. By discussing slave breeding as an aspect of economic or agricultural history, white historians and the readers of their histories have kept these emotions at bay. For many Americans, this emotional distancing has been necessary because incorporating historical images of a brutal and exploitative practice like the breeding of slaves raises uncomfortable questions about historical identity in American culture. If the United States is a republic of laws, a land of freedom, and a nation of rational economic actors, then slave breeding must be ignored, denied, or explained away if this collective sense of self is to retain its affirmative qualities.

As the chapters in this book have demonstrated, African Americans have articulated a different perspective on the significance of slave breeding in the history of slavery and of the relevance of slavery to the American republic. The violent and coercive sexual schemes that white and black abolitionists sensationally associated with slave breeding, the memories of slave breeding that former slaves sometimes shared with the outside world during the late nineteenth to the early twentieth century, the crafting of historical narratives—be they by amateur historians or a nascent black intelligentsia—and the publication, production, and presentation of novels, plays, music, and art by African

Americans has ensured that slave breeding has remained an important part of how black Americans understand racial violence, sexual exploitation, and the external pressures placed on black families since slavery.

Still, prominent black Americans often complain that white Americans refuse to engage with African American interpretations of U.S. history. In 2001, Harvard University law professor Charles Ogletree said as much when he challenged Americans to finally confront the legacy of slavery. Ogletree claimed, "The history of slavery in America has never been fully addressed in a public forum."[13] Implicit in Ogletree's remarks is not only frustration about a lack of engagement with the meaning of slavery in American history but also an explanation for why African Americans have more often than not kept stories about the brutalities experienced by the enslaved alive in historical memory. For decades, African Americans were prohibited from participating in any sort of "public forum," much less one that included whites. And when black Americans did find themselves engaged in a "public forum" with white people, they knew that the racial etiquette of Jim Crow America demanded silence on issues that might embarrass, hurt, or anger white American perceptions of their ancestors.

In the 1990s, the former North Carolina civil rights leader and minister Carl Wesley Matthews analyzed a document called the "Willie Lynch Letter." A late-eighteenth-century slave owner reportedly wrote the document, which was reputed to contain details on how best to control and breed slaves. The letter, which had been in circulation since the 1970s, became an Internet sensation during the 1990s and is now featured on scores of black studies and African American history Web sites. That the letter is a hoax is beside the point; the real issue for many who read it is that it confirmed suspicions about the existence of coercive breeding schemes in American slavery. Summarizing the historical implications of the "Willie Lynch Letter," Matthews stated: "We are the offspring of test tube babies. We have been broken, bred, and cross-bred. We have been bred in the bone. We have been reborn. And we have been recycled [laughter]. We are the product of recycling."[14] Matthews combined history with memory, fact with fiction, and humor with biting analysis to highlight the myriad ways in which violence, sex, and slavery have been used to justify the implementation of programs of human management, biological knowledge, and technology that have targeted black Americans since slavery.

While the "Willie Lynch Letter" is a hoax, Matthews's assessment of its significance reminds us of just how easy it has been to marginalize African American perspectives on slavery. This is especially so if the disciplinary angle at which one enters this discussion is political, agricultural, or economic in focus. From these approaches, slave breeding is the stuff of fiction, and more recent debates about an apology or reparations for slavery are irrelevant.

The human dimensions of historical experience and emotion are lost if the memories of African American people are not taken seriously and incorporated into our understandings of the past. Few topics in American history underscore this as boldly as slave breeding. By recognizing that individuals draw on myriad sources to understand the significance of the past in relation to the present, and to write histories that are both scholarly and compassionate, a more inclusive, democratic history—one that incorporates its abuses and its triumphs—might be possible. Such histories will certainly enrich national debate about the ongoing legacy of slavery. They will also provide us with opportunities to address what the historian Ira Berlin has termed the "perplexing connection between slavery and race and the relation of both to the intractable problems of race and class in the twenty-first century."[15] As an engagement with slave breeding in African American culture reminds us, the study of interracial sex, violence, and memory in United States history has never been more relevant.

# NOTES

## Introduction

1. Rawick, *The American Slave*, North Carolina Narratives, 15, pt. 2:274. Hereafter cited as *AS*.

2. John L. Caughey, "Individuals and Their Cultures," in Caughey, *Negotiating Cultures and Identities*, 7.

3. *AS*, North Carolina Narratives, 15, pt. 2:275.

4. Ibid., 270, 274. For a provocative reinterpretation of the worldview of the master class in the antebellum South see Fox-Genovese and Genovese, *The Mind of the Master Class*, 3.

5. *AS*, North Carolina Narratives, 15, pt. 2:271.

6. In *Centering Woman*, Beckles explores how enslaved women in the Caribbean navigated the power dynamics of plantation society to develop a semblance of social hierarchy among themselves. For antebellum observations of this nature see Weld, *American Slavery as It Is*, 174–75.

7. *AS*, North Carolina Narratives, 15, pt. 2:274–75.

8. Fogel and Engerman, *Time on the Cross*, 78–79. See similarly Lowe and Campbell, "The Slave-Breeding Hypothesis"; Kotlikoff and Pinera, "Old South's Stake"; Genovese, *The Political Economy of Slavery*, 281; Tadman, *Speculators and Slaves*, 124–25; Cooper and Terrill, *The American South*, 206. Historians have vigorously debated the profitability of slavery in the American South. For a sampling of this debate see Woodman, "The Profitability of Slavery"; Thomas and Bean, "The Fishers of Men"; Temperley, "Capitalism, Slavery and Ideology"; Ransom and Sutch, "Capitalist without Capital"; Thornton, "Slavery, Profitability, and the Market Process"; and Ransom, *Conflict and Compromise*, 9–10, 43–46.

9. Boles, *Black Southerners*, 69. Claire Robertson has argued that her data reveals that New World slave owners were interested in "production," not "reproduction. See Robertson, "Africa in the Americas? Slavery and Women, the Family, and the Gender Division of Labor," in Gaspar and Hine, *More Than Chattel*, 26.

10. D'Emilio and Freedman, *Intimate Matters*, xii–xii, xviii–xix; Teresa de Lauretis, "The Violence of Rhetoric: On Representation and Gender," in Lancaster and di Leonardo, *The Gender Sexuality Reader*; Povinelli, *The Empire of Love*, 7–10.

11. Mia Bay, "Looking Backward in Order to Go Forward: Black Women Historians and Black Women's History," in D. G. White, *Telling Histories*, 182–99.

12. Genovese and Fox-Genovese, "Slavery, Economic Development, and the Law";

Ransom and Sutch, "Capitalists without Capital," 138; Carr, *What Is History?* 9–10; J. C. Scott, *Domination and the Arts of Resistance,* 53; Bevir, "Objectivity in History," 329; Tetlock, "Theory-Driven Reasoning"; Hodgson, *How Economics Forgot History,* 3–4; Joan W. Scott, "Women's History," in Burke, *New Perspectives on Historical Writing,* 60–61; Zahedieh, *The Capital and the Colonies,* 94.

13. ILGALLAT-L Archives, July 11, 2000, http://archiver.rootsweb.ancestry.com/th/read/ILGALLAT/2000-07/0963333532 (accessed September 15, 2011).

14. Gordon-Reed, *Thomas Jefferson and Sally Hemings;* Gordon-Reed, *The Hemingses of Monticello.*

15. Wood is quoted in Peter Wood, "Jefferson-Hemings Revisited," *Chronicle of Higher Education,* September 1, 2011, http://chronicle.com/blogs/innovations/jefferson-hemings-revisited/30273 (accessed September 1, 2011); R. F. Turner, *The Jefferson-Hemings Controversy,* 31, 33 (see 126 for "junk science").

16. On this point I am in agreement with H. White, *Tropics of Discourse,* 51–53; Novick, *That Noble Dream,* 6; and Trouillot, *Silencing the Past,* 5–6.

17. Robert O'Meally, "On Burke and the Vernacular: Ralph Elison's Boomerang of History," in Fabre and O'Meally, *History and Memory in African-American Culture,* 245.

18. David W. Blight, "W. E. B. Du Bois and the Struggle for American Historical Memory," in Fabre and O'Meally, *History and Memory in African-American Culture,* 53; Susan Willis, "Memory and Mass Culture," in Fabre and O'Meally, *History and Memory in African-American Culture,* 187.

19. Dorothy Nelkin and Susan Lindee, "The Media-Fed Gene: Stories of Gender and Race," in Terry and Urla, *Deviant Bodies,* 398.

20. *Jet,* February 1, 1988, 18.

21. Mike Bianchi, "Dusty's Remarks Shouldn't Inflame Hot-Button Topic," *Orlando Sentinel,* July 11, 2003, http://articles.orlandosentinel.com/2003-07-11/sports/0307110305_1_dusty-baker-ira-berlin-white-people (accessed September 27, 2011).

22. Elizabeth Nunez, e-mail correspondence with author, October 12, 2010. I thank Professor Nunez for responding to my questions. On Washington "buying" his slaves' teeth see Chadwick, *The General and Mrs. Washington,* 148. For the history of medical experimentation on black Americans see H. A. Washington, *Medical Apartheid.*

23. Mda, *Cion,* 36–37.

24. Zakes Mda, e-mail correspondence with the author, July 21, 2011. I thank Professor Mda for responding to my questions.

25. Abercrombie, *Pathways of Memory and Power,* 21.

26. Herbert Gutman and Richard Sutch, "Victorians All! The Sexual Mores and Conduct of Slaves and Their Masters," in David et al., *Reckoning with Slavery,* 154.

27. Gutman, *The Black Family in Slavery and Freedom,* 148–50. See also Conrad and Meyer, "Economics of Slavery"; C. Morris, "The Articulation of Two Worlds," 993. A recent summation of this historiography can be found in Boswell, *Her Act and Deed,* 161 n. 19.

28. Higman, *Slave Populations of the British Caribbean*, 349.

29. C. Morris, *Becoming Southern*, 71; C. Morris, "The Articulation of Two Worlds," 993.

30. Analysis and quotations in this paragraph are from C. Morris, *Becoming Southern*, 70–72.

31. Hartman, *Scenes of Subjection*, 3, 5. See also R. Richardson, *Black Masculinity and the U.S. South*. Richardson is also interested in exploring historical legacies and connections. Her focus, however, is on black masculinity, using a geographical focus on the South to delve into the construction of black male identities since the nineteenth century.

32. My thinking on this point is indebted to Glassberg, "Public History and the Study of Memory"; Kammen, "Public History and the Uses of Memory"; Irene Carlota Silber, "Commemorating the Past in Postwar El Salvador," in Walkowitz and Knauer, *Memory and the Impact of Political Transformation*, 214; and Tyrell, *Historians in Public*. See also the special issue "The Public Life of History" in *Public Culture* 20, no. 2 (2008).

33. Donoghue, *Black Breeding Machines*, 327.

34. The rhetoric used in this debate was more often than not sensational. See, for example, *Extracts from the Evidence Delivered Before a Select Committee of the House of Commons*, 27–29; and *The Debate on the Motion for the Abolition of the Slave-Trade*, 116.

35. Wood quoted in Beckles, *Natural Rebels*, 101. On the historical debate about slave breeding in the Caribbean see Bennett, "The Problem of Slave Labor Supply"; Lowenthal and Clark, "Slave Breeding in Barbuda"; B. C. Richardson, *Caribbean Migrants*, 57; Higman, *Slave Populations of the British Caribbean*, 348–49; McCaw-Binns, "Safe Motherhood in Jamaica," 255; Bergad, *Comparative Histories*, 106; P. Levine, *The British Empire*, 19–20. For a study that breaks away from demographic and socio-historical analysis and uses insights from psychology see Kempadoo, *Sexing the Caribbean*, 40.

36. C. Snyder, *Slavery in Indian Country*, 182.

37. Alexander, *History of the Colored Race*, 180.

38. Faux, *Memorable Days in America*, 49.

39. Olmstead, *A Journey in the Seaboard Slave States*, 2:353; Olmstead, *A Journey to the Back Country*, 285. In 1862, Olmstead turned to census data to support his earlier claims for the existence of slave breeding in portions of the South. See his *The Cotton Kingdom*, 58.

40. See, for example, Neal, *Unburdened by Conscience*, 72; Enrico Dal Lago and Constantina Katsari, "Ideal Models of Slave Management in the Roman World and in the Ante-Bellum American South," in Dal Lago and Katsari, *Slave Systems*, 188–211; and Glymph, *Out of the House of Bondage*, 48.

41. Plantation Manual, 1857–58, James Henry Hammond, James Henry Hammond Papers (Container 35, Reel 18), Manuscript Division, Library of Congress, LC-MS-24695-1; Faust, *James Henry Hammond and the Old South*, 88–91; Fogel and Engerman, *Time on the Cross*, 84–85.

42. The encouragement of slave-breeding practices was often reinforced by racist

beliefs that the slave was naturally able to breed prolifically. See, for example, Weston, *The Progress of Slavery in the United States*, 82. Success in mating slaves who promised to breed prodigiously was not always guaranteed, as Thomas Foster noted in the wake of slavery's abolition. See his "Norman and Saxon Blood Royal," 328. For antebellum examples see Hazard, "On the General Management of Negroes"; Hammond, "Overseers."

43. The William Massie Papers, 1747–1919, Center for American History, University of Texas at Austin, Box 2 E505.

44. Volume 15, Register of Negroes, 1836–1866, Massie Papers, Box 2Q85.

45. Barbour County (Ala.) Agriculture Society, Report, 1846, in Breeden, *Advice to Masters*, 6.

46. For a contrasting view see Genovese, *The Political Economy of Slavery*.

47. Quoted in Breeden, *Advice to Masters*, 13.

48. Marx and Engels, *The Communist Manifesto*, 26.

49. Tadman, *Speculators and Slaves*, 121–27; T. D. Morris, *Southern Slavery and the Law*, 92; Donald L. Yates, "Plantation-Style Social Control: Oppressive Social Structures in the Slave Plantation System," in Durant and Knottnerus, *Plantation Society and Race Relations*, 31; W. Johnson, *Soul by Soul*, 58; W. Johnson, *The Chattel Principle*, 1; Sharifa Ahjum, "The Law of the White Father: Psychoanalysis, 'Paternalism,' and the Historiography of Cape Slave Women," in Campbell, Miers, and Miller, *Women and Slavery*, 100.

50. Moynihan, *The Negro Family*.

51. Rawick, *From Sundown to Sunup*; Genovese, *Roll, Jordan, Roll*; Blassingame, *The Slave Community*; Gutman, *The Black Family in Slavery and Freedom*.

52. D. G. White, *Ar'n't I a Woman?* 98; T. Hunter, *To 'Joy My Freedom*, 11.

53. Hine, "Rape and the Inner Lives of Black Women."

54. Mitchell, *Righteous Propagation*, 13; Matterson, *For the Freedom of Her Race*, 83–84; McGuire, *At the Dark End of the Street*.

55. Elsa Barkley Brown, "To Catch the Vision of Freedom: Reconstructing Southern Black Women's Political History, 1865–1880," in Gordon et al., *African American Women and the Vote*, 66–67, 68.

56. Ibid., 68. See also Parks, *Fierce Angels*.

57. Malone, *Sweet Chariot*, 260; Stevenson, *Life in Black and White*, 205, 206–57 passim. See also Dunaway, *The African-American Family*; her "Theoretical Reprise" (268–88) provides a useful overview of some of the literature reviewed above and some provocative suggestions for future research.

58. Stevenson, *Life in Black and White*, 232.

59. Schwartz, *Birthing a Slave*, 5.

60. Betts, *Thomas Jefferson's Farm Book*, 46.

61. Schwartz, *Birthing a Slave*, 11, 16, 23, 68, 71.

62. Ibid., 22–23. See also Neal, *Unburdened by Conscience*, 75–76.

63. P. H. Collins, *Black Feminist Thought*, 136.

64. J. Carson, *Silent Voices*, 2.

65. Nelson, *Straight, No Chaser*, 97. Historians have recently broached similar issues, particularly in relation to the internal slave trade. See, for example, W. Johnson, *Soul by Soul*, 86–88; and Deyle, *Carry Me Back*, 48, 68, 172.

66. Bridgewater, "Reproductive Freedom as Civil Freedom," 411–12. See also Bridgewater, "Un/Re/Dis Covering Slave Breeding."

67. Bridgewater, *Breeding a Nation*.

68. Arendt, *Between Past and Future*, 48; Huggins, *Black Odyssey*; Edward E. Baptist, "'Stol' and Fetched Here: Slave Migration, Ex-Slave Narratives, and Vernacular History," in Baptist and Camp, *New Studies in the History of American Slavery*, 243–74.

69. On the growth of "sentiment" in nineteenth-century literature about slavery see Levecq, *Slavery and Sentiment*.

70. C. R. Wilson, *Baptized in Blood*; Blight, *Race and Reunion*.

71. Quote found in Baptist, "'Stol' and Fetched Here," 253. Interdisciplinarity is also important to the study of slavery and race in the United States because, to borrow from the philosopher Pierre Bourdieu, the "horizon of the past and of the future are . . . tied together in a single consciousness." Bourdieu quoted in Adjaye, *Time in the Black Experience*, 5.

## Chapter 1. American Abolitionism and Slave-Breeding Discourse

1. *The Eclectic Review*, March 1841, 342; *The Economist*, August 24, 1844, 1139; *The Anti-Slavery Reporter*, June 1, 1846, 95–96. See also Rodriguez, *Slavery in the United States*, 1:308.

2. Victoria E. Bynum, "Misshapen Identity: Memory, Folklore, and the Legend of Rachel Knight," in P. Morton, *Discovering the Women in Slavery*, 30.

3. C. Tate, *Domestic Allegories of Political Desire*, 171.

4. V. Smith, *Self-Discovery and Authority*, 41. Sentimentalism also involved taking literary risks, as the author might run the risk of reifying racial and sexual stereotypes in the minds of white readers. On this point see Fionnghuala Sweeney, "'Mask in Motion': Dialect Spaces and Class Representation in Frederick Douglass' Atlantic Rhetoric," in Braxton and Diedrich, *Monuments of the Black Atlantic*, 38.

5. This chapter builds on the important insights of Welter, "The Cult of True Womanhood"; Kerber, *Women of the Republic*, chapter 9; C. Dixon, *Perfecting the Family*; Vergne, *Shaping the Discourse on Space*; Cott, *Public Vows*; McBride, *Impossible Witnesses*; Rice, *Radical Narratives of the Black Atlantic*; Sweet, *Bodies Politic*; Lightner, *Slavery and the Commerce Power*.

6. A recent special edition of the *William and Mary Quarterly* provides excellent analysis of abolitionist historiography and presents important new research. See *William and Mary Quarterly*, 3rd ser., 56, no. 4 (2009).

7. Of a vast historiography, some of the most compelling analyses in recent years include Drescher, *Capitalism and Antislavery*; Blackburn, *The Overthrow of Colonial Slavery*, chap. 8; Carey, *British Abolitionism*; C. L. Brown, *Moral Capital*.

8. Philip D. Morgan, "Ending the Slave Trade: A Caribbean and Atlantic Context" in D. R. Peterson, *Abolitionism and Imperialism in Britain, Africa, and the Atlantic*, 101–2.

9. *Abridgement of the Minutes, 1789*, 50.

10. Hochschild, *Bury the Chains*, 323. Typical examples of the pros and cons of schemes to "breed" slaves were articulated by Ranby, *Doubts on the Abolition of the Slave Trade*, 67–68; Fitzpatrick, *Suggestions on the Slave Trade*; and Renny, *An History of Jamaica*, 311.

11. Wilberforce, *A Letter on the Abolition of the Slave Trade*, 243. British abolitionists linked images of life and death in their political discourse to emphasize the immoral nature of the commerce in which slave traders engaged. V. Brown, *The Reaper's Garden*, 175–76.

12. See the introduction to this book for further details and citations.

13. Increase and Decrease of Slaves and Stock, 1822/23, 1160/7/10, and Increase and Decrease of Slaves and Stock, 1832, 1160/7/12, Georgia Estate, MS 1160/7/8–19, Special Collection, University of Aberdeen, Scotland.

14. Blackburn, *The Making of New World Slavery*, 519; Fogel, *The Slavery Debates*, 55; Hartnett, *Democratic Dissent*, 50; Klein, *The Atlantic Slave Trade*, 22.

15. McBride, *Impossible Witnesses*, 63; Deyle, "An 'abominable' New Trade," 833–35.

16. Newman, *The Transformation of American Abolitionism*, 1, 2. Historical works dealing with the early years of American abolitionism during the Revolutionary War and early republic include D. B. Davis, *The Problem of Slavery*; Nash, *Race and Revolution*; Nash and Soderlund, *Freedom by Degrees*; Soderlund, *Quakers and Slavery*; Dillon, *The Abolitionists*; Zilversmit, *The First Emancipation*; and S. White, *Somewhat More Independent*. For studies of the politics, philosophies, and protest tactics of American abolitionism after the 1830s see Abzug, *Cosmos Crumbling*; Blackett, *Building an Antislavery Wall*; Kraditor, *Means and Ends in American Abolitionism*; L. Perry, *Radical Abolitionism*; P. Goodman, *Of One Blood*; and Harrold, *The Abolitionists and the South*. On the role of women in the abolitionist movement see Yee, *Black Women Abolitionists*; Jeffrey, *The Great Silent Army of Abolitionism*; Pierson, *Free Hearts and Free Homes*; Portnoy, *Their Right to Speak*; and Salerno, *Sister Societies*.

17. Lightner, *Slavery and the Commerce Power*, 171–72.

18. "The Legal Basis of American Slavery," *Massachusetts Quarterly Review* 3 (June 1848): 289.

19. See Walters, "The Erotic South," 177 n. 1, in which Walters notes the hostility encountered when presenting his research findings. Since the early 1970s, however, historical analysis of slavery and sexuality has grown increasingly sophisticated and nuanced. See Baptist, "'Cuffy,' 'Fancy Maids,' and 'One-Eyed Men'"; E. West, *Chains of Love*; Pierson, "'Slavery Cannot Be Covered Up'"; Stephanie M. H. Camp, "The Pleasures of Resistance: Enslaved Women and Body Politics in the Plantation South, 1830–1861," in Baptist and Camp, *New Studies in the History of American Slavery*, 87–124; Fraser, *Courtship and Love*.

More recent social histories have provided excellent insights into the socioeconomic importance of the internal slave trade. See Tadman, *Speculators and Slaves*; W. Johnson, *Soul by Soul*; Gudmestad, *A Troublesome Commerce*; W. Johnson, *The Chattel Principle*; Deyle, *Carry Me Back*; Deyle, "An 'abominable' New Trade."

20. Beecher, *Freedom and War*, 421. See also Brewster, *Slavery and the Constitution*, 9. See also C. Dixon's *Perfecting the Family*, 38–39, 42–43; Cott, *Public Vows*, 34; and Bergad, *Comparative Histories*, 105–7.

21. Walters, "The Erotic South," 179, 183, 187; Pierson, "'Slavery Cannot Be Covered Up,'" 384–85, 387, 396, 399; C. Morris, "The Articulation of Two Worlds," 988, 993–94; Glymph, *Out of the House of Bondage*, 5, 53–54, 136; Levecq, *Slavery and Sentiment*, 8, 20, 192.

22. Norbert Finzsch, "'The Aborigines . . . were never annihilated, and still they are becoming extinct': Settler Imperialism and Genocide in Nineteenth-Century America and Australia," in A. D. Moses, *Empire, Colony, Genocide*, 254; Smithers, "The 'Pursuits of the Civilized Man,'" 247.

23. Bay, *The White Image in the Black Mind*, 16–17; Rael, *Black Identity and Black Protest*, 5, 15.

24. Wheatley's 1773 poem "On the Death of an Infant" was reprinted in *The Poetical Magazine*, November 1809, 369.

25. *Narrative of the Life of Moses Grandy*, 40.

26. Painter, *Sojourner Truth*, 159; O. Gilbert, *Narrative of Sojourner Truth*, 12. Henry Watson provided readers of his 1849 memoir with insight into the mixture of emotions experienced by slaves in the auction room: "Some were in tears; others were apparently cheerful," and many had grease applied to the mouth "so as to make it appear that they are well and hearty." Watson, *Narrative*, 7, 12. See similarly *Narrative of the Life of Moses Grandy*, 31.

27. Quarles, *Black Abolitionists*, 17, 211; Harding, *There Is a River*, 127; Condit and Lucaites, *Crafting Equality*, 72; Stauffer, *The Black Hearts of Men*, 15–17.

28. *A Narrative of Some Remarkable Incidents in the Life of Solomon Bayley, Formerly a Slave, in the State of Delaware, North America*, 591.

29. H. Watson, *Narrative*, 5.

30. Ibid., iii–iv, 26, 38.

31. Ibid., 32.

32. Yellin and Van Horne, *The Abolitionist Sisterhood*, 164; 164; Sterling, *Black Foremothers*, xxvi; G. T. Tate, *Unknown Tongues*, 125; Salerno, *Sister Societies*; Stewart, *William Lloyd Garrison at Two Hundred*, 56.

33. Grace and Sarah M. Douglass to William Lloyd Garrison, May 27, 1839, in F. Berry, *From Bondage to Liberation*, 143. See also Stauffer, *The Black Hearts of Men*, 110.

34. Quoted in Cott et al., *Root of Bitterness*, 253.

35. *Monthly Review*, July 1839, 313; *Slavery Illustrated in Its Effects Upon Woman and Domestic Society*, 37–38, 65; Cheever, *God against Slavery*, 225; Eiselein, *Literature and Humanitarian Reform*, 21.

36. Economic and social historians have focused a great deal of their energy on analyzing abolitionist claims about the breeding and sale of slaves from the upper to the lower South. See the introduction to this book for further discussion of this point.

37. *Monthly Review*, July 1839, 312.

38. *An Address Delivered by the Rev. Theodore Parker before the New York City Anti-Slavery Society*, 43. See similarly R.L.C., "Our Concern with American Slavery," *The Christian Reformer; or Unitarian Magazine and Review*, September 1853, 556; Marjoribanks, *Travels*, 363; "The Foreign Policy of the United States," *Westminster Review*, July 1855, 97.

39. "Hebrew and American Slavery Compared," *Christian Spectator*, July 1863, 392.

40. M. A. Morrison, *Slavery and the American West*, 88; Glover, *Southern Sons*, 88, 182; *The Proslavery Argument*, 237.

41. Genovese, *Roll, Jordan, Roll*, 3–4; Tadman, *Speculators and Slaves*, 179; Bay, *The White Image in the Black Mind*, 135–36; Ford, *Deliver Us from Evil*, 7–8.

42. Genovese, *Roll, Jordan, Roll*, 4, 178, 338–40, 402; Ford, *Deliver Us from Evil*, 497.

43. Weld, *American Slavery as It Is*, 182; *Slavery Illustrated in Its Effects upon Woman and Domestic Society*, 9, 14; Weld, *Slavery and the International Slave Trade*, 13–14.

44. Dew quoted in *The Proslavery Argument*, 359.

45. Elizabeth Margaret Chandler quoted posthumously in Rubens, *"Liberty,"* 52. White women who took an active part in the abolition movement spoke in similarly sentimental terms, lamenting the bondage of "my poor brothers and sisters" and the physical and mental abuse heaped on the enslaved. Sarah M. Grimke explained leaving her native South Carolina in such terms: "I left my native state on account of slavery, and deserted the home of my fathers to escape the sound of the lash and the shriek of tortured victims." See *The Evangelical Repository* 18 (1859): 502. Statements of a similar nature can be found throughout abolitionist rhetoric, highlighting both the sentimentalism infused into abolitionists' writing and speechmaking and the limits of liberal notions of human equality in antebellum America. Unlike the "tortured victims" Grimke described, she had the ability to make choices; she chose to leave a region that millions could not.

46. Weld, *American Slavery as It Is*, 182. On the expulsion of "the great and growing evil" of free blacks in Virginia, see Link, *Roots of Secession*, 155; Klarman, *Unfinished Business*, 36; Ashwood, *Slavery, Capitalism, and Politics*, 78–79.

47. C. Phillips, *Missouri's Confederate*, 151–52. See also Wubben, *Civil War Iowa and the Copperhead Movement*, 7–8; James F. Brooks, "Violence, Justice, and State Power in the New Mexican Borderlands, 1780–1880," in White and Findlay, *Power and Place*, 40–41; M. A. Morrison, *Slavery and the American West*, 33; Huston, *Stephen A. Douglass*, 63–64; Bergad, *Comparative Histories*, 263; Hammond, *Slavery, Freedom, and Expansion*.

48. M. A. Morrison, *Slavery and the American West*, 88; *The Proslavery Argument*, 237. See also p. 331. Similar arguments had been on the rise since the 1830s. See *A Review, in Part, of "The New-York Humbugs." By David Meredith, M.D. in Which the Bold Denuncia-*

*tions of the Author Are Brought to the Test of Reason and Philosophy* (1838), 7, New York Historical Society.

49. M. A. Morrison, *Slavery and the American West*, 113.

50. Channing, *A Letter to the Honorable Henry Clay*, 36.

51. *The Anti-Slavery Record*, 9. Steven Deyle notes that the "slave trade tied Virginia slaveholders' own frontiers to the Southwest via this [slave] trade." See Deyle, "An 'abominable' New Trade," 834.

52. Freehling, *The Road to Disunion*; Finkelman, *Slavery and the Founders*; Jaffa, *Crisis of the House Divided*; J. J. Ellis, *Founding Brothers*; Feagin, *Racist America*, 11; Epps, *Democracy Reborn*, 6; Mason, *Slavery and Politics*; Howe, *What Hath God Wrought*; Forbes, *The Missouri Compromise and Its Aftermath*; Beeman, *Plain, Honest Men*.

53. *Eclectic Review*, July 1835, 114.

54. Channing, *A Letter to the Honorable Henry Clay*, 37.

55. *Congressional Globe* 12 (1843), 195. See also J. R. Giddings, *Speeches in Congress*, 474.

56. Parker, *Defects*, 86.

57. Seaman, *Essays on the Progress of Nations*, 215. See also p. 117, in which Seaman doubts the ability of abolitionism to form the basis for a successful political party at the national level. It should also be noted that slight variations in abolitionist rhetoric can be seen throughout the antebellum period, with some anti-slavery advocates referring to "slave-breeding" or "slave-rearing" states of the upper South and the "slave-consuming" states of the lower South. See, for example, *Proceedings of the New-England Anti-Slavery Convention*, 31, 65; "The Disruption of Family Ties," *Anti-Slavery Record*, March 1836, 33; Price, *Slavery in America*, 271–72; Rubens, "Liberty," 182.

58. Seaman, *Essays on the Progress of Nations*, 425. See also Dewey, *Discourse on Slavery*, 13–14.

59. *Address of John Quincy Adams*, 16.

60. Porter, *Early Negro Writing*, 460.

61. Ibid., 464. See also *Narrative of the Adventures and Escape of Moses Roper*, 72; Henson, *Father Henson's Story*, 30; Mars, *Life of James Mars*, 21.

62. See also F. Douglass, *Frederick Douglass Papers*, 2:26; Heglar, *Life and Adventures of Henry Bibb*, 38, 189–90.

63. Porter, *Early Negro Writing*, 466. See also C. Dixon, *Perfecting the Family*, 50; Houchins, *Spiritual Narratives*; Cott et al., *Root of Bitterness*, 253, 255, 260–61.

64. Potter, *The Impending Crisis*; Waugh, *On the Brink of Civil War*, 190–91; H. Hamilton, *Prologue to Conflict*, xiv.

65. P. S. Foner and Branham, *Lift Every Voice*, 322–23.

66. Cheever, *God against Slavery*, 226; See similarly Johnston, *Notes on North America*, 2:354; *Friends' Intelligencer*, January 17, 1857, 699; Beecher, *Freedom and War*, 421. See also Brewster, *Slavery and the Constitution*, 9; C. Dixon, *Perfecting the Family*, 38–39; 42–43; Cott, *Public Vows*, 34; and Bergad, *Comparative Histories*, 105–7. African American historian Benjamin Quarles made a similar point when he argued that black

abolitionists were highly critical of "the disparity between the rhetoric and the reality, between their country's high professions of liberty and equality and the existence of slavery and the high wall of color." Quarles, *Black Abolitionists*, 122.

67. Johnston, "Notes on North America," 48; G. Smith, *The True Office of Civil Government*, 6–8.

68. For the abolitionist fear that compromise politics would extend not only slavery but also slave-breeding practices into the Southwest and West see Cheever, *God against Slavery*, 225; Henry, *Plain Reasons*, 17. Henry Clay attempted to moderate anti-slavery and Free Soil fears that the slave South wanted to extend slave-breeding practices westward, insisting that the increase in slave numbers in the upper South reflected little more than the kind, paternal care of the slave master. *Remarks of Mr. Clay, Kentucky*, 14.

69. For the "new slave breeding Guinea" see R. Hildreth, *Archy Moore*, 351. Similar claims can be found in M. Hall, *Two-Fold Slavery*, 24–26; Marjoribanks, *Travels*, 320, 322; Boynton and Mason, *Journey through Kansas*, 131; Olmstead, *A Journey in the Seaboard Slave States*, 283; M'Carter, *Border Methodism and Border Slavery*, 8; Helper, *Impending Crisis*, 54; and H. Wilson, *No Rights, No Duties*, 5.

70. M. Hall, *Two-Fold Slavery*, 27. See similarly J. D. Long, *Pictures of Slavery*, 39–40; Brewster, *Slavery and the Constitution*, 9.

71. On the opposite side of the Atlantic, the *North British Review* lamented that it is "painful to dwell upon the scenes which must be of almost daily occurrence in a slave-breeding state, whose sensitive beings are literally treated like every other description of domestic animal, endowed indeed with instincts and appetites, but utterly destitute of parental or filial affection, beyond the period when it is required for the continuation and preservation of the species. . . . How many cherished ties were ruthlessly severed, must be left to the imagination." *North British Review*, February 1857, 300.

72. M. Hall, *Two-Fold Slavery*, 29. See similarly "Slavery," *Dublin University Magazine*, December 1856, 684; *Evangelical Christendom*, November 1, 1862, 562; J. D. Long, *Pictures of Slavery*, 2; M'Carter, *Border Methodism and Border Slavery*, 61; R. Hildreth, *Archy Moore*, 325; Cairnes, *The Slave Power*, 127–28; Marjoribanks, *Travels*, 321–22. See also Elliot, *Sinfulness of American Slavery*, 1:330; Mann, *Slavery*, 82; Jay, *Miscellaneous Writings on Slavery*, 129–30; "Politics, Sociology, and Travels," *Westminster Review* 72 (July 1859): 151; *Revelations of a Slave Smuggler*, 52.

73. The former slave Henry Bibb's famous words, "where I should have received moral, mental, and religious instruction, I received stripes without number, the object of which was to degrade and keep me in subordination," embody this perception on the part of former slaves and black abolitionists. Heglar, *Life and Adventures of Henry Bibb*, 13.

74. F. Douglass, *My Bondage and My Freedom*, 411–12. See similarly *Narrative of the Life of Moses Grand*, 35; Sprague, *His Promised Land*, 26.

75. My thinking on this point is indebted to Thavolia Glymph's brilliant *Out of the House of Bondage* (especially pp. 3–4). The analysis that follows is an attempt to expand on Glymph's insights.

76. Clinton, *The Plantation Mistress*; D. G. White, *Ar'n't I a Woman*; Fox-Genovese, *Within the Plantation Household*; Weiner, *Mistresses and Slaves*; Glymph, *Out of the House of Bondage*, 5–6.

77. F. Douglass, *My Bondage and My Freedom*, 48.

78. F. Douglass, *Frederick Douglass Papers*, 2:54, 96. On these issues, Douglass's condemnation of the slave South intensified as political divisions between North and South widened. In 1850 he remarked that "there is nothing in piracy, nothing in lewdness, that is not to be found in the slave system—indeed, slavery is a system of lewdness and piracy." Ibid., 263. See also F. Douglass, *My Bondage and My Freedom*, 80; *Narrative of the Life of Moses Grandy*, 36–37; Henson, *Father Henson's Story*, 15.

79. *A Narrative of the Adventures and Escape of Moses Roper, From American Slavery*, 44. See similarly *Narrative of the Life of Moses Grandy*, 36; and Garnet, "To the Slaves of the United States of America," 1843, in Garnet, *A Memorial Discourse*, 45.

80. J. Jones, *Labor of Love, Labor of Sorrow*, 38; E. West, *Chains of Love*, 34, 36; Schwartz, *Birthing a Slave*, 13; Fraser, *Courtship and Love*, chap. 2.

81. Yellin and Van Horne, *The Abolitionist Sisterhood*, 117.

82. Sanchez-Eppler, *Touching Liberty*, 135; Kaplan, *The Erotics of Talk*, 104.

83. Child, *Incidents in the Life of a Slave Girl*, 79–80. For analysis of Jacobs's life see Yellin, *Harriet Jacobs*. For an account that echoes the emotions experienced by Wheatley, Jacobs, and generation after generation of enslaved women but was penned by a former male slave, see Green, *Narrative of the Life of J. D. Green*, 9–10, 19.

84. Nellie Y. McKay, "The Narrative Self: Race, Politics, and Culture in Black American Women's Autobiography," in S. Smith and Watson, *Women, Autobiography, Theory*, 97–98; Sidonie Smith and Julia Watson, introduction, in S. Smith and Watson, *Before They Could Vote*, 14.

85. V. Smith, *Self-Discovery and Autobiography*, 12.

86. H. A. Jacobs, *Incidents in the Life of a Slave Girl*, 5. All subsequent references to *Incidents in the Life of a Slave Girl* are from this edition.

87. Ibid., 8.

88. Ibid., 27.

89. Ibid., 39. See also 32.

90. Ibid., 49. Sarah Parker Remond expressed similar sentiments. She exclaimed in 1859: "The slave woman was the victim of the heartless lust of her master, and the children she bore were his property." Cott et al., *Root of Bitterness*, 258.

91. *Narrative of the Life of Moses Grandy*, 6, 16–17; *Experience and Personal Narrative of Uncle Tom Jones*, 10, 14; Henson, *Father Henson's Story*, 13, 15, 30, 42; Green, *Narrative of the Life of J. D. Green*, 20–21; Frederick Douglass, "The Nature of Slavery," December 1, 1850, in Brotz, *African-American Social and Political Thought 1850–1920*, 216.

92. Typical of the recollections of former slaves in antebellum America, J. D. Green recalled that at the age of twenty "my master told me I must marry Jane, one of the slaves." After five months of marriage, Jane gave birth to a child who was "nearly white," the father being the child's master. Green, *Narrative of the Life of J. D. Green*, 22.

93. Ripley, *Black Abolitionist Papers*, 24. See also pp. 253–54, 268, 348, 409. See also Frederick Douglass, "The Present and Future of the Colored Race in America," June 1863, in Brotz, *African-American Social and Political Thought*, 268.

94. Purvis, *Appeal to Forty Thousand Citizens*, 14. See also Henson, *Father Henson's Story*, 6.

95. On this point see *Slavery Illustrated in Its Effects upon Woman and Domestic Society*, 22–23; W. W. Brown, *The Black Man*, 33–35.

96. Frederick Douglass, "What Are the Colored People Doing for Themselves?" July 14, 1848, in Brotz, *African-American Social and Political Thought*, 208; F. Douglass, *Papers*, 4:83, 173–74.

97. Delany, *Condition, Elevation, Emigration, and Destiny*, 14.

98. *Memoir of Old Elizabeth, a Coloured Woman*, 14.

99. *Slavery Illustrated in Its Effects upon Woman and Domestic Society*, 37.

100. Harding, *There Is a River*, 127 ("humble, grateful slave"); Quarles, *Black Abolitionists*, 47, 49, 118; William E. Gienapp, "Abolitionism and the Nature of Antebellum Reform," in D. M. Jacobs, *Courage and Conscience*, 41.

101. Condit and Lucaites, *Crafting Equality*, 72.

102. Frederick Douglass, "An Address to the Colored People of the United States," September 29, 1848, in Brotz, *African-American Social and Political Thought*, 210.

103. Whipple, *The Story-Life of Lincoln*, 640.

## Chapter 2. Slavery, the Lost Cause, and African American History

1. Elmore, *Lincoln's Gettysburg Address*, 233.

2. Pollard, *The Lost Cause* (1st ed.), 45–46; Pollard, *The Lost Cause Regained*, 156.

3. *Historical Magazine* 10, no. 5 (1866): 153. Pollard responded to his critics in Pollard, *The Lost Cause* (2nd ed.).

4. Towns, *Enduring Legacy*, esp. chap. 6.

5. Blight, *Race and Reunion*, 38.

6. Cash, *The Mind of the South*, 129–31; Catton, *The Coming Fury*, 456; Woodward, *Origins of the New South*, 79–80, 84; E. Foner, *Reconstruction*, 34; Williamson, *The Crucible of Race*, 155–57; Silber, *The Romance of Reunion*, 18–19, 62; Blight, *Race and Reunion*, 79–81; Gardner, *Blood and Irony*, 55–62, 208; B. E. Baker, *What Reconstruction Meant*, 69–70.

7. Quoted in Woodward, *The Burden of Southern History*, 140.

8. Sumner accused South Carolina senator Andrew Butler of taking up with "the harlot, slavery" and of being unable to control his drooling. See C. Dixon, *Perfecting the Family*, 79–80; Rodriguez, *Slavery in the United States*, 1:202. On the significance of the Battle of Gettysburg see Gallagher, *Lee and His Army*, 83; McPherson, *Battle Cry of Freedom*.

9. Pierce, *Memoir and Letters of Charles Sumner*, 4:141.

10. Escott, *"What Shall We Do with the Negro?"*

11. Doesticks and Butler, *What Became of the Slaves*, 9, 15; McKaye, *The Mastership and Its Fruits*, 6; Conway, *Testimonies Concerning Slavery*, 19.

12. *Report of the Commissioner of Agriculture for the Year 1865*, 130.

13. Greeley, *The American Conflict*, 1:70–71.

14. *Scribner's Monthly*, December 1875, 274. See also Pike, *First Blows of the Civil War*, 391.

15. *New Englander and Yale Review* 37 (1878): 90.

16. Calman, *Life and Labours of John Ashworth*, 294.

17. Julie Roy Jeffrey provides a brilliant historical analysis of abolitionist memories and remembrance in her *Abolitionists Remember*. See also W. Phillips, *Speeches, Lectures, and Letters* (1872 ed.), 64.

18. Pillsbury, *Acts of the Anti-Slavery Apostles*, 15.

19. Karl Marx famously argued that "in the United States, after the conversion of the neutral territory between the wage labor states of the North and the slave labor states of the South in a slave breeding region for the South, where the slave thus raised for market had become an element of annual production," the slave market supplied coerced labor power. Marx, *Capital*, 2:559. Volume 2 of *Capital* was originally published in German as *Das Kapital* in 1886. See similar arguments in Simons, "Economic Aspects of Chattel Slavery," 164; and Von Holst, *Constitutional and Political History*, 1:352.

20. Albion W. Tourgee, a Radical Republican, lawyer, and novelist, played his part in keeping slave breeding in popular consciousness. His novel *Hot Plowshares* tied the memory of territorial expansion to slave breeding when he asked rhetorically: "Was slave-breeding and slave-trading to become as much a part of our internal economy as stock-raising or sheep-farming?" (325).

21. A. Hildreth, *History of the United States*, 6:697; Beecher, *Patriotic Addresses*, 469; W. Phillips, *Speeches, Lectures, and Letters* (1872 ed.), 63; Tuckerman and Jay, *William Jay and the Constitutional Movement*, 151; Schuricht, *History of the German Element in Virginia*, 1:29; Lowell, *Writings of James Russell Lowell*, 5:141.

22. H. Wilson, *Rise and Fall of the Slave Power*, 1:100; Lee and Thorpe, *The Civil War*, 44, 59; Bogart, *Economic History of the United States*, 253; Keifer, *Slavery and Four Years of War*, 1:40.

23. Rhodes, *History of the United States*, 1:27.

24. Ibid.

25. Ibid., 310. See also Fischer, *The Gun and the Gospel*, 11; Keifer, *Slavery and Four Years of War*, 1:40; and Fite, *History of the United States*, 299.

26. Rhodes, *History of the United States*, 1:311. See also George, *The Political History of Slavery*, 14.

27. Thomas Foster, writing in the popular *Gentleman's Magazine*, scoffed at suggestions of slave breeding. In language that typified the social Darwinian ethos of the age, Foster insisted that the laws of "natural selection" worked against the idea of slave breeding. He explained: "There have been some cases in which men have been treated in some respects like animals under domestication, as, for instance, in certain

slave-breeding districts. But even in such cases the influence of the affections, though restrained, was not destroyed; and the process of selection which slave-breeders would have liked to carry out systematically was considerably interrupted. Besides, slave-breeders were unable to hasten the growth of individual specimens of their art, so that in the lifetime of a single slave-breeder not more than two or three generations of slaves could be dealt with, and in two or three generations selection can produce no very marked results. Nor again, can the effect of natural selection be noted in the case of the more civilized races of man; seeing that multitudes of relations, other than those which are involved in ordinary natural selection, come into action among communities of men." Foster, "Norman and Saxon Blood Royal," 328.

28. Phelps, *My Study*, 192; Kelsey, "The Evolution of Negro Labor," 73; W. H. Collins, *Domestic Slave Trade*, 69–71. On the representation of mixed-race people and miscegenation laws after the Civil War see Williamson, *New People*, 95–96, 134–35; Wald, *Crossing the Line*; Moran, *Interracial Intimacy*; Talty, *Mulatto America*, 20; Pascoe, *What Comes Naturally*.

29. For claims that the Association for the Study of Negro Life and History peddled a steady stream of historical propaganda see the editorial commentary in the *Mississippi Valley Historical Review* 12, no. 4 (1926): 628–29. It should be noted that Woodson was determined that the association and its publications not be used as vehicles of propaganda, but should involve serious scholarship. See Dagbovie, *The Early Black History Movement*, 61. For further historical analysis see Adeleke, *Without Regard to Race*, 6–7; Cook, *Troubled Commemoration*, 161.

30. Moore, "Some Recollections of Slavery," 23.

31. Ibid., 24.

32. Ibid., 25.

33. Mallard, *Plantation Life before Emancipation*, 113.

34. At the American Historical Association's annual meeting in 1911, Columbia University historian James H. Robinson claimed that the historical profession had made great strides since the mid-nineteenth century in becoming "scientifically presentable." "The Meeting of the American Historical Association at Indianapolis," *American Historical Review* 16, no. 3 (1911): 470–72. For analysis of the "objectivity question" in history see Novick, *That Noble Dream*.

35. Dunning, *Essays on the Civil War*, 204–7. Dunning argued that African Americans were, at best, possessed of enough intelligence to mimic whites. He wrote that the freedmen "wandered aimlessly but happy through the country, found endless delight in hanging about the towns and Union camps, and were fascinated by the pursuit of the white man's culture in the schools which optimistic northern philanthropy was establishing whenever it was possible" (11). Examples of other notable histories from the Dunning school include Garner, *Reconstruction in Mississippi*; W. L. Fleming, *Civil War and Reconstruction in Alabama*; Reynolds, *Reconstruction in South Carolina*; W. W. Davis, *The Civil War and Reconstruction in Florida*; J. G. Hamilton, *Reconstruction in North Carolina*; Thompson, *Reconstruction in Georgia*; and Staples, *Reconstruction in Arkansas*.

36. See, for example, the 1868 testimony of Elizabeth Keckley, a former Virginia slave, in Mintz, *African American Voices*, 151; McBride, *Impossible Witness*, 4–9; Camp, *Closer to Freedom*, 51; Baptist, "'Stol' and Fetched Here': Slave Migration, Ex-Slave Narratives, and Vernacular History," in Baptist and Camp, *New Studies in the History of American Slavery*, 243–65; Stephanie M. H. Camp, "The Pleasures of Resistance," in Baptist and Camp, *New Studies in the History of American Slavery*, 87–113; Fraser, *Courtship and Love*, 85; Glymph, *Out of the House of Bondage*, 31, 93–94.

37. *The Story of Mattie J. Jackson: A True Story* (Lawrence: Printed at Sentinel Office, 1866) in *Six Women's Slave Narratives*, 4.

38. *Memoir of Old Elizabeth, a Coloured Woman* (Philadelphia: Collins, Printer, 1863) in *Six Women's Slave Narratives*, 14–15.

39. Ibid., 18. In 1889, Bethany Veney provided one of the clearest postbellum literary examples of how she resisted the debasement of the slave auction block. She wrote of how "One after the another the crowd felt my limbs, asked me all manner of questions, to which I replied in the ugliest manner I dared." *The Narrative of Bethany Veney, a Slave Woman* (Worcester, Mass., 1889) in *Collected Black Women's Narratives*, 30.

40. H. Mattison, *Louisa Picquet, the Octoroon: Or Inside Views of Southern Domestic Life* (New York: Published by the author, 1861), in *Collected Black Women's Narratives*, 5. See also W. Johnson, "The Slave Trader," 17–18; Baptist, "'Cuffy,' 'Fancy Maids,' and 'One-Eyed Men'"; A. Davis, "'Don't Let Nobody Bother Yo' Principle'"; A. P. Long, *The Great Southern Babylon*, 2.

41. Steward, *Twenty-Two Years a Slave*, 131.

42. Preston, "Genesis of the Underground Railroad"; Okur, "Underground Railroad in Philadelphia"; Harrold, "On the Borders of Slavery and Race"; Switala, *Underground Railroad in Pennsylvania*.

43. Still, *The Underground Rail Road*, 2.

44. Ibid., 75.

45. Ibid., 76.

46. Ibid., 314–15.

47. Ibid., 315–16; Still, *An Address on the Voting and Laboring*, 5–6; Siebert, *The Underground Railroad*, 228.

48. H. C. Bruce, *The New Man*, 130.

49. Ibid.

50. J. P. Green, *Recollections*, 85.

51. F. Jones, *Days of Bondage*, 6–7.

52. Ibid., 7.

53. Ibid., 9–10.

54. Ibid., 10.

55. Ibid., 18.

56. James, *Wonderful Eventful Life*, 20.

57. Crummell, *The Race-Problem in America*, 8.

58. Bolding, *"What of the Negro Race,"* 15.

59. Hurley, *The Negro in America*, 3.

60. Ibid., 2.

61. Ibid., 5.

62. On the African American use of social Darwinian, eugenic, and "racial destiny" discourse see Lewis, *W. E. B. Du Bois: Biography*, 286–87; Mitchell, *Righteous Propagation*, esp. chapter 7.

63. Hurley, *The Negro in America*, 8.

64. Mia Bay, "'The World Was Thinking Wrong about Race': The *Philadelphia Negro* and Nineteenth Century Science," in Katz and Sprague, *W. E. B. Du Bois, Race, and the City*, 54; Mitchell, *Righteous Propagation*, 203, 215.

65. K. Miller, *Race Adjustment*, 130. For a reactionary African American interpretation of these issues—one that places the burden of responsibility for racial uplift on black women—see Thomas, *The American Negro*.

66. *Appendix to the Souvenir Presented to James M. Ashley on Emancipation Day, September 2, 1893*, v.

67. Williamson, *New People*; Kennedy, *Interracial Intimacies*; Pascoe, *What Comes Naturally*.

68. Charles W. Chesnutt, "What Is a White Man?" in McElrath, Leitz, and Crisler, *Charles W. Chesnutt*, 72–73; Mitchell, *Righteous Propagation*, 215–16. For more detail on lynching, see chapter 3 of this book.

69. P. H. Collins, *Black Sexual Politics*, 336; Bay, *To Tell the Truth Freely*, 103.

70. Mitchell, *Righteous Propagation*, 12.

71. Ibid., 87; Higginbotham, *Righteous Discontent*, chap. 7; Wolcott, *Remaking Respectability*, 17.

72. Archibald H. Grimké, "The Sex Question and Race Segregation," in *American Negro Academy Occasional Papers*, 4–5.

73. F. L. Hunter, "Slave Society on the Southern Plantation," 7. See also Duvall, *The Building of a Race*, 7–9, 57, 60.

74. H. C. Bruce, *The New Man*, 123.

## Chapter 3. Black History and Slave Breeding in the Early Twentieth Century

1. U. B. Phillips, *American Negro Slavery*, 377.

2. Ibid., 222.

3. Ibid., 306.

4. Reinhart, "The Negro"; MacLeod, "Economic Aspects of Indigenous American Slavery," 642.

5. U. B. Phillips, *American Negro Slavery*, 514.

6. Lewis, *W. E. B. Du Bois: Reader*, 196.

7. Bowers, *The Tragic Era*, 51; K. Miller, "Eugenics and the Negro."

8. Horsman, *Race and Manifest Destiny*, 2, esp. chap. 7; Bederman, *Manliness and Civilization*, 30, 178; Jacobson, *Whiteness of a Different Color*, 207–10; Stern, *Eugenic Nation*, 168–71.

9. On the complexities of race, sex, and color at the turn of the century see Spickard, *Mixed Bloods*; Jacobson, *Whiteness of a Different Color*; Wald, *Crossing the Line*; Guterl, *The Color of Race*; Talty, *Mulatto America*.

10. Dagbovie, *The Early Black History Movement*, 84.

11. W. J. Moses, *Afrotopia*, 24; Bay, *The White Image in the Black Mind*, 221–23; Rael, *Black Identity and Black Protest*, 222; Dagbovie, *The Early Black History Movement*, 32; S. G. Hall, *Faithful Account of the Race*, 22, 152.

12. Dagbovie, "Black Women Historians," 241.

13. Dreer, "What Does the Innocent Teacher Impart as History?" 482.

14. Ibid., 480.

15. See, for example, the documents in part 1 of Broderick and Meier, *Negro Protest Thought*.

16. Greener quoted in J. D. Smith, "A Different View of Slavery," 301. See also Conyers, *Charles H. Wesley*, 133.

17. W. C. Bruce, *The Negro Problem*, 3–4.

18. J. E. Johnson, *The Negro Problem*, v. See also Wickliffe, "Negro Suffrage a Failure," 798; Winston, "An Unconsidered Aspect of the Negro Question," 267; and Shannon, *Racial Integrity*. It should be noted that this work was published by the Methodist Episcopal Church, South, a branch of the Methodist Episcopal Church that had long held pro-slavery and strong racial segregationist positions.

19. B. T. Washington, *The Negro Problem*, 10, 79, 108; W. E. B. Du Bois, "The Immediate Program of the American Negro," *The Crisis*, April 1915, 310–12.

20. H. T. Kealing, "The Characteristics of the Negro People," in B. T. Washington, *The Negro Problem*, 174.

21. J. B. Perry, *A Hubert Harrison Reader*, 72. For analysis see the insightful J. B. Perry, *Hubert Harrison*, 181.

22. Buehler, *Increasing the Power of the Federal Government*, 1.

23. Fleming quoted in J. D. Smith, "A Different View of Slavery," 305.

24. Reuter, "Why the Presence of the Negro Constitutes a Problem," 294.

25. Myrdal, *An American Dilemma*, 2:786.

26. B. F. Robinson, "War and Race Conflicts in the United States," 311.

27. On the historical exclusion or marginalization of black women in academia see D. K. King, "Multiple Jeopardy, Multiple Consciousness," 55.

28. C. West, *Race Matters*, 83; Dyson, *Race Rules*, 80; Pinn and Hopkins, *Loving the Body*, 4–5.

29. Lewis, *W. E. B. Du Bois: Biography*, 156–57.

30. Du Bois, *Suppression of the African Slave-Trade*.

31. Lewis, *W. E. B. Du Bois: Biography*, 157.

32. Ibid., 139–40.

33. Du Bois, *Suppression of the African Slave-Trade*, 154; Du Bois, "The Study of the Negro Problem," 3.

34. Du Bois, "The Conservation of Race."

35. See Michele Mitchell's wonderful analysis in *Righteous Propagation*.

36. Du Bois, "The Conservation of Race," 10.

37. Ibid., 12.

38. K. Miller, "A Review of Hoffman's Race Traits," 20.

39. Du Bois, *The Negro American Family*, 26. See also Ballagh, *A History of Virginia*.

40. Du Bois, *The Negro American Family*, 21.

41. Roman, *American Civilization and the Negro*, 155–56.

42. Brawley, *A Short History of the American Negro*, 53.

43. Du Bois, *Suppression of the African Slave-Trade*, 154; *American Political Science Review* 12 (November 1918): 722; *The Crisis*, January 1911, 13–14; February 1911, 10; March 1911, 6; April 1911, 6, 30; August 1911, 157–58; March 1915, 231–33; September 1915, 223–24.

44. Du Bois, *Darkwater*, 164. See also Lewis, *W. E. B. Du Bois: Biography*, 148–49; Griffin, "Black Feminists and Du Bois," 35–36; Rabaka, "W. E. B. Du Bois and 'The Damnation of Women'"; Balfour, "Representative Women"; Du Bois, *The Philadelphia Negro*, 358–67.

45. Du Bois, *Darkwater*, 165.

46. Ibid., 166.

47. Ibid., 169.

48. Ibid., 172, 180.

49. Ibid., 186.

50. Having said that, it should also be noted that Du Bois's analysis of miscegenation also fixated at times on value-laden observations of lower-class and working-class examples of black-white "miscegenation," something that provides insight into his own class prejudices.

51. Dagbovie, "Black Women Historians," 251; Welter, "The Cult of True Womanhood," 151–74.

52. P. J. Giddings, *When and Where I Enter*, 87.

53. David Levering Lewis observes that Du Bois drew liberally on the social Darwinian and biologized language of late-nineteenth- and early-twentieth-century America. See Lewis, *W. E. B. Du Bois: Biography*, 148–49.

54. Griffin, "Black Feminists and Du Bois," 35–36; Rabaka, "W. E. B. Du Bois and 'The Damnation of Women'"; Balfour, "Representative Women"; Du Bois, *The Philadelphia Negro*, 358–67.

55. In *Darkwater* (1920), Du Bois called for the "honoring of motherhood"—a status denied during slavery—and warned black men not to "shirk" their duty as patriarch and protector. Du Bois, *Darkwater*, 107.

56. Du Bois, "Race Relations in the United States," 9–10. See also Archibald H. Grimké, "The Shame of America: Or the Negro's Case against the Republic," in *American Negro Academy Occasional Papers*, 8–12. In the early twentieth century the social sciences and humanities produced a massive literature on black-white race mixing. A sampling of the key works from this period—works that Du Bois no doubt read—includes Shannon, *Racial Integrity*; Reuter, *The Mulatto in the United States*; Hankins, *The*

*Racial Basis for Civilization*; and Herskovits, *The American Negro*. For a brilliant historical analysis of these and similar scholarship, see V. J. Williams, *The Social Sciences and Theories of Race*.

57. W. E. B. Du Bois, "Worlds of Color," *Foreign Affairs* 3, no. 3 (1925): 423–44; W. E. B. Du Bois, "The Shape of Fear," *North American Review* 223, no. 831 (1926): 296–97; Du Bois, "Race Relations in the United States," 7, 10.

58. *The Crisis* 40, no. 2 (February 1933), 44. See also Cobb, "The Negro as a Biological Element."

59. Du Bois provided the following data in his "Race Relations in the United States":

| Year | Population | Percent increase over decade |
|------|-----------|------------------------------|
| 1790 | 757,208 | |
| 1800 | 1,002,037 | 32.3 |
| 1810 | 1,377,808 | 37.5 |
| 1820 | 1,771,636 | 28.6 |
| 1830 | 2,328,642 | 31.4 |
| 1840 | 2,873,648 | 23.4 |
| 1850 | 3,633,808 | 26.6 |
| 1860 | 4,441,830 | 22.1 |
| 1870 | 4,880,009 | 9.9 |
| 1880 | 6,580,793 | 34.9 |
| 1890 | 7,488,676 | 13.5 |
| 1900 | 8,833,994 | 18.0 |
| 1910 | 9,827,763 | 11.2 |
| 1920 | 10,463,131 | 6.5 |
| 1930 | 11,891,143 | 13.6 |

60. Ibid, 8. Du Bois referred to "hypocritical America" on p. 10, where he explained: "There is reason to believe that over 70 percent of these so-called Negroes are descendants of American whites and that 40 percent of them have as much white blood as Negro. Such intermingling of blood took place, moreover, mainly during slavery and mainly at the demand of white folk. Assuming that there is today no such demand from whites, it is difficult to see how in the future there could come from self-respecting, educated persons of Negro descent, any demand for this mingling of blood which would bring as much miscegenation in the near future as in the past."

61. Du Bois, "The Position of the Negro," 553.

62. Ibid., 560, 563, 569.

63. Du Bois, *Black Reconstruction*, 11, 45. I would like to thank David Barber for reminding me of the importance of Du Bois's analysis of slave breeding in *Black Reconstruction*.

64. Ibid., 45.

65. Ibid.; see also pp. 3, 33, 90, 431.

66. See chapter 2 for background biographical information on Woodson.

67. Dagbovie, *The Early Black History Movement*, xi, 181.

68. Ibid., 181.

69. Ibid., 83.

70. Brodie, *Thomas Jefferson*, 355–60; Gordon-Reed, *Thomas Jefferson and Sally Hemings*; Gordon-Reed, *The Hemingses of Monticello*; C. E. Walker, *Mongrel Nation*.

71. Woodson, "The Beginnings of the Miscegenation," 351. See also Cobb, "Physical Constitution of the American Negro," 347; Dagbovie, *The Early Black History Movement*, 181–82.

72. Woodson, *The Negro in Our History*, 102.

73. Woodson and Wesley, *The Story of the Negro Retold*, 99. See similarly Zikle, "Soil Exhaustion"; Lathrop, "Texas vs. Louisiana, 1849," 93–97.

74. Foucault, *The History of Sexuality*, 12, 82–92 passim; Vostral, *Under Wraps*, 38.

75. Foucault, *The History of Sexuality*, 44; Lemert and Bhan, *The Voice of Anna Julia Cooper*, 207.

76. Woodson, *The Mis-Education of the Negro*.

77. Ibid., 84–86, 140–41.

78. Ibid., 102.

79. The historical study of human "agency" among the enslaved exploded in the 1970s and 1980s. Some of the most important works to emerge during this period include Rawick, *From Sundown to Sunup*; Blassingame, *The Slave Community*; Genovese, *Roll, Jordan, Roll*; Gutman, *The Black Family in Slavery and Freedom*; Raboteau, *Slave Religion*; Joyner, *Down by the Riverside*; and Stuckey, *Slave Culture*.

80. Ernest W. Burgess in Frazier, *The Negro Family in the United States*, xi.

81. Frazier, *The Negro Family in the United States*, 960.

82. Ibid., 482.

83. In a subsequent study Frazier clarified his position on the gendered nature of African American families, arguing that only when a male head of household existed did black families in slavery achieve some degree of permanence and stability. See Frazier, *The Negro in the United States* (rev. ed., 1957), 308.

84. Ibid., 45–46.

85. Ibid., 39.

86. Ibid., 185–86.

87. For analysis of this point see Caron, *Who Chooses?*

88. Frazier, *The Negro in the United States*, 567–68.

89. Lemert and Bhan, *The Voice of Anna Julia Cooper*, 207.

## Chapter 4. The Theater of Memory

1. Edmonds, *Breeders*, in *Six Plays for a Negro Theater*, 99.

2. Tucker, *Telling Memories among Southern Women*, 215; Sommerville, *Rape and Race in the Nineteenth-Century South*, 147; S. A. Hill, *Black Intimacies*, 62.

3. Huggins, *Voices from the Harlem Renaissance*, 9; Lewis, *When Harlem Was in Vogue*,

17, 47, 305; H. A. Baker, "Modernism and the Harlem Renaissance," 84–97; Hutchinson, *Harlem Renaissance in Black and White*, 440–41.

4. Logan, *Howard University*, 394–96; E. P. Walker, "Krigwa"; Conner, *Pittsburgh in Stages*, 119.

5. Mary P. Burrill, *Aftermath*, in Hatch and Shine, *Black Theater USA*, 176–77.

6. Wood, *Lynching and Spectacle*, 1; Markovitz, *Legacies of Lynching*, xxvi; Ifill, *On the Courthouse Lawn*, 144; Drain, *Twentieth-Century Theatre*, 3.

7. On the issue of audience and early-twentieth-century black drama see Huggins, *Harlem Renaissance*, 292; Barrios, *Black Theatre Movement*, 100–103; Corbould, *Becoming African American*, 9, 130.

8. Holloway, *Passed On*, 60–61.

9. As Matthew Frye Jacobson reminds us, the imagery of the threatening black man needing to be contained and controlled by legal and extra-legal means cuts across generations of white native-born and immigrant Americans. See Jacobson, *Roots Too*, 332.

10. Van DeBurg, *Slavery and Race*, 123.

11. Carter, "Cultural History Written with Lightning," 347; Van DeBurg, *Slavery and Race*, 116. Writing of the controversy that has been reignited over the past twenty years by claims that Thomas Jefferson fathered at least one child with the slave Sally Hemings, Sarah Chinn contends that "a deep vein of denial" characterizes the American—particularly the white American—reluctance to engage with the darker aspects of its history. Chinn, *Technology and the Logic of American Racism*, 164.

12. *Crisis* quoted in Van DeBurg, *Slavery and Race*, 124.

13. Brundage, *Lynching in the New South*, 17, 40–41; D. M. Scott, *Contempt and Pity*, 12.

14. Shay, *Judge Lynch*, 69, 73; McGovern, *Anatomy of a Lynching*, 2; Brundage, *Lynching in the New South*, 9–11; Stephen Kantrowitz, "White Supremacist Justice and the Rule of Law: Lynching, Honor, and the State in Ben Tillman's South Carolina," in Spierenburg, *Men and Violence*, 241. W. Fitzhugh Brundage observes that only after "white supremacy was securely entrenched" did the number of lynchings decrease. Brundage, *Under the Sentence of Death*, 40.

15. Shay, *Judge Lynch*, 84, 88–89; Brundage, *Lynching in the New South*, 58–59; Amanda Frisken, "'A Shameless Prostitute and a Negro': Miscegenation Fears in the Election of 1872," in Schultz, *Fear Itself*, 133; Madison, *A Lynching in the Heartland*, 14–15.

16. Dubey, *Black Women Novelists*, 19; Donoghue, *Black Breeding Machines*.

17. Dollard, *Caste and Class in a Southern Town*, 324. See also G. C. Wright, *Life behind the Veil*, 75; Kantrowitz, "White Supremacist Justice and the Rule of Law," 218; Waldrep, *The Many Faces of Judge Lynch*, 16–17.

18. G. C. Wright, *Racial Violence in Kentucky*, 22, 43; J. L. Morgan, *Laboring Women*, 7.

19. P. J. Giddings, *Ida*, 24.

20. Wells, *A Red Record*, in Royster, *Southern Horrors*, 75.

21. Wells quoted in Schechter, *Ida B. Wells-Barnett and American Reform*, 87.

22. Wells, *A Red Record*, 94.

23. Smith quoted in Brundage, *Lynching in the New South*, 65.

24. Robyn Wiegman, "The Anatomy of Lynching," in Jenkins and Hine, *A Question of Manhood*, 350; Wood, *Lynching and Spectacle*, 98.

25. Quoted in Ifill, *On the Courthouse Lawn*, 145.

26. Stephens, *Plays of Georgia Douglas Johnson*, 2. See also Patton and Honey, *Double-Take*, 152–53.

27. Stephens, *Plays of Georgia Douglas Johnson*, 139–53.

28. Peterson, *Early American Playwrights and Dramatic Writers*, 119. On the color-conscious nature of African American class tensions see Gatewood, *Aristocrats of Color*; and Lake, *Blue Veins and Kinky Hairs*.

29. Fahy, "Exotic Fantasies, Shameful Realities"; Childs, *Modernism and Eugenics*; Whalan, *Race, Manhood, and Modernism in America*.

30. Munby, *Public Enemies, Public Heroes*, 26–27, 51; Conor, *The Spectacular Modern Woman*, 119–21; Koritz, *Culture Makers*, 56–57.

31. Kelves, *In the Name of Eugenics*, 75; Dyer, *Roosevelt and the Idea of Race*, 144–50; J. P. Jackson and Weidman, *Race, Racism, and Science*, 115–17; Stern, *Eugenic Nation*.

32. Bogle, *Toms, Coons, Mulattoes, Mammies, and Bucks*, 9–10; Krasner, *Resistance, Parody and Double Consciousness*, 157.

33. Myrtle Smith Livingston, *For Unborn Children*, in Hatch and Shine, *Black Theater USA*, 189–91.

34. Mitchell, *Righteous Propagation*, 15. See also Smithers, *Science, Sexuality, and Race*, 112.

35. Schwartz, *Birthing a Slave*, 10. See also Ross, "African-American Women and Abortion"; Caron, *Who Chooses?*

36. Krasner, *Resistance, Parody and Double Consciousness*, 160.

37. L. W. Levine, *Black Culture and Black Consciousness*, 234.

38. For lynching plays written by women see Perkins and Stephens, *Strange Fruit*.

39. Perkins, *Black Female Playwrights*, 53–56.

40. Demastes, *Realism and the American Dramatic Tradition*, 96.

41. Burrill, *Aftermath*, 176–77.

42. Ibid., 180.

43. Ibid., 182.

44. Krasner, *A Beautiful Pageant*, 145; Hill and Hatch, *History of African American Theatre*, 216–18, quote on 218.

45. Craig, *Black Drama of the Federal Theatre Era*, 20; Hutchinson, *Harlem Renaissance in Black and White*, 188; Fraden, *Blueprints for a Black Federal Theatre*, 101; Krasner, *A Beautiful Pageant*, 61; 155; 249.

46. Spence quoted in Hamalian, *Lost Plays of the Harlem Renaissance*, 466.

47. Goggin, *Carter G. Woodson*; Corbould, *Becoming African Americans*, 114.

48. Randolph Edmonds, "Review: Return of the Plantation Tradition," *Phylon* 10, no. 1 (1949): 90.

49. Efflong, *In Search of a Model for African-American Drama*, 5–6.

50. Sanders, *Development of Black Theater*, 19.

51. See Edmonds, preface, in Edmonds, *Six Plays for a Negro Theatre*, 7–8; Sanders, *Development of Black Theater*, 19–20.

52. Koch, *American Folk Plays*, xvi; Sanders, *Development of Black Theater*, 20–21.

53. *Negro History Bulletin* 2 (1938): 30.

54. *Opportunity* 13 (January 1935): 189; *Players Magazine* 16–17 (1940): np; Koch, *Carolina Folk-Plays*, xxv; Henderson, *Pioneering a People's Theatre*, 11; Peterson, *The African American Theater Directory*, 47; Conner, *Pittsburgh in Stages*, 121–22.

55. Edmonds, *Breeders*, 86.

56. Ibid.

57. Ibid., 87.

58. Ibid., 92.

59. Ibid., 95.

60. Ibid., 99.

61. Ibid.

62. Ibid., 101.

## Chapter 5. The WPA Narratives and Slave Breeding

1. Paul D. Escott, "The Art and Science of Reading WPA Slave Narratives," in C. T. Davis and Gates, *The Slave's Narrative*, 43; Escott, *Slavery Remembered*, 10–11, 45.

2. Lomax quoted in L. M. Hill, "Ex-Slave Narratives," 64.

3. Escott, *Slavery Remembered*, 45.

4. Hine, "Rape and the Inner Lives of Black Women," 96.

5. All references to the WPA narratives in this chapter come from Rawick, ed., *The American Slave*, 19 vols.; Rawick, ed., *The American Slave*, Supplemental Series 1, 12 vols.; and Rawick, ed., *The American Slave*, Supplemental Series 2, 10 vols.

6. Yetman, "Ex-Slave Interviews," 182; Escott, "The Art and Science of Reading WPA Slave Narratives," 41; C. Vann Woodward, "History from Slave Sources," in C. T. Davis and Gates, *The Slave's Narrative*, 51; Spindel, "Assessing Memory," 248.

7. Cox, *Race Relations*, 258.

8. *AS*, Arkansas Narratives, 11, pt. 7:189.

9. Botkin quoted in R. L. Baker, *Homeless, Friendless, and Penniless*, 8; Yetman, "Ex-Slave Interviews," 187.

10. See, for example, Blassingame, *The Slave Community*; Rawick, *From Sundown to Sunup*; Botkin, *Lay My Burden Down*; Genovese, *Roll, Jordan, Roll*; Gutman, *The Black Family in Slavery and Freedom*; Stuckey, *Slave Culture*; Berlin and Morgan, *Cultivation and Culture*; Camp, *Closer to Freedom*; Kaye, *Joining Places*. The use of the phrase "culture as resistance"—that is, resistance through such devices as song, folktales, dress, and family and slave community festivities—should be distinguished from the "culture of resistance"—deliberate acts designed to undermine the socioeconomic viability of slavery—analyzed by scholars such as Herbert Aptheker and Gerald Mullin. See Aptheker, *Negro Slave Revolts in the United States*; Mullin, *Fight and Rebellion*; Ira Berlin,

"The Quest for Freedom: Runaway Slaves and the Plantation South," in Boritt and Hancock, *Slavery, Resistance, Freedom*, 1–20.

11. Camp, *Closer to Freedom*, 75; see also 70, 99, 102.

12. Dylan Penningroth's recent cautionary note about narratives of slave resistance is important. Noting the power dynamic that existed between the enslaved and enslavers, Penningroth argues the following about slavery's "raw realties": "the system was about making black people work for white people, and the whites had all the guns." Dylan Penningroth, "My People, My People: The Dynamics of Community in Southern Slavery," in Baptist and Camp, *New Studies in the History of American Slavery*, 167.

13. Hurmence, *My Folks Don't Want Me to Talk about Slavery*, 36; *AS*, Alabama and Indiana Narratives, 6:427.

14. Novick, *That Noble Dream*. See also chapter 2 of this book.

15. Trauma, and traumatic events, lay at the very heart of how many former slaves remembered, and chose to remember, enslavement. Trauma has also played a significant role in how the descendants of slaves have narrated and understood antebellum slavery in relation to their twentieth-century experiences. My thinking about trauma and memory has been shaped by Kai Erikson, "Notes on Trauma and Community," in Caruth, *Trauma*, 183–84; Connie M. Kristiansen, Carolyn Gareau, Jennifer Mittleholt, Nancy H. DeCourville, and Wendy E. Hovestad, "The Sociopolitical Context of the Delayed Memory Debate," in L. M. Williams and Banyard, *Trauma and Memory*, 331–72; James Ritchie, "Culture, Personality and Prejudice," in P. Watson, *Psychology and Race*, 325; Edkins, *Trauma and the Memory of Politics*, 16; Ferguson, *Self-Identity and Everyday Life*, 113.

16. *AS*, Arkansas Narratives, 8, pt. 1:311–12; see also *AS*, Virginia Narratives, 16:11, 15; *AS*, North Carolina Narratives, 15, pt. 2:139–40; *AS*, North Carolina Narratives, 14, pt. 1:140–41.

17. *AS*, Arkansas Narratives, 8, pt. 1:312. See similarly Hurmence, *My Folks Don't Want Me to Talk about Slavery*, 41.

18. *AS*, Texas Narratives, Supp. Ser. 2, 8, pt. 7:3332.

19. *AS*, Texas Narratives, Supp. Ser. 2, 2, pt. 1:303.

20. *AS*, Kentucky Narratives, 7:34.

21. *AS*, Arkansas Narratives, 11, pt. 7:246.

22. *AS*, Georgia Narratives, 13, pt. 3:174. See also *AS*, Kansas Narratives, 16:3; *AS*, North Carolina Narratives, 14, pt. 1:172–73; *AS*, North Carolina Narratives, 15, pt. 2:14; North Carolina Narratives, Supp. Ser. 1, 11:173–74.

23. Cutler quoted in Metcalf and Barnhart, *America in So Many Words*, 106.

24. S. B. Little, "Report on Mares and Colts," *Farmer's Monthly Visitor*, January 15, 1839, 182. There is ample evidence to demonstrate that nineteenth-century writers increasingly engaged in a loose mixture of "stud" metaphors to refer to horse breeding, slave sexuality, and plantation management in the United States and abroad. See, for example, Stirling, *Letters from the Slave States*, 315; Buckingham, *The Slave States of America*, 1:259; Henningsen, *The White Slave*, 1:108.

25. Cardyn, "Sexualized Racism/Gendered Violence," 714.

26. Follett, *The Sugar Masters*, 59.

27. Munro, *Elements of the Anatomy of the Human Body*, 2:159. The term "bucking" was also used in the American South, usually to refer to the disciplining of slaves. "Bucking," I would argue, also denoted the sadomasochistic sexual nature of such discipline. Cardyn, "Sexualized Racism/Gendered Violence," 715.

28. Curzon, *Gender Shifts*, 147.

29. M. Morton, *The Lover's Tongue*, 65

30. David Dalby, "Americanisms That May Once Have Been Africanisms," in Dundes, *Mother Wit from the Laughing Barrel*, 151.

31. St. Clair, *A Soldier's Recollections*, 1:115.

32. Parent and Wallace, "Childhood and Sexual Identity under Slavery," 387.

33. Mencken, "Designations for Colored Folk," 169; Kennedy, *Nigger*, 66, 84

34. *AS*, South Carolina Narratives, 14, pt. 1:22.

35. *AS*, North Carolina Narratives, 15, pt. 2:98.

36. Graff, *What Is Marriage For?* 17; Regosin, *Freedom's Promise*, 99.

37. *AS*, Texas Narratives, 5, pt. 3:223. Newspaper reports from the late nineteenth century contain similar accounts and were a staple of British journalism. See, for example, the *Liverpool Daily Post*, February 3, 1863; *The Times* (London), November 27, 1865, GD 1/912/1, America—Newspaper Clippings, National Archives of Scotland.

38. *AS*, Texas Narratives, Supp. Ser. 2, 6, pt. 5:1950.

39. *AS*, Texas Narratives, Supp. Ser. 2, 2, pt. 1:105.

40. *AS*, Arkansas Narratives, 9:3.

41. *AS*, Texas Narratives, Supp. Ser. 2, 2, pt. 2:303–5.

42. *AS*, North Carolina Narratives, 15, pt. 2:417.

43. *AS*, Texas Narratives, 4, pt. 1:180.

44. *AS*, Texas Narratives, Supp. Ser. 2, 6, pt. 5:1963–64. See also *AS*, Texas Narratives, 4, pt. 1:203; *AS*, Texas Narratives, 5, pt. 3:44–45.

45. *AS*, North Carolina Narratives, 15, pt. 2:434.

46. *AS*, Alabama Narratives, 6:222.

47. *AS*, Georgia Narratives, 24, pt. 4:360–61.

48. *AS*, Alabama and Indiana Narratives, 6:58.

49. Ibid., 60.

50. *AS*, Texas Narratives, 5, pt. 3:190.

51. Ibid., 191–92.

52. Ibid., 191.

53. *AS*, Alabama and Indiana Narratives, 6:72.

54. Ibid., 73. See also *AS*, North Carolina Narratives, 14, pt. 1:330; ibid., 327–28; *AS*, Arkansas Narratives, Supp. Ser. 2, 8, pt. 4:141–42; *AS*, Georgia Narratives, 13, pt. 4:310.

55. *AS*, Arkansas Narratives, 2, pt. 1:49, 54.

56. Ibid., 52.

57. The historiography on slave families since the 1970s is enormous. A small sampling includes Rawick, *From Sundown to Sunup*; Genovese, *Roll, Jordan, Roll*; Gutman, *The Black Family in Slavery and Freedom*; Blassingame, *The Slave Community*; Malone, *Sweet Chariot*; Brenda E. Stevenson, "Distress and Discord in Virginia Slave Families, 1830–1860," in Bleser, *In Joy and in Sorrow*, 103–24; and E. West, "The Debate on the Strength of Slave Families."

58. W. Johnson, *Soul by Soul*; Deyle, *Carry Me Back*.

59. Calomiris and Pritchett, "Preserving Slave Families for Profit."

60. Works Project Administration, *Slave Narratives*, 213; Wahl, "Jurisprudence of American Slave Sales," 159.

61. *AS*, Georgia Narratives, 12, pt. 1:124.

62. On the concept of romantic love and its relationship to race see Lystra, *Searching the Heart*, 28; Hodes, *White Women, Black Men*, 14; Singer, *The Nature of Love*, 2:27–33.

63. Lankford, *Bearing Witness*, 192. See also *AS*, South Carolina Narratives, 2, pt. 1:331.

64. *AS*, North Carolina Narratives, 15, pt. 2:310. See also *AS*, Unwritten History of Slavery, 18:171.

65. E. West, *Chains of Love*, 45; D. R. Berry, "Swing the Sickle for the Harvest Is Ripe," 54–59; F. S. Foster, *'Til Death or Distance Do Us Part*, 23.

66. Killion and Waller, *Slavery Times*, 3. See similarly *AS*, Indiana Narratives, Supp. Ser. 1, 5:68.

67. Killion and Waller, *Slavery Times*, 29; Perdue, Barden, and Philips, *Weevils in the Wheat*, 26.

68. *AS*, Alabama and Indiana Narratives, 6:155.

69. Ibid., 156. Similar examples can be found in Killion and Waller, *Slavery Times*, 16, 22, 45.

70. *AS*, Kentucky Narratives, 16:72. See also *AS*, Maryland Narratives, 16:7; *AS*, Unwritten History of Slavery, 18:101; Heglar, *Rethinking the Slave Narrative*, 26; D. B. Davis, *Inhuman Bondage*, 201.

71. Hall quoted in Hurmence, *My Folks Don't Want Me to Talk about Slavery*, 51.

72. *AS*, South Carolina Narratives, 3, pt. 4:147.

73. Ibid., 148.

74. This hotly debated aspect of slave societies has been observed in both the Caribbean and mainland Americas. See Stephen Small and James Walvin, "African Resistance to Enslavement," in Tibbles, *Transatlantic Slavery*, 43; Helene Lecaudrey, "Behind the Mask: Ex-Slave Women and Interracial Sexual Relations," in P. Morton, *Discovering the Women in Slavery*, 260–77; Browne, *Creole Economies*, 180.

75. *AS*, Texas Narratives, 5, pt. 4:174.

76. Ibid., 176–77.

77. *AS*, Georgia Narratives, 12, pt. 1:228.

78. Ibid., 12, pt. 2:50.

79. Goodell, *American Slave Code*, 84–85; Wahl, "Jurisprudence of American Slave Sales," 159.

80. *AS*, Florida Narratives, 17:167. See also *AS*, South Carolina Narratives, 3, pt. 4:148; Fraser, *Courtship and Love*, 60.

81. *AS*, North Carolina Narratives, 15, pt. 2:97.

82. *AS*, Texas Narratives, Supp. Ser. 2, 6, pt. 5:1964.

83. Perdue, Barden, and Philips, *Weevils in the Wheat*, 185.

84. *AS*, Missouri Narratives, 11:163.

85. Ibid., 277. For a different perspective on the significance of slave auctions see the Slavery Collection, E. H. Stokes Letters Received—1859–1861, Box 5, Folder A, Series IV, New York Historical Society.

86. *AS*, Missouri Narratives, 11:44.

87. Berry quoted in Perdue, Barden, and Philips, *Weevils in the Wheat*, 30–31. See also *AS*, Kentucky Narratives, 16:23; *AS*, Arkansas Narratives, XI, 7, 246.

88. Berry quoted in Perdue, Barden, and Philips, *Weevils in the Wheat*, 30.

89. *AS*, Missouri Narratives, 11:311.

90. Perdue, Barden, and Philips, *Weevils in the Wheat*, 207.

91. Ibid., 205.

92. *AS*, Arkansas Narratives, 8, pt. 1:210. See similarly *AS*, North Carolina Narratives, 15, pt. 2:317.

93. *AS*, Georgia Narratives, 12, no. 2:304; *AS*, Arkansas Narratives, 9, pt. 3:92; *AS*, South Carolina Narratives, 14, pt. 1:39.

94. Mitchell, *Righteous Propagation*, 115, 218–19.

95. Ibid., 10.

96. Genovese, *Roll, Jordan, Roll*, part 2; Gutman, *The Black Family in Slavery and Freedom*, 217, 325; Blassingame, *The Slave Community*, 187; Malone, *Sweet Chariot*, 234, 241; 119, 235, Stevenson, *Life in Black and White*. On deflecting questions of paternity see Kaye, *Joining Places*, 81.

97. Hurmence, *My Folks Don't Want Me to Talk about Slavery*, 93.

98. C. H. Johnson, *God Struck Me Dead*, 19–20. See also Raboteau, *Slave Religion*, 133, passim; and Genovese, *Roll, Jordan, Roll*, 211, 247, passim. In recent decades, African American churches have redoubled the conservative rhetoric about sexual morality. Responding to the rise of AIDS, black ministers often preach against sexual promiscuity in general, and homosexuality in particular. See Baer and Singer, *African American Religion*, 93.

99. C. H. Johnson, *God Struck Me Dead*, 90. See also p. 40.

100. *AS*, Tennessee Narratives, 16:2.

101. *AS*, Ohio Narratives, 16:61.

102. Meier, *Negro Thought in America*; S. L. Smith, *Sick and Tired*, 109; Banta, *Barbaric Intercourse*, 284; Mitchell, *Righteous Propagation*, 109–12.

103. Raboteau, *Slave Religion*, 299.

104. *AS*, South Carolina Narratives, 14, pt. 1:293.

105. On the topic of political empowerment and Christianity in African American life see F. C. Harris, *Something Within*, 70.

106. Perdue, Barden, and Philips, *Weevils in the Wheat*, 25.

107. *AS*, South Carolina Narratives, 2, pt. 2:5. See, similarly, *AS*, Kansas Narratives, 16:4.

108. *AS*, Arkansas Narratives, 9, pt. 4:302.

109. C. E. Walker, *Deromanticizing Black History*, xvii.

110. *AS*, Alabama Narratives, 1:370.

111. Durant quoted in Smithers, *Science, Sexuality, and Race*, 112.

112. *AS*, South Carolina Narratives, 14, pt. 4:184; *AS*, Georgia Narratives, 4, pt. 2:13. See also W. King, *Stolen Childhood*, 94, 97; Schwartz, *Born in Bondage*, 80–81.

113. W. King, *Stolen Childhood*, 60. See also E. West, *Chains of Love*; Fraser, *Courtship and Love*; D. R. Berry, *"Swing the Sickle for the Harvest Is Ripe,"* 10.

114. West, *Chains of Love*, 26.

115. W. King, *Stolen Childhood*, 16.

116. *AS*, Arkansas Narratives, 10, pt. 6:283.

117. *AS*, Oklahoma Narratives, 7:15.

118. *AS*, Missouri Narratives, 11:164.

119. *AS*, Arkansas Narratives, 9, pt. 3:337.

120. *AS*, Missouri Narratives, 11:78.

121. *AS*, North Carolina Narratives, 15, pt. 2:3.

122. *AS*, Alabama Narratives, 1:137.

123. *AS*, South Carolina Narratives, 3, pt. 3:23–24.

124. *AS*, Arkansas Narratives, 8, pt. 1:78.

125. Ibid., 171.

126. *AS*, Georgia Narratives, 13, pt. 4:112.

127. *AS*, Missouri Narratives, 11:277.

128. *AS*, Arkansas Narratives, 8, pt. 2:175. See also *AS*, Tennessee Narratives, 16:34, 60; *AS*, Arkansas Narratives, 10, pt. 6:295; and *AS*, Arkansas Narratives, 11, pt. 7:91.

129. *AS*, Georgia Narratives, 13, pt. 3:293.

130. *AS*, Arkansas Narratives, 11, pt. 7:68.

131. *AS*, Georgia Narratives, 12, pt. 2:203.

132. Ibid., 152. See also *AS*, South Carolina Narratives, 3, pt. 4:216; *AS*, Mississippi Narratives, 7:54; *AS*, Texas Narratives, 4, pt. 2:112; *AS*, Arkansas Narratives, 8, pt. 1:217; *AS*, Tennessee Narratives, 16:44; *AS*, Ohio Narratives, 16:67.

133. *AS*, North Carolina Narratives, 14, pt. 1:186.

134. *AS*, Arkansas Narratives, 8, pt. 1:151.

135. Ibid., 152. See also *AS*, Arkansas Narratives, 11, pt. 7;30; *AS*, Georgia Narratives, 13, pt. 3:301; *AS*, North Carolina Narratives, 14, pt. 1:90.

136. As sex researchers M. S. Kimmel and J. Fracher observe, "how we are sexual—where, when, how often, with whom, and why—has to do with cultural learning, with meanings transmitted in a cultural setting." Such observations applied to former slaves and their descendants as much as they related to other segments of the American popu-

lation. M. S. Kimmel and J. Fracher, "Hard Issues and Soft Spots: Counseling Men About Sexuality" in Kimmel and Fracher, *Men's Lives*, 473.

137. In this respect, the work of theorists of "symbolic interactionism," or how individual subjectivity is constructed in relation to the broader social environment, help us to tease out the historical significance of the slave narratives in new and more insightful ways. On "symbolic interactionism" see Blumer, *Symbolic Interactionism*, 1–4; Ferguson, *Self-Identity and Everyday Life*, 111–12.

138. Blumer, *Symbolic Interactionism*, 1–2. I am not suggesting here that there existed a clear link between antebellum slavery and Jim Crow racism; however, in the memories of former slaves the connections drawn between slave masters and Ku Klux Klan members, for instance, offered a means of making sense of the past in the context of the present. On this point my thinking has been assisted by Ferguson, *Self-Identity and Everyday Life*, 111–12.

139. Blumer, *Symbolic Interactionism*, 4.

140. Rüsen, "Making Sense of Time," 17, 89; M. Gilbert, *On Social Facts*, 62; Climo and Cattell, *Social Memory and History*, 25–26; Lemert, *Social Things*, 53–54.

141. Reddick, "A New Interpretation for Negro History," 18.

## Chapter 6. Sex, Violence, and the Quest for Civil Rights

1. McGuire, *At the Dark End of the Street*, xvii–xviii.

2. Hine, "Rape and the Inner Lives of Black Women," 96.

3. Marisa Chappell, Jenny Hutchinson, and Brian Ward, "'Dress Modestly, Neatly . . . as if You Were Going to Church': Respectability, Class, & Gender in the Montgomery Bus Boycott & the Early Civil Rights Movement," in Ling and Monteith, *Gender and the Civil Rights Movement*, 84; McGuire, *At the Dark End of the Street*, xx.

4. Duvall, *The Building of a Race*, 6; Zieger and Gall, *American Workers, American Unions*, 126.

5. Sullivan, *Lift Every Voice*, 105–8, 304.

6. Huddle, *Marcus Garvey*.

7. Aptheker, *Documentary History of the Negro People*, 571.

8. Mary McLeod Bethune, "Full Integration—America's Newest Challenge," in Houck and Dixon, *Rhetoric, Religion, and the Civil Rights Movement*, 51.

9. This is a position shared by historians of the civil rights movement. See A. D. Morris, *Origins of the Civil Rights Movement*, 5; Allison Calhoun-Brown, "Will the Circle Be Unbroken? The Political Involvement of Black Churches since the 1960s," in O. A. Johnson and Stanford, *Black Political Organizations in the Post-Civil Rights Era*, 14.

10. Charlayne Hunter Gault, "'Heirs to a Legacy of Struggle': Charlayne Hunter Integrates the University of Georgia," in Collier-Thomas and Franklin, *Sisters in Struggle*, 81.

11. Robert H. Walkup, "Not Race but Grace," sermon delivered at the First Presbyterian Church, Starkville, Mississippi, September 30, 1962, in Houck and Dixon, *Rhetoric, Religion, and the Civil Rights Movement*, 473.

12. Houck and Dixon, *Rhetoric, Religion, and the Civil Rights Movement*, 468.

13. D. Levine, *Bayard Rustin and the Civil Rights Movement*, 25.

14. Ibid., 63; D'Emilio, *Lost Prophet*, 11; Podair, *Bayard Rustin*, 2–5.

15. D'Emilio, *Lost Prophet*, 74.

16. Ibid., 151.

17. McGuire, *At the Dark End of a Street*, 188.

18. Sargent, *The Civil Rights Revolution*, 86.

19. *The Papers of Martin Luther King, Jr.* were published in 6 volumes and edited by Clayborne Carson. The quote is from 1:109–10; see also 5:508.

20. Ibid., 1:280–82, 2:413. See also Oates, *Let the Trumpet Sound*, 31.

21. C. Carson, *Papers of Martin Luther King, Jr.*, 3:280–83 (see also 300, 322–24, 341); Oates, *Let the Trumpet Sound*, 100; Fairclough, *Martin Luther King, Jr.*, 4; J. M. Washington, *A Testament of Hope*, 116, 136–37; M. L. King, *Stride toward Freedom*, 100, 183.

22. Chappell, *A Stone of Hope*, 88.

23. C. Carson, *Papers of Martin Luther King, Jr.*, 4:171–72, 5:288; J. M. Washington, *A Testament of Hope*, 150; Chappell, *A Stone of Hope*, 188.

24. M. L. King, *Why We Can't Wait*, 13.

25. Ibid., 13–14.

26. C. Carson, *Papers of Martin Luther King, Jr.*, 3:286, 5:252–53 (see also 5:144, 280); Oates, *Let the Trumpet Sound*, 302.

27. C. Carson, *Papers of Martin Luther King, Jr.*, 5:266; Chappell, *A Stone of Hope*, 59.

28. J. M. Washington, *A Testament of Hope*, 75.

29. C. Carson, *Papers of Martin Luther King, Jr.*, 5:509; J. M. Washington, *A Testament of Hope*, 579.

30. C. Carson, *Papers of Martin Luther King, Jr.*, 5:510; Fairclough, *Martin Luther King, Jr.*, 8, 59, 90–91.

31. McGuire, *At the Dark End of the Street*, 4.

32. On this point see ibid., ix, 199, and especially chapter 5.

33. C. Carson, *Papers of Martin Luther King, Jr.*, 3:90–91.

34. Fairclough, *To Redeem the Soul of America*, 32.

35. C. Carson, *Papers of Martin Luther King, Jr.*, 4:170, 5:500.

36. Lischer, *The Preacher King*, 72.

37. C. Carson, *Papers of Martin Luther King, Jr.*, 4:170, 5:500; Lischer, *The Preacher King*, 259.

38. C. Carson, *Papers of Martin Luther King, Jr.*, 5:501.

39. Ibid., 500.

40. Broderick and Meier, *Negro Protest Thought*, 270.

41. Breitman, *Malcolm X Speaks*, 10; Karim, *The End of White World Supremacy*, 87.

42. Malcolm X, *Autobiography*, 124. See similarly Baldwin, *The Fire Next Time*, 68.

43. Karim, *The End of White World Supremacy*, 11.

44. Breitman, *Malcolm X Speaks*, chapter 3; Terrill, *Malcolm X*, 139.

45. R. F. Williams, *Negroes with Guns*, 63, 84. For a wonderful analysis of Williams's

life see Tyson, *Radio Free Dixie*; Arsenault, *Freedom Riders: 1961 and the Struggle for Racial Justice*, 81.

46. Broderick and Meier, *Negro Protest Thought*, 329, 331.

47. Marsh, *The Beloved Community*, 2, 49–50.

48. Fleming quoted in Collier-Thomas and Franklin, *Sisters in Struggle*, 209. For further analysis of this point see Barnett, "Invisible Southern Black Women Leaders," 173–75.

49. Ladner quoted in Barber, *A Hard Rain Fell*, 97. See similarly Mumia Abu-Jamal, "A Life in the Party: An Historical and Retrospective Examination of the Projections and Legacies of the Black Panther Party," in Cleaver and Katsiaficas, *Liberation, Imagination, and the Black Panther Party*, 41.

50. For analysis of this literature and the sexual politics of the civil rights movement see K. Anderson, *Changing Woman*.

51. Kathleen Neal Cleaver, "Women, Power, and Revolution," in Cleaver and George, *Liberation, Imagination, and the Black Panther Party*, 123.

52. P. J. Giddings, *When and Where I Enter*, 5–6; D. K. King, "Multiple Jeopardy, Multiple Consciousness," 42; Barnett, "Invisible Southern Black Women Leaders," 165; Cheryl Townsend Gilkes, "'If It Wasn't for the Women . . .': African American Women, Community Work, and Social Change," in Zinn and Dill, *Women of Color in U.S. Society*, 230.

53. D. K. King, "Multiple Jeopardy, Multiple Consciousness," 53.

54. Ransby, *Ella Baker*, 5, 21–22; Charron, *Freedom's Teacher*, 42, 43; Gill, *Beauty Shop Politics*, 10–12, 90, 106.

55. Cornelius, *Slave Missions and the Black Church*, 42; Ramsey, *Reading, Writing, and Segregation*, 90.

56. Charron, *Freedom's Teacher*, 42.

57. Forsythe interviewed in M. Foster, *Black Teachers on Teaching*, 25.

58. Quoted in Barnett, "Invisible Southern Black Women Leaders," 173.

59. Quoted in Anne Standley, "The Role of Black Women in the Civil Rights Movement," in Crawford, Rouse, and Woods, *Women in the Civil Rights Movement*, 195.

60. Houck and Dixon, *Rhetoric, Religion, and the Civil Rights Movement*, 732.

61. *The Negro Family: The Case for National Action*.

62. Herman, *Romance of American Psychology*, 204; Margaret Cerullo and Marla Erlien, "Beyond the 'Normal Family': A Cultural Critique of Women's Poverty," in Dujon and Withorn, *For Crying Out Loud*, 94; Gottheimer, *Ripples of Hope*, 275.

63. Ransby, *Ella Baker*, 21.

64. P. Morton, *Disfigured Images*, 115; M. M. Wright, *Becoming Black*, 132; Roth, *Separate Roads to Feminism*, 85–86.

65. D. G. White, *Too Heavy a Load*, 200.

66. Carmichael in Barber, *A Hard Rain Fell*, 102.

67. K. Mills, *This Little Light of Mine*, 274.

68. Breines, *The Trouble between Us*, chap. 5; L. M. Anderson, *Black Feminism in Contemporary Drama*, 12.

69. P. H. Collins, *Black Feminist Thought*, 173; P. H. Collins, *From Black Power to Hip Hop*, 12. See also James Smethurst, "Retraining the Heartworks: Women in Atlanta's Black Arts Movement," in Gore, Theoharis, and Woodard, *Want to Start a Revolution?* 217–18.

70. McGuire, *At the Dark End of the Street*, 114.

71. M. L. King, *Where Do We Go from Here?* 101.

## Chapter 7. Slave Breeding in Literature, Film, and New Media

1. L. Goodman, *Contemporary Feminist Theater*, 53, 115; Canning, *Feminist Theaters in the U.S.A.*, 30.

2. Flannery, *Feminist Literacies*, 152.

3. W. J. Harris, *The Leroi Jones/Amiri Baraka Reader*, 224.

4. Aldon Morris, "Centuries of Black Protest: Its Significance for America and the World," in H. Hill and Jones, *Race in America*, 53; Stephen Ward, "The Third World Women's Alliance: Black Feminist Radicalism and Black Power Politics," in Joseph, *The Black Power Movement*, 130.

5. Boothe, *Why Are So Many Black Men in Prison?*; Baxandall and Gordon, *Dear Sisters*, 197.

6. Seale, *Seize the Time*, 153.

7. Kirby, *Media-Made Dixie*, 115. Steven Spielberg's *Amistad* is one of the best-known examples of this more recent tendency among Hollywood filmmakers. See McCrisken and Pepper, *American History and Contemporary Hollywood Film*, chap. 2; Wasser, *Steven Spielberg's America*, 167–69. For the cinematic portrayal of slavery and race over the past century see, for example, Wallace-Sanders, *Mammy*, 141; Ed Guerrero, "Black Violence as Cinema: From Cheap Thrills to Historical Agonies," in Slocum, *Violence and American Cinema*, 222. The plantation genre of slavery films reinforced images of contented and loyal slaves working happily for slave masters and mistresses. These were films with direct politico-economic implications, reminding audiences that the labor systems developed in the Jim Crow South were both normal and "natural." See C. J. Robinson, *Forgeries of Memory and Meaning*, 298.

8. McCrisken and Pepper, *American History and Contemporary Hollywood Film*, 39.

9. On Kara Walker see the wonderful Du Bois Shaw, *Seeing the Unspeakable*; Lister et al., *New Media*, 9.

10. Clarence Gohdes, "On the Study of Southern Literature," *William and Mary Quarterly*, 2nd ser., 16, no. 1 (1936): 86.

11. Boney, "The American South," 290.

12. Caldwell, "Erskine Caldwell," 358 ("grotesque exaggeration"); Gray, "Southwestern Humor," 4. See also Christopher D. Geist, "In Depth," 1; and Keely, "Poverty, Sterilization, and Eugenics."

13. Yerby, *The Foxes of Harrow*; Glasrud and Champion, "'The Fishes and the Poet's Hands.'" It is important to recognize a narrative tension in this chapter that reflects a divide among literary scholars since the nineteenth century. This tension centers on a disagreement over how African American experiences are representative and interpretive. On one hand, readers will recognize the *racial realism* that black literary giants from Alain Locke to Amiri Baraka have emphasized in portraying the trials and tribulations of African American people. At other times, the so-called *anomalous fiction* of writers like Frank Yerby blur the contours of racial realism through their use of dramatic love stories, lush costume dramas, and characterizations that appear overly contrived. I would like to suggest that racial realism and anomalous fiction—applied to both literary and cinematic forms of narration—make up a scholarly binary that does not do justice to the significance of representations of sex and slavery (and particularly slave breeding) in twentieth-century literature and film. Instead, if we take a less rigid cultural approach to novels, films, performative dance, and folklore we will see how racial realism and anomalous fiction overlap in ways that defy academic classification and reflect the subjective historical experiences of writers, performers, and audiences.

14. Kirby, *Media-Made Dixie*, 103.

15. D. T. Turner, "Frank Yerby as Debunker," 569; B. Jackson, "A Survey Course in Negro Literature," 635.

16. Yerby, *Foxes*, 110.

17. Ibid., 93.

18. Ibid., 146.

19. Ibid., 178.

20. Ibid., 122.

21. Ibid., 179.

22. For analysis of such portrayals see Kirby, *Media-Made Dixie*; Adams, *Wounds of Returning*; Lassiter and Crespino, *Myth of Southern Exceptionalism*.

23. Walker quoted in Worley and Perry, *African-American Literature*, 458.

24. M. Walker, *Jubilee*, 4.

25. A. P. Davis, Redding, and Joyce, *The New Cavalcade*, 2:359.

26. Irons, "The Shaping of Activist Recruitment and Participation."

27. G. Brooks, "The Mother," in *Black Voices*, 461; Alice Walker, "Women," in Worley and Perry, *African-American Literature*, 467–68; Dandridge, ed., *Black Women's Blues*, 297. See also Rita Dove's evocative poem "Motherhood" in A. P. Davis, Redding, and Joyce, *The New Calvacade*, 2:885.

28. Talbot, *Mondo Mandingo*. The account that follows can be found on pp. 9–11.

29. Ibid., 6.

30. Bargainnier, "The Falconhurst Series," 298.

31. Ibid., 298–99; Ryan, *Calls and Responses*, 22, 61.

32. Talbot, *Mondo Mandingo*, 27.

33. Ollie Harrington, "The Last Days of Richard Wright," *Ebony*, February 1961, 84.

34. Van Deburg, *Slavery and Race*, 149; Seidel, *The Southern Belle in the American Novel*, 165; Styron, "Nat Turner Revisited," 72; Server, *Encyclopedia of Pulp Fiction Writers*, 145; Ryan, *Calls and Responses*, 68.

35. Bargainnier, "The Falconhurst Series," 299.

36. Of course, Onstott was by no means the first or only novelist to address these themes in American society. See, for example, Stowe, *Uncle Tom's Cabin*; T. Williams, *Cat on a Hot Tin Roof*; T. Williams, *Suddenly Last Summer*. For analysis of homosexuality in southern literature see Poteet, *Gay Men in Modern Southern Literature*.

37. A. Goldberg, *Sex, Religion, and the Making of Modern Madness*, 60, passim; M. Douglass, *Purity and Danger*, 117, 178.

38. My analysis has been informed by the insights of Koven, *Slumming*, 198; and Gordon-Reed, *The Hemingses of Monticello*, 367–68.

39. Sherrill, *Gothic Politics in the Deep South*, 34; Ashmore, *Hearts and Minds*, 299.

40. S. Ellis, *The Mask of Anarchy*, 192.

41. Onstott, *Mandingo*, 164–67.

42. Ibid., 52.

43. Ibid., 91–94.

44. Ibid., 114.

45. Lois Weaver, "Performing Butch/Femme Theory," in Rapi and Chowdhry, *Acts of Passion*, 138.

46. Onstott, *Mandingo*, 68, 335, 339–41. See similarly Charles Johnson's novel *Oxherding Tale*, especially his description of the white slave mistress Flo Hatfield. For further analysis of this point see Seidel, *The Southern Belle in the American Novel*.

47. Onstott, *Mandingo*, 570.

48. Bargainnier, "The Falconhurst Series," 305.

49. Onstott, *Mandingo*, 167–68.

50. Ibid., 576.

51. Ibid., 587, 581.

52. W. W. Dixon, *Visions of the Apocalypse*, 38.

53. *The Plantation System in Southern Life* (Coronet Instructional Films, 1950).

54. Benshoff and Griffith, *America on Film*, 83; W. W. Dixon, *American Cinema in the 1940s*, 12.

55. Bogle, *Toms, Coons, Mulattoes, Mammies, and Bucks*, 158; Lubin, *Romance and Rights*, 59.

56. W. W. Dixon, *American Cinema in the 1940s*, 13.

57. Vera and Gordon, *Screen Saviors*, 64.

58. Bogle, *Toms, Coons, Mulattoes, Mammies, and Bucks*, 191.

59. *Mandingo* was also adapted to the stage; it opened on Broadway in May 1961. *Jet*, June 1, 1961, 60.

60. The quote "sex, sadism, and miscegenation" is from Earl F. Bargainnier's insightful analysis of the Falconhurst series. "The Falconhurst Series," 298.

61. Paul Talbot provides an engrossing account of the making of the movie in chapter 5 of *Mondo Mandingo*.

62. Talbot, *Mondo Mandingo*, 102.

63. Ibid., 109.

64. Coincidentally, Ali had been offered the role of Mede but turned it down on religious grounds. See ibid., 97.

65. Ibid., 121.

66. Ibid., 128–29.

67. *Biography News* 2 (1975): 146; Kenneth Robinson, "Black Comedy," *The Spectator* 325 (1975): 387; *New York Magazine*, September 13, 1976, 17; *Films and Filming* 32 (1975): 42–43; "Mandingo," *Films in Review* 26 (1975): 311; Richard Schickel, "Cold, Cold Ground," *Time*, May 12, 1975, 58.

68. *Jet*, May 1, 1975, 62.

69. *Jet*, May 12, 1977 ("Readers Rap"), 6. For Norton's declaration that *Mandingo* "was fictitious" see *Jet*, March 3, 1977, 32. Norton's parents expressed mixed emotions about his role in the film. Norton joked that his mother "threw up her hands" and "cried, 'Oh my God! How can I ever go to church again?'" Norton's father, by contrast, "loved the flick." *Jet*, August 26, 1976, 46.

70. *Jet*, June 5, 1975, 64.

71. *Jet*, July 10, 1975, 56.

72. *Jet*, January 4, 1979, 61.

73. Feagin, *Racist America*, 131.

74. Katherine Q. Seelye, "Celebrating Secession without Slaves," *New York Times*, November 29, 2010.

75. Mark Goodall, "Shockumentary Evidence: The Perverse Politics of the Mondo Film," in Dennison and Lim, *Remapping World Cinema*, 125.

76. L. W. Levine, *Black Culture and Black Consciousness*, 310–12; Dance, *Shuckin' and Jivin'*, 5, 165.

77. L. S. Levine, *Black Culture and Black Consciousness*, 332.

78. Dance, *Shuckin' and Jivin'*, 53.

79. Ibid., 105, 107.

80. Ibid., 102–3.

81. Ibid., 166; Spalding, *Encyclopedia of Black Folklore and Humor*, 65–66.

82. Dance, *Shuckin' and Jivin'*, 185.

83. See also Dundes, *Mother Wit*, 599, (603) (604).

84. Abrahams, *Deep Down in the Jungle*, 109; R. L. Baker, "Lady Lil and Pisspot Pete"; Ronald L. Baker and Simon J. Bonner, "'Letting Out Jack': Sex and Aggression in Manly Recitations," in Bronner, *Manly Traditions*, 328.

85. Dance, *Shuckin' and Jivin'*, 193.

86. Aaron Smith, "Technology Trends among People of Color," *Pew Internet*, September 17, 2010, http://pewinternet.org/Commentary/2010/September/Technology-Trends-Among-People-of-Color.aspx (accessed November 1, 2010).

87. U.S. National Slavery Museum, http://www.usnationalslaverymuseum.org (accessed November 3, 2010).

88. http://wearerespectablenegroes.blogspot.com (accessed October 21, 2010).

89. Carmen Van Kerckhove, "Amusement Park Allows Visitors to Be Slave for a Day," http://www.racialicious.com/2008/01/07/amusement-park-allows-visitors-to-be-slave-for-a-day (accessed December 20, 2009).

90. Perkins-Valdez, *Wench*.

91. Du Bois Shaw, *Seeing the Unspeakable*, 1. See also R. Richardson, "Kara Walker's Old South and New Terrors."

92. Shaw, *Seeing the Unspeakable*, 38.

93. Ifill, *On the Courthouse Lawn*, 136.

94. I. Perry, *Prophets of the Hood*, 51.

## Epilogue

1. Franklin, *From Slavery to Freedom*, 177–80.

2. Franklin, *From Slavery to Freedom* (2nd ed.), 176–80.

3. Franklin and Moss, *From Slavery to Freedom* (8th ed.), 131–32.

4. "Professor Sir John Elliot: Interview Transcript, March 7, 2008," *Making History*, http://www.history.ac.uk/makinghistory/resources/interviews/Elliott_John.html (accessed September 12, 2011); David Brooks, "The Return of History," *New York Times*, March 25, 2010, A27; Rok Spruk, "Economics and the Return of History?" *Capitalism & Freedom*, March 29, 2010, http://rspruk.blogspot.com/2010/03/economics-and-return-of-history.html (accessed March 29, 2010).

5. Eleanor Bright Fleming, "When Sorry Is Enough: The Possibility of a National Apology for Slavery," in Gibney et al., *The Age of Apology*, 105; R. L. Brooks, *Atonement and Forgiveness*, 207.

6. "Should the Government Apologize for Slavery?" *Jet*, July 14, 1997, 8; Yamamoto, *Interracial Justice*, 55; *Congressional Record: Proceedings and Debates of the 106th Congress, Second Session*, Vol. 146, Pt. 10, July 10, 2000 to July 17, 2000 (Washington, D.C.: U.S. Government Printing Office, 2000), 14371; Fobanjong, *Understanding the Backlash*, 114; Nobles, *The Politics of Official Apologies*, 137.

7. M. L. King, *Why We Can't Wait*, 23–24.

8. Lowery quoted in "Should the Government Apologize for Slavery?" *Jet*, July 14, 1997, 9. Since 1989, Representative Don Conyers Jr. (D-Mich.) has regularly introduced a bill for compensation for slavery.

9. In the 1990s, President Clinton expressed reservations about an apology for slavery because it would open the possibilities of reparations. See Roy L. Brooks, "Not Even an Apology?" in R. L. Brooks, *When Sorry Isn't Enough*, 312.

10. Data quoted in Michael Dawson, "The Price of Slavery," *Harvard Magazine*, May–June, 2003.

11. Liliane Weissberg, introduction, in Ben-Amos and Weisberg, *Cultural Memory and the Construction of Identity*, 15.

12. E. B. Fleming, "When Sorry Is Enough," 95.

13. Quoted in Tamar Lewin, "Calls for Slavery Restitution Getting Louder," *New York Times,* June 4, 2001.

14. http://www.youtube.com/watch?v=wO4B__iRWFs. See also Matthews's Web site, http://carlwesleymatthews.com/index.html.

15. Ira Berlin, "Coming to Terms with Slavery in the Twenty-First-Century," in Horton and Horton, *Slavery and Public History,* 4.

# BIBLIOGRAPHY

**Primary Sources—Manuscripts**

HISTORICAL SOCIETY OF PENNSYLVANIA

Papers of the Pennsylvania Society for Promoting the Abolition of Slavery.

LIBRARY COMPANY OF PHILADELPHIA

Great Britain. Colonial Office. *Papers Relative to the West Indies, Part I: Jamaica, 1839.* London, 1839.

LIBRARY OF CONGRESS, MANUSCRIPT DIVISION

Plantation Manual, 1857–58. James Henry Hammond. James Henry Hammond Papers (Container 35, Reel 18), LC-MS-24695-1.

MUSEUM OF THE CONFEDERACY, RICHMOND, VIRGINIA

Papers Related to Richmond Slave Traders, 1851–1863, African American Collection, NU-960212.

NATIONAL ARCHIVES OF SCOTLAND

GD 1/912/1, America—Newspaper Clippings.

NEW YORK HISTORICAL SOCIETY

Slavery Collection, 1709–1864.
*A Review, in Part, of "The New-York Humbugs." By David Meredith, M.D. in Which the Bold Denunciations of the Author are Brought to the Test of Reason and Philosophy* (1838).

UNIVERSITY OF ABERDEEN, ARCHIVES AND SPECIAL COLLECTIONS

Account of Increase and Decrease of Slaves, 1832, Gordons of Buthlaw and Cairness: Estate and Family Papers, MS 1160/7/12.
Essay on Slavery and Copy of Lectures on Moral Philosophy and Logic, James Beattie Papers, MS 30/49.

UNIVERSITY OF TEXAS AT AUSTIN, CENTER FOR AMERICAN HISTORY

William Massie Papers.

## Select Filmography

*Addio Zio Tom* [Goodbye Uncle Tom]. Euro International Films Production, 1971.

*Band of Angels*. Warner Brothers, 1951.

*The Birth of a Nation*. Epoch Film Company, 1915.

*Gone with the Wind*. Loew's, 1939.

*Guess Who's Coming to Dinner*. Columbia Pictures, 1967.

*Imitation of Life*. Universal Pictures, 1934 & 1959.

*Japanese War Bride*. Twentieth-Century Fox, 1952.

*The Jazz Singer*. Warner Brothers, 1927.

*Lost Boundaries*. Warner Brothers, 1949.

*Mandingo*. Paramount Pictures, 1975.

*The Plantation System in Southern Life*. Coronet Instructional Films, 1950.

*Quadroon*. Presidio, 1972.

## Printed Primary Sources

*Abridgement of the Minutes of the Evidence Taken Before a Committee of the Evidence Taken before a Committee of the Whole House, to Whom It Was Referred to Consider of the Slave-Trade, 1789*. London, 1789.

*An Address Delivered by the Rev. Theodore Parker before the New York City Anti-Slavery Society*. New York: American Anti-Slavery Society, 1854.

*Address of John Quincy Adams, to His Constituents of the Twelfth Congressional District, at Braintree, September 17th, 1842*. Boston: J. H. Eastburn, 1842.

Alexander, William T. *History of the Colored Race in America*. Kansas City, Mo.: Palmetto, 1887.

American and Foreign Anti-Slavery Society. Annual Reports.

*American Negro Academy Occasional Papers, Nos. 1–22*. New York: Arno Press, 1969.

*The Anti-Slavery Record: Volume III for 1837*. New York: American Anti-Slavery Society, 1838.

*Appendix to the Souvenir Presented to James M. Ashley on Emancipation Day, September 2, 1893*. Philadelphia: Publishing House of the A.M.E. Church, 1894.

Aptheker, Herbert., ed. *A Documentary History of the Negro People in the United States, 1933–1945*. Secaucus, N.J.: The Citadel Press, 1974.

Baldwin, James. *The Fire Next Time*. 1962. Reprint, New York: Vintage Books, 1991.

Ballagh, James C. *A History of Virginia*. Baltimore: Johns Hopkins Press, 1902.

Baxandall, Rosalyn, and Linda Gordon, eds. *Dear Sisters: Dispatches from the Women's Liberation Movement*. New York: Perseus Books Group, 2000.

Beecher, Henry Ward. *Freedom and War, Discourses on Topics Suggested by the Times*. Boston: Ticknor & Fields, 1863.

———. *Patriotic Addresses in America and England from 1850 to 1885, on Slavery, the Civil War, and the Development of Civil Liberty in the United States*. New York: Fords, Howard, & Hulbert, 1891.

Betts, Edwin M., ed. *Thomas Jefferson's Farm Book.* Chapel Hill: University of North Carolina Press, 2001.

Bogart, Ernest L. *The Economic History of the United States.* New York: Longmans, Green, 1907.

Bolding, B. J. *"What of the Negro Race": Bolding vs. Hassarl.* Chambersburg, Pa.: The Democratic News, 1906.

Bowers, Claude G. *The Tragic Era: The Revolution after Lincoln.* Cambridge, Mass.: Houghton Mifflin, 1929.

Boynton, C. B., and T. B. Mason. *Journey through Kansas: With Sketches of Nebraska: Describing the Country, Climate, Soil, Mineral, Manufacturing, and Other Resources.* Cincinnati: Moore, Wilstach, Keys, 1855.

Branagan, Thomas. *A Preliminary Essay, on the Oppression of the Exiled Sons of Africa: Consisting of Animadversions on the Impolicy and Barbarity of the Deleterious Commerce and Subsequent Slavery of the Human Species.* Philadelphia: Printed by the author, 1804.

Brawley, Benjamin Griffith. *A Short History of the American Negro.* Rev. ed. New York: Macmillan, 1919.

Breeden, James O., ed. *Advice to Masters: The Ideal in Slave Management in the Old South.* Westport, Conn.: Greenwood, 1980.

Breitman, George, ed. *Malcolm X Speaks: Selected Speeches and Statements.* New York: Grove Press, 1990.

Brewster, Frances E. *Slavery and the Constitution: Both Sides of the Question.* Philadelphia, 1850.

Brooks, Gwendolyn. "The Mother." In *Black Voices: An Anthology of Afro-American Literature,* ed. Abraham Chapman, 61. New York: New American Library, 1968.

Brotz, Howard, ed. *African-American Social and Political Thought, 1850–1920.* New Brunswick, N.J.: Transaction, 1992.

Brown, William Wells. *The Black Man: His Antecedents, His Genius, and His Achievements.* 2nd ed. New York: Thomas Hamilton, 1863.

———. *Narrative of William W. Brown, a Fugitive Slave, Written by Himself* (1843), in *Slave Narratives.* New York: Library of America, 2000.

Bruce, Henry Clay. *The New Man: Twenty-Nine Years a Slave, Twenty-Nine Years a Free Man.* York, Pa.: Anstadt and Sons, 1895.

Bruce, William Cabell. *The Negro Problem.* Baltimore: John Murphy & Co., 1891.

Buckingham, James S. *The Slave States of America.* 2 vols. London: Fisher, Son, 1842.

Buehler, Ezra Christian, ed. *Increasing the Power of the Federal Government.* New York: Noble & Noble, 1940.

Cairnes, J. E. *The Slave Power: Its Character, Career and Probable Designs.* London: Macmillan, 1863.

Calman, Andrew L. *Life and Labours of John Ashworth.* Manchester: Tubbs & Brook, 1875.

Carson, Clayborne, ed. *The Papers of Martin Luther King, Jr.* 6 vols. Berkeley: University of California Press, 1992–2008.

Carson, Josephine. *Silent Voices: The Southern Negro Woman Today.* New York: Delacorte Press, 1969.

Caughey, John L., ed. *Negotiating Cultures and Identities: Life History Issues, Methods, and Readings.* Lincoln: University of Nebraska Press, 2006.

Channing, William E. *A Letter to the Honorable Henry Clay, on the Annexation of Texas to the United States.* Boston: James Munroe & Company, 1837.

Cheever, George Barrell. *God against Slavery: And the Freedom and Duty of the Pulpit to Rebuke It, as a Sin Against God.* New York: Joseph H. Ladd, 1857.

Child, L. Maria, ed. *Incidents in the Life of a Slave Girl: Written by Herself.* Boston: Published for the author, 1861.

Clay, Henry. *Remarks of Mr. Clay, Kentucky, on Introducing His Proposition to Compromise, on the Slavery Question.* Washington, D.C.: Jno. T. Towers, 1850.

Cobb, W. Montague. "The Negro as a Biological Element in the American Population." *Journal of Negro Education* 8, no. 3 (1939): 336–48.

———. "The Physical Constitution of the American Negro." *Journal of Negro Education* 3, no. 3 (1934): 340–88.

*Collected Black Women's Narratives.* New York: Oxford University Press, 1988.

Collier-Thomas, Bettye, and V. P. Franklin, eds. *Sisters in Struggle: African American Women in the Civil Rights–Black Power Movement.* New York: New York University Press, 2001.

Collins, Winfield H. *The Domestic Slave Trade of the Southern United States.* New York: Broadway, 1904.

Crummell, Alexander. *The Race-Problem in America.* Washington, D.C.: Judd & Detweiler, 1889.

Dance, Daryl Cumber. *Shuckin' and Jivin': Folklore from Contemporary Black Americans.* Bloomington: Indiana University Press, 1978.

Dandridge, Rita B., ed. *Black Women's Blues: A Literary Anthology, 1934–1988.* New York: G. K. Hall, 1992.

Davis, Arthur P., J. Saunders Redding, and Joyce Ann Joyce, eds. *The New Cavalcade: African American Writing from 1760 to the Present.* 2 vols. Washington, D.C.: Howard University Press, 1992.

Davis, W. W. *The Civil War and Reconstruction in Florida.* New York: Columbia University, 1913.

*The Debate on the Motion for the Abolition of the Slave-Trade, in the House of Commons, on Monday the Second of April, 1792.* London: W. Woodfall, 1792.

Delany, Martin Robinson. *The Condition, Elevation, Emigration, and Destiny of the Colored People of the United States.* 1852; New York: Arno Press and the New York Times, 1968.

Dewey, Orville. *Discourse on Slavery and the Annexation of Texas.* New York: Charles E. Frances & Company, 1844.

Doesticks, Q. K. Philander, and Price M. Butler. *What Became of the Slaves on a Georgia Plantation? Great Auction Sale of Slaves, at Savannah, Georgia, March 2d & 3d, 1859. A Sequel to Mrs. Kemble's Journal* (Savannah, Ga., 1863). Housed in the Daniel A. P. Murray Collection, Library of Congress.

Douglass, Frederick. *The Frederick Douglass Papers: Series One: Speeches, Debates, and Interviews.* Ed. John W. Blassingame. 5 vols. New Haven: Yale University Press, 1979–92.

———. *My Bondage and My Freedom.* New York: Miller, Orton, 1857.

Douglass, Mary. *Purity and Danger: An Analysis of Concepts of Pollution and Taboo.* 1966. Reprint, New York: Routledge, 2003.

Drake, Richard. *Revelations of a Slave Smuggler: Being the Autobiography of Capt. Rich'd Drake, an African Trader for Fifty Years-From 1807 to 1857; During Which Period he was Concerned in the Transportation of Half a Million Blacks from African Coasts to America.* New York: Andrew & Filmer, 1860.

Du Bois, W. E. B. *The Autobiography of W. E. B. DuBois: A Soliloquy on Viewing My Life from the Last Decade of Its First Century.* Reprint, New York: International Publishers, 1968.

———. *Black Reconstruction in America, 1860–1880.* 1935. Reprint, New York: The Free Press, 1992.

———. "The Conservation of Race." In *The American Negro Academy Occasional Papers, No. 2.* Washington, D.C.: Published by the Academy, 1897.

———. *Darkwater: Voices from Within the Veil.* New York: Harcourt, Brace and Howe, 1920.

———. *The Negro American Family.* Atlanta: The Atlanta University Press, 1908.

———. *The Philadelphia Negro: A Social Study.* Elijah Anderson & Isabel Eaton, eds. Philadelphia: University of Pennsylvania Press, 1995.

———. "The Position of the Negro in the American Social Order: Where Do We Go From Here?" *Journal of Negro Education* 8, no. 3 (June 1939): 351–70.

———. "Race Relations in the United States." *Annals of the American Academy of Political and Social Science* 140 (November 1928): 6–10.

———. "The Study of the Negro Problem." *Annals of the American Academy of Political and Social Sciences* 11 (January 1898): 1–23.

———. *The Suppression of the African Slave-Trade to the United States of America, 1638–1870.* New York: Longman, Green, 1896.

Dunning, William Archibald. *Essays on the Civil War and Reconstruction and Related Topics.* New York: Macmillan, 1898.

Duvall, C. H. *The Building of a Race.* Boston: Everett Press, 1919.

Edmonds, Randolph. "Review: Return of the Plantation Tradition." *Phylon* 10, no. 1 (1949): 90–92.

———. *Six Plays for a Negro Theater.* Boston: Walter H. Baker, 1934.

Efflong, Philip U. *In Search of a Model for African-American Drama: A Study of Selected Plays by Lorraine Hansberry, Amiri Baraka, and Ntozake Shange.* Lanham, Md.: University Press of America, 2000.

Elliot, Charles. *Sinfulness of American Slavery: Proved from Its Evil Sources; Its Injustices; Its Wrongs; Its Contrariety to Many Scriptural Commands, Prohibitions, and Principles, and to the Christian Spirit; and From Its Evil Effects; Together with Observations on Emancipation, and the Duties of American Citizens in Regard to Slavery*. 2 vols. Cincinnati: L. Swormstedt & J. H. Power, 1851.

*Experience and Personal Narrative of Uncle Tom Jones, Who was Forty Years a Slave. Also the Surprising Adventures of Wild Tom, of the Island Retreat, a Fugitive Negro from South Carolina*. Boston: Farwell & Co., 1858.

*Extracts from the Evidence Delivered Before a Select Committee of the House of Commons, in the Years 1790 and 1791; on the Part of the Petitioners for the Abolition of the Slave-Trade*. London: L. Wayland, 1791.

Fahy, Thomas. "Exotic Fantasies, Shameful Realities: Race in the Modern American Freak Show." In *A Modern Mosaic: Art and Modernism in the United States*, ed. Townsend Ludington, 67–92. Chapel Hill: University of North Carolina Press, 2000.

Faux, William. *Memorable Days in America: Being a Journal of a Tour to the United States, Principally Undertaken to Ascertain, by Positive Evidence, the Condition and Probable Prospects of British Emigrants; Including Accounts of Mr. Birkbeck's Settlement in the Illinois: And Intended to Show Men and Things as they are in America*. London: W. Simpkin and R. Marshall, 1823.

Fischer, Hugh Dunn. *The Gun and the Gospel: Early Kansas and Chaplain Fischer*. 2nd ed. New York: Medical Century Company, 1899.

Fite, Emerson D. *History of the United States*. 2nd ed. New York: Henry Holt, 1919.

Fitzpatrick, Sir Jeremiah. *Suggestions on the Slave Trade: For the Consideration of the Legislature of Great Britain*. London: John Stockdale, 1797.

Fleming, William L. *Civil War and Reconstruction in Alabama*. New York: Columbia University Press, 1905.

Foner, Philip S., and Robert J. Branham, eds. *Lift Every Voice: African American Oratory, 1787–1900*. Tuscaloosa: University of Alabama Press, 1998.

Foster, Thomas. "Norman and Saxon Blood Royal." *The Gentleman's Magazine*, January–June 1880, 328–42.

Foucault, Michel. *The History of Sexuality*. Vol. 1, *An Introduction*. London: Viking, 1986.

Frazier, E. Franklin. *The Negro Family in the United States*. Chicago: University of Chicago Press, 1939.

———. *The Negro in the United States*. Rev. ed. 1949. New York: Macmillan, 1957.

Garner, J. W. *Reconstruction in Mississippi*. New York: Macmillan, 1901.

Garnet, Henry Highland. *A Memorial Discourse; By Rev. Henry Highland Garnet, Delivered in the Hall of the House of Representatives, Washington City, D.C. On Sabbath, February 12, 1865. With an Introduction, by James McCune Smith, M.D.* Philadelphia: Joseph M. Wilson, 1865.

George, James Z. *The Political History of Slavery in the United States*. New York: Neale Publishing Company, 1915.

Giddings, Joshua R. *Speeches in Congress*. Boston: John P. Jewett, 1858.

Gilbert, Olive, ed. *Narrative of Sojourner Truth: A Bondswoman of Olden Time, with a History of Her Labors and Correspondence Drawn from Her "Book of Life."* 1850; New York: Penguin, 1998.

Goodell, William. *The American Slave Code in Theory and Practice: Its Distinctive Features Shown by Its Statutes, Judicial Decisions, and Illustrative Facts*. New York: American and Foreign Anti-Slavery Society, 1853.

Greeley, Horace. *The American Conflict: A History of the Great Rebellion in the United States of America, 1860–'64*. 2 vols. Hartford: O. D. Case, 1866.

Green, Jacob D. *Narrative of the Life of J. D. Green, a Runaway Slave from Kentucky*. Huddersfield: Henry Fielding, 1864.

Green, John P. *Recollections of the Inhabitants, Localities, Superstitions, and Ku Klux Outrages of the Carolinas*. N.p., 1880.

Hall, Marshall. *The Two-Fold Slavery of the United States: With a Project of Self-Emancipation*. London: Adam Scott, Charterhouse Square, 1854.

Hamilton, J. G. de Roulhac. *Reconstruction in North Carolina*. Raleigh, N.C.: Presses of Edwards & Broughton, 1914.

Hammond, James Henry. "Overseers." *Carolina Planter* 1 (1844): 25–26.

Hankins, Frank H. *The Racial Basis for Civilization: A Critique of the Nordic Doctrine*. New York: Knopf, 1926.

Harris, William J., ed. *The Leroi Jones/Amiri Baraka Reader*. New York: Avalon, 1999.

Hatch, James V., and Ted Shine, eds. *Black Theater USA: Plays by African Americans, the Early Period, 1847–1938*. New York: Free Press, 1996.

Hazard, W. W. "On the General Management of Negroes." *Southern Agriculturalist* 4 (1831): 350–54.

Heglar, Charles J., ed. *The Life and Adventures of Henry Bibb: An American Slave*. 1850. Madison: University of Wisconsin Press, 2001.

Helper, Hinton Rowan. *The Impending Crisis of the South: How to Meet It*. New York: A. B. Burdick, 1860.

Henningsen, Charles F. *The White Slave: Or, the Russian Peasant Girl*. 3 vols. London: Henry Colburn, 1845.

Henry, Caleb S. *Plain Reasons for the Great Republican Movement: What We Want; Why We Want It; and What Will Come If We Fail*. 2nd ed. New York: Dix, Edwards, 1856.

Herskovits, Melville. *The American Negro: A Study of Racial Crossing*. 1928. Reprint, Bloomington: Indiana University Press, 1968.

Hildreth, Andrew. *The History of the United States of America*. 6 vols. New York: Harper & Brothers, 1880.

Hildreth, Richard. *Archy Moore, the White Slave; or, Memoirs of a Fugitive*. New York: Miller, Orton & Mulligan, 1856.

Houchins, Sue E., ed. *Spiritual Narratives*. New York: Oxford University Press, 1988.

Houck, Davis W., and David E. Dixon, eds. *Rhetoric, Religion, and the Civil Rights Movement, 1954–1965*. Waco, Tex.: Baylor University Press, 2006.

Hunter, Frances L. "Slave Society on the Southern Plantation." *Journal of Negro History* 7, no. 1 (1922): 1–10.

Hurley, Rev. R. F. *The Negro in America: The Influence of His Presence Upon the Material, Social, Moral and Political Development of the Nation, and the Identity of His Interests with the Interests of Other Americans.* Columbia, S.C.: Published by the author, 1899.

Hurmence, Belinda, ed. *My Folks Don't Want Me to Talk about Slavery: Twenty-One Oral Histories of Former North Carolina Slaves.* Winston-Salem: John F. Blair, 1984.

Jacobs, Harriet A. *Incidents in the Life of a Slave Girl: Written by Herself.* 1861. Reprint edited with an introduction by Jean Fagan Yellin. Cambridge: Harvard University Press, 1987.

James, Thomas. *Wonderful Eventful Life of Rev. Thomas James, by Himself.* Rochester, N.Y.: Post-Express Printing Co., 1887.

Jay, William. *Miscellaneous Writings on Slavery.* Boston: John P. Jewitt, 1853.

Johnson, Charles. *Oxherding Tale: A Novel.* New York: Scribner, 1982.

Johnson, Clifton H., ed. *God Struck Me Dead: Religious Conversion Experiences and Autobiographies of Ex-Slaves.* Philadelphia: Pilgrim Press, 1969.

Johnson, Julia E., ed. *The Negro Problem.* New York: H. W. Wilson, 1921.

Johnson, Ollie A., III, and Karin L. Stanford, eds. *Black Political Organizations in the Post–Civil Rights Era.* New Brunswick, N.J.: Rutgers University Press, 2002.

Johnston, James F. W. "Notes on North America." *The London Quarterly Review* 2 (July 1851): 48.

———. *Notes on North America: Agricultural, Economical, and Social.* 2 vols. Boston: Charles C. Little and James Brown, 1851.

Jones, Friday. *Days of Bondage: Autobiography of Friday Jones, Being a Brief Narrative of His Trials and Tribulations in Slavery.* Washington, D.C.: Commercial Pub. Co., 1883.

Juge, M. A. *The American Planter; or the Bound Labor Interest in the United States.* New York: Long and Brother, 1854.

Karim, Benjamin, ed. *The End of White World Supremacy: Four Speeches.* New York: Merlin House, 1971.

Keifer, Joseph W. *Slavery and Four Years of War: A Political History of Slavery in the United States.* 2 vols. New York: Putnam, 1900.

Kelsey, Carl. "The Evolution of Negro Labor." *Annals of the American Academy of Political and Social Science* 21 (January 1903): 55–76.

Killion, Ronald, and Charles Waller, eds. *Slavery Times When I Was Chillun Down on Marster's Plantation: Interviews with Georgia Slaves.* Savannah: Beehive Press, 1973.

King, Martin Luther, Jr. *Stride toward Freedom: The Montgomery Story.* 1958. Reprinted with introduction by Clayborne Carson. Boston: Beacon Press, 2010.

———. *Where Do We Go from Here? Chaos or Community?* Boston: Beacon Press, 1968.

———. *Why We Can't Wait.* 1963. Reprint, New York: Signet Classics, 2000.

Koch, Frederick. *American Folk Plays.* New York: D. Appleton, 1939.

———. *Carolina Folk-Plays: First, Second, and Third Series.* New York: Henry Holt, 1941.

Lake, Obiagele. *Blue Veins and Kinky Hairs: Naming and Color Consciousness in African America*. Westport, Conn.: Praeger, 2003.

Lankford, George E. *Bearing Witness: Memories of Arkansas Slavery from the 1930s WPA Collections*. Fayetteville: University of Arkansas Press, 2006.

Lee, Guy C., and Francis N. Thorpe, eds. *The Civil War: The National View*. Philadelphia: G. Barrie & Sons, 1906.

Long, John Dixon. *Pictures of Slavery in Church and State: Personal Reminiscences, Biographical Sketches, Etc., Etc.* Philadelphia: Published by the author, 1857.

Lowell, James R. *The Writings of James Russell Lowell: Political Essays*. 5 vols. Boston: Houghton Mifflin, 1900.

MacLeod, William Christie. "Economic Aspects of Indigenous American Slavery." *American Anthropologist* 30, no. 4 (1928): 632–50.

Mallard, Robert Quarterman. *Plantation Life before Emancipation*. Richmond: Whittet & Shepperson, 1892.

Mann, Horace. *Slavery: Letters and Speeches*. Boston: B. B. Mussey & Co., 1851.

Marjoribanks, Alexander. *Travels in South and North America*. 5th ed. London: Simpkin, Marshall, 1854.

Mars, James. *The Life of James Mars, a Slave Born and Sold in Connecticut. Written by Himself*. Hartford: Lockwood and Company, 1868.

Marx, Karl. *Capital: A Critique of Political Economy*. 2 vols. New York: Modern Library of America, 1906.

Marx, Karl, and Friedrich Engels. *The Communist Manifesto*. 1848. Reprint edited by Eric Hobsbawm, London: Verso, 1998.

M'Carter, J. Mayland. *Border Methodism and Border Slavery: Being a Statement and a Review of the Philadelphia Annual Conference Concerning Slavery*. Philadelphia: Collins, 1858.

McElrath, Joseph R., Robert C. Leitz III, and Jesse S. Crisler, eds. *Charles W. Chesnutt: Essays and Speeches*. Stanford: Stanford University Press, 1999.

McKaye, James. *The Mastership and Its Fruits: The Emancipated Slave Face to Face with His Old Master. A Supplement Report to Hon. Edwin M. Stanton, Secretary of War*. New York: Loyal Publications Society, 1864.

*Memoir of Old Elizabeth, a Coloured Woman*. Philadelphia: Collins, 1863.

Mencken, H. L. "Designations for Colored Folk." *American Speech*, 19, no. 3 (1944): 161–74.

Miller, Kelly. "Eugenics and the Negro." *Scientific Monthly*, July 1917, 57–59.

———. *Race Adjustment: Essays on the Negro in America*. Washington, D.C.: Neale, 1908.

———. "A Review of Hoffman's Race Traits and Tendencies of the American Negro." *American Negro Academy Occasional Papers, No. 1* (1969): 3–36.

Mintz, Steven, ed. *African American Voices: A Documentary Reader, 1619–1877*. Oxford: Wiley-Blackwell, 2009.

Mitchell, Margaret. *Gone with the Wind*. New York: Macmillan, 1936.

Moore, M. V. "Some Recollections of Slavery: By a Former Slaveholder." *New England Magazine* 10, no. 1 (1891): 23–28.

Morrison, Toni. *Beloved: A Novel.* New York: Plume, 1987.

Moynihan, Daniel Patrick. *The Negro Family: A Case for National Action.* Washington, D.C.: Government Printing Office, 1965.

Munro, Alexander. *Elements of the Anatomy of the Human Body in Its Sound State; with Occasional Remarks on Physiology, Pathology, and Surgery.* 2 vols. Edinburgh: Maclachlan & Stewart, 1825.

Myrdal, Gunnar. *An American Dilemma: The Negro Problem and Modern Democracy.* 2 vols. 1944. Reprint, New Brunswick, N.J.: Transaction, 2009.

*A Narrative of the Adventures and Escape of Moses Roper, From American Slavery.* Philadelphia: Merrihew and Gun, 1838.

*Narrative of the Life of Moses Grandy, Formerly a Slave in the United States of America.* Boston: Oliver Johnson, 1844.

*A Narrative of Some Remarkable Incidents in the Life of Solomon Bayley, Formerly a Slave, in the State of Delaware, North America; Written by Himself, and Published for His Benefit; to Which are Prefixed, a Few Remarks by Robert Hurnard.* 2nd ed. London: Printed for Harvey & Darton, Gracechurch St., 1825.

*The Negro Family: The Case for National Action.* Washington, D.C.: U.S. Government Printing Office, 1965.

Nelson, Jill. *Straight, No Chaser: How I Became a Grown-Up Black Woman.* New York: Penguin Books, 1997.

Olmstead, Frederick Law. *The Cotton Kingdom: A Traveller's Observations on Cotton and Slavery in the American Slave States.* Vol. 1. 2nd ed. New York: Mason Brothers, 1862.

———. *A Journey in the Seaboard Slave States in the Years 1853–1854, with Remarks on Their Economy.* 2 vols. New York: Putnam, 1856.

———. *A Journey to the Back Country.* New York: Mason Brothers, 1861.

Onstott, Kyle. *Mandingo.* Richmond: Denlinger, 1957.

Perdue, Charles L., Jr., Thomas E. Barden, and Robert K. Philips, eds. *Weevils in the Wheat: Interviews with Virginia Ex-Slaves.* Bloomington: Indiana University Press, 1980.

Perkins, Kathy A., and Judith L. Stephens, eds. *Strange Fruit: Plays on Lynching by American Women.* Bloomington: Indiana University Press, 1998.

Perkins-Valdez, Dolen. *Wench: A Novel.* New York: Harper Collins, 2010.

Perry, Jeffrey B., ed. *A Hubert Harrison Reader.* Middletown, Conn.: Wesleyan University Press, 2001.

Peterson, Bernard L., Jr. *Early American Playwrights and Dramatic Writers: A Biographical Directory and Catalog of Plays, Films, and Broadcasting Scripts.* Westport, Conn.: Greenwood, 1990.

Phelps, Austin. *My Study: And Other Essays.* New York: Scribner, 1886.

Phillips, Ulrich Bonnell. *American Negro Slavery: A Survey of the Supply, Employment and Control of Negro Labor as Determined by the Plantation Regimes.* New York: D. Appleton, 1918.

Phillips, Wendell. *Speeches, Lectures, and Letters.* Boston: Lee & Shephard, 1872.

———. *Speeches, Lectures, and Letters.* Ed. Rev. Theodore C. Peasr. Cambridge, Mass.: John Wilson & Sons, 1891.

Pierce, Edward L., ed. *Memoir and Letters of Charles Sumner.* 4 vols. Boston: Roberts Brothers, 1893.

Pike, James Shepherd. *First Blows of the Civil War: The Ten Years of Preliminary Conflict in the United States. From 1850 to 1860.* New York: American News Co., 1879.

Pillsbury, Parker. *Acts of the Anti-Slavery Apostles.* Concord, N.H.: Clague, Wegman, Schlicht, 1883.

Pollard, Edward A. *The Lost Cause: A New Southern History of the War of the Confederates.* New York: E. B. Treat, 1866.

———. *The Lost Cause: A New Southern History of the War of the Confederates.* 2nd ed. New York: E. B. Treat, 1890.

———. *The Lost Cause Regained.* New York: G. W. Carleton & Co., 1868.

Porter, Dorothy B., ed. *Early Negro Writing, 1760–1837.* Boston: Beacon Press, 1971.

Price, Thomas. *Slavery in America: With Notices of the Present State of Slavery and the Slave Trade throughout the World.* London: G. Wightman, 1837.

*Proceedings of the New-England Anti-Slavery Convention, Held in Boston on the 27th, 28th and 29th of May, 1834.* Boston: Printed by Garrison & Knapp, 1834.

*The Proslavery Argument; as Maintained by the Most Distinguished Writers of the Southern States, Containing the Several Essays, on the Subject of Chancellor Harper, Governor Hammond, Dr. Simms, and Professor Dew.* Charleston: Walker, Richards & Co., 1852.

Purvis, Robert. *Appeal to Forty Thousand Citizens, Threatened with Disfranchisement, to the People of Pennsylvania.* Philadelphia: Merrihew and Gunn, 1838.

Ranby, John. *Doubts on the Abolition of the Slave Trade, by an Old Member of Parliament.* London: John Stockdale, 1790.

Rawick, George P., ed. *The American Slave: A Composite Autobiography.* 19 vols. Westport, Conn.: Greenwood, 1972.

———, ed. *The American Slave: A Composite Autobiography,* Supplemental Series 1. 12 vols. Westport, Conn.: Greenwood, 1977.

———, ed. *The American Slave: A Composite Autobiography,* Supplemental Series 2. 10 vols. Westport, Conn.: Greenwood, 1979.

Reddick, L. D. "A New Interpretation for Negro History." *Journal of Negro History* 22, no. 1 (1937), 17–28.

Reinhart, James M. "The Negro: Is He a Biological Inferior?" *American Journal of Sociology* 33, no. 2 (1927): 248–61.

Renny, Robert. *An History of Jamaica.* London: J. Cawthorn, 1807.

*Report of the Commissioner of Agriculture for the Year 1865.* Washington, D.C.: U.S. Government Printing Office, 1866.

Reuter, Edward B. *The Mulatto in the United States: Including a Study of the Mixed-Blood Races Throughout the World.* 1918. Reprint, New York: Negro Universities Press, 1969.

————. "Why the Presence of the Negro Constitutes a Problem in the American Social Order." *Journal of Negro Education* 8, no. 3 (1939): 291–98.

*Revelations of a Slave Smuggler: Being the Autobiography of Capt. Richard Drake, an African Trader for Fifty Years—From 1807 to 1857; During Which Period He was Concerned in the Transportation of Half a Million Blacks from African Coasts to America, with a Preface by His Executor, rev. Henry Byrd West, of the protestant Home Mission.* New York: Robert M. Dewitt, 1860.

Reynolds, J. S. *Reconstruction in South Carolina, 1865–1877.* Columbia, S.C.: State Co., 1905.

Rhodes, James Ford. *History of the United States from the Compromise of 1850.* 4 vols. New York: Harper & Brothers, 1892–1919.

Ripley, C. Peter, ed. *The Black Abolitionist Papers.* 5 vols. Chapel Hill: University of North Carolina Press, 1985–92.

Robinson, Bernard F. "War and Race Conflicts in the United States." *Phylon* 2, no. 4 (1943): 311–18, 321–27.

Roman, Charles Victor. *American Civilization and the Negro: The Afro-American in Relation to National Progress.* Philadelphia: F. A. Davis, 1916.

Royster, Jacqueline Jones, ed. *Southern Horrors and Other Writings: The Anti-Lynching Campaign of Ida B. Wells, 1892–1900.* Boston: Bedford Books, 1997.

Rubens, Julius. *"Liberty."* New York: American Anti-Slavery Society, 1839.

Sanders, Leslie C. *The Development of Black Theater in America: From Shadows to Slaves.* Baton Rouge: Louisiana State University Press, 1998.

Schuricht, Herrmann. *History of the German Element in Virginia.* 2 vols. Baltimore: Theo. Kroh, 1898–1900.

Seale, Bobby. *Seize the Time: The Story of the Black Panther Party and Huey P. Newton.* 1970. Reprint, Baltimore: Black Classic Press, 1991.

Seaman, Ezra Champion. *Essays on the Progress of Nations, in Productive Industry, Civilization, Population, and Wealth; Illustrated by Statistics of Mining, Agriculture, Manufactures, Commerce, Banking, Revenues, Internal Improvements, Emigration, Mortality, and Population.* New York: Baker & Scribner, 1846.

Shannon, Alexander Harvey. *Racial Integrity and Other Features of the Negro Problem.* Nashville: M. E. Church, South, 1907.

Siebert, Wilbur H. *The Underground Railroad: From Slavery to Freedom.* New York: Macmillan, 1898.

Simons, A. M. "Economic Aspects of Chattel Slavery." *International Socialist Review* 4 (July 1903–June 1904): 257–75.

*Six Women's Slave Narratives.* New York: Oxford University Press, 1988.

*Slavery Illustrated in Its Effects upon Woman and Domestic Society.* Boston: Isaac Knapp, 1837.

Smith, Gerrit. *The True Office of Civil Government: A Speech in the City of Troy.* New York: S. W. Benedict, 1851.

South Carolina. House of Representatives. *Special Committee on Slavery and the Slave Trade.* Columbia, S.C., 1867.

Sprague, Stuart Seely, ed. *His Promised Land: The Autobiography of John P. Parker, Former Slave and Conductor on the Underground Railroad.* New York: Norton, 1996.

Staples, Thomas. *Reconstruction in Arkansas, 1862–1874.* New York: Columbia University, 1923.

St. Clair, Thomas Staunton. *A Soldier's Recollections of the West Indies and America, with a Narrative of the Expedition to the Island of Walcheren,* 2 vols. London: Richard Bentley, 1834.

Stephens, Judith L. *The Plays of Georgia Douglas Johnson: From the New Negro Renaissance to the Civil Rights Movement.* Champaign: University of Illinois Press, 2006.

Steward, Austin. *Twenty-Two Years a Slave, and Forty Years a Freeman; Embracing a Correspondence of Several Years, While President of Wilberforce Colony, London, Canada West.* Rochester, N.Y.: William Alling, 1857.

Still, William. *An Address on the Voting and Laboring, Delivered at Concert Hall, Tuesday Evening, March 10, 1874.* Philadelphia: Jas. B. Rogers, 1874.

———. *The Underground Rail Road: A Record of Facts, Authentic Narratives, &c., Narrating the Hardships, Hair-breadth Escapes and Death Struggles of the Slaves in their Efforts for Freedom, as Related by Themselves and Others, or Witnessed by the Author; Together with Sketches of Some of the Largest Stockholders, and Most Liberal Aiders, of the Road.* Philadelphia: Porter & Coates, 1872.

Stirling, James. *Letters from the Slave States.* London: John W. Parker & Son, 1857.

Stowe, Harriet Beecher. *Uncle Tom's Cabin: Or, Life among the Lowly.* Boston: John P. Jewett, 1852.

Strickland, S. *Negro Slavery Described by a Negro: Being the Narrative of Ashton Warner a Native of St. Vincent's.* London: Samuel Maunder, 1831.

Thomas, William Hannibal. *The American Negro: What He Was, What He Is, and What He May Become: A Critical and Practical Discussion.* New York: Macmillan, 1901.

Thompson, C. Mildred. *Reconstruction in Georgia.* New York: Columbia University Press, 1915.

Tourgee, Albion W. *Hot Plowshares: A Novel.* New York: Fords, Howard, & Hulbert, 1883.

Tuckerman, Bayard, and John Jay. *William Jay and the Constitutional Movement for the Abolition of Slavery.* New York: Dodd, Mead, 1894.

Tyler, Ron, and Lawrence R. Murphy, eds. *The Slave Narratives of Texas.* Abilene, Tex.: State House Press, McMurry University, 2006.

Von Holst, Hermann. *The Constitutional and Political History of the United States: 1750–1833, State Sovereignty and Slavery.* 8 vols. Chicago: Callaghan & Company, 1889.

Walker, Margaret. *Jubilee.* Boston: Houghton Mifflin, 1966.

Washington, Booker T., ed. *The Negro Problem: A Series of Articles by Representative American Negroes of To-Day.* New York: James Pott & Company, 1903.

Washington, James M., ed. *A Testament of Hope: The Essential Writings and Speeches of Martin Luther King, Jr.* New York: Harper Collins, 1991.

Watson, Henry. *Narrative of Henry Watson, a Fugitive Slave.* 2nd ed. Boston: Bella Marsh, 1849.

Weld, Theodore Dwight. *American Slavery as It Is: Testimony of a Thousand Witnesses.* New York: Published by the American Anti-Slavery Society, 1839.

———. *Slavery and the International Slave Trade in the United States of North America.* London: T. Ward & Co., 1841.

Wells, Ida B. *A Red Record: Lynchings in the United States, 1892-1893-1894.* Chicago, 1997.

Weston, George M. *The Progress of Slavery in the United States.* Washington, D.C.: Published by the author, 1857.

Whipple, Wayne. *The Story-Life of Lincoln: A Biography Composed of Five Hundred True Stories Told by Abraham Lincoln and His Friends.* Philadelphia: John C. Winston, 1908.

Whiteley, Henry. *Excessive Cruelty to Slaves: Three Months in Jamaica, in 1832: Comprising a Residence of Seven Weeks on a Sugar Plantation.* London, 1833. Held in the Library Company of Philadelphia.

Wickliffe, John C. "Negro Suffrage a Failure: Shall We Abolish It?" *The Forum* 17 (1892): 797–804.

Wilberforce, William. *A Letter on the Abolition of the Slave Trade: Addressed to Freeholders and other Inhabitants of Yorkshire.* London: Luke Hansard & Sons, 1807.

Williams, Robert F. *Negroes with Guns.* 1962. Reprint, Detroit: Wayne State University Press, 1998.

Wilson, Henry. *History of the Rise and Fall of the Slave Power in America.* 3 vols. Boston: James R. Osgood & Company, 1872–77.

———. *No Rights, No Duties: Or, Slaveholders, As Such, Have no Rights; Slaves, as Such, Owe no Duties.* Boston: Printed for the author, 1860.

Winston, Robert W. "An Unconsidered Aspect of the Negro Question." *South Atlantic Quarterly* 1, no. 3 (1902): 265–68.

Woodson, Carter G. "The Beginnings of the Miscegenation of the Whites and Blacks." *Journal of Negro History* 3, no. 4 (1918): 335–53.

———. *The Mis-Education of the Negro.* Washington, D.C.: Associated Publishers, 1933.

———. *The Negro in Our History.* 2nd ed. Washington, D.C.: Associated Publishers, 1922.

Woodson, Carter G., and Charles H. Wesley. *The Story of the Negro Retold.* Washington, D.C.: Associated Publishers, 1935.

Works Project Administration. *Slave Narratives: A Folk History of Slavery in the United States from Interviews with Former Slaves.* 1941. Reprint, Charleston, S.C.: Bibliolife, 2006.

Worley, Demetrice A., and Jesse Perry Jr., eds. *African-American Literature: An Anthology.* 2nd ed. Lincolnwood, Ill.: NTC Publishing Group, 1998.

X, Malcolm. *The Autobiography of Malcolm X.* With Alex Haley. 1964. Reprint, New York: Ballantine, 1999.

Yerby, Frank. *The Foxes of Harrow.* New York: Dial Press, 1947.

**Secondary Sources**

Abercrombie, Thomas Alan. *Pathways of Memory and Power: Ethnography and History among an Andean People.* Madison: University of Wisconsin Press, 1998.

Abrahams, Roger D. *Deep Down in the Jungle: Negro Narrative Folklore from the Streets of Philadelphia.* New York: Aldine de Gruyter, 1970.

Abzug, Robert. *Cosmos Crumbling: American Reform and the Religious Imagination.* New York: Oxford University Press, 1994.

Adams, Jessica. *Wounds of Returning: Race, Memory, and Property on the Postslavery Plantation.* Chapel Hill: University of North Carolina Press, 2007.

Adeleke, Tunde. *Without Regard to Race: The Other Martin Delany.* Jackson: University Press of Mississippi, 2003.

Adjaye, Joseph K. *Time in the Black Experience.* Santa Barbara, Calif.: Greenwood, 1994.

Anderson, Karen. *Changing Woman: A History of Racial Ethnic Women in Modern America.* New York: Oxford University Press, 1996.

Anderson, Lisa M. *Black Feminism in Contemporary Drama.* Bloomington: University of Illinois Press, 2008.

Aptheker, Herbert. *Negro Slave Revolts in the United States, 1526–1860.* New York: International Publishers, 1939.

Arendt, Hannah. *Between Past and Future: Eight Exercises in Political Thought.* New York: Penguin, 1993.

Arsenault, Raymond. *Freedom Riders: 1961 and the Struggle for Racial Justice.* New York: Oxford University Press, 2006.

Ashmore, Harry S. *Hearts and Minds: The Anatomy of Racism from Roosevelt to Reagan.* New York: McGraw Hill, 1982.

Ashwood, John. *Slavery, Capitalism, and Politics in the Antebellum Republic: The Coming of the Civil War.* Cambridge: Cambridge University Press, 2008.

Baer, Hans E., and Merrill Singer. *African American Religion: Varieties of Protest and Accommodation.* 2nd ed. Knoxville: University of Tennessee Press, 2002.

Baker, Bruce E. *What Reconstruction Meant: Historical Memory in the American South.* Charlottesville: University of Virginia Press, 2007.

Baker, Houston A., Jr. "Modernism and the Harlem Renaissance." *American Quarterly* 39, no. 1 (1987): 84–97.

Baker, Ronald L. *Homeless, Friendless, and Penniless: The WPA Interviews with Former Slaves Living in Indiana.* Bloomington: Indiana University Press, 2000.

———. "Lady Lil and Pisspot Pete." *Journal of American Folklore* 100, no. 396 (1987): 191–99.

Balfour, Katherine L. "Representative Women: Slavery, Citizenship, and Feminist Theory in Du Bois's 'Damnation of Women.'" *Hyptia* 20, no. 3 (2005): 127–48.

Banta, Martha. *Barbaric Intercourse: Caricature and the Culture of Conduct, 1841–1936.* Chicago: University of Chicago Press, 2003.

Baptist, Edward E. "'Cuffy,' 'Fancy Maids,' and 'One-Eyed Men': Rape, Commodification, and the Domestic Slave Trade in the United States." *American Historical Review* 106, no. 5 (2001): 1619–50.

Baptist, Edward E., and Stephanie M. H. Camp, eds. *New Studies in the History of American Slavery.* Athens: University of Georgia Press, 2006.

Barber, David. *A Hard Rain Fell: SDS and Why It Failed.* Jackson: University Press of Mississippi, 2008.

Bargainnier, Earl F. "The Falconhurst Series: A New Popular Image of the Old South." *Journal of Popular Culture* 10, no. 2 (1976): 298–314.

Barnett, Bernice McNair. "Invisible Southern Black Women Leaders in the Civil Rights Movement: The Triple Constraints of Gender, Race, and Class." *Gender and Society* 7, no. 2 (1993): 162–82.

Barrios, Olga. *The Black Theatre Movement in the United States and in South Africa.* Valencia: Universitat de Valencia, 2008.

Bay, Mia. *To Tell the Truth Freely: The Life of Ida B. Wells.* New York: Hill & Wang, 2009.

———. *The White Image in the Black Mind: African American Ideas about White People, 1830–1925.* New York: Oxford University Press, 2000.

Beckles, Hilary McD. *Centering Woman: Gender Discourses in Caribbean Slave Society.* Princeton, N.J.: Markus Wiener, 1999.

———. *Natural Rebels: A Social History of Enslaved Black Women in Barbados.* New Brunswick, N.J.: Rutgers University Press, 1989.

Bederman, Gail. *Manliness and Civilization: A Cultural History of Gender and Race in the United States, 1880–1917.* Chicago: University of Chicago Press, 1996.

Beeman, Richard. *Plain, Honest Men: The Making of the American Constitution.* New York: Random House, 2009.

Ben-Amos, Dan, and Liliane Weisberg, eds. *Cultural Memory and the Construction of Identity.* Detroit: Wayne State University Press, 1999.

Bennett, J. Harry, Jr. "The Problem of Slave Labor Supply at the Codrington Plantations." *Journal of Negro History* 36, no. 4 (1951): 406–41.

Benshoff, Harry M., and Sean Griffith. *America on Film: Representing Race, Class, Gender, and Sexuality at the Movies.* Malden, Mass.: Blackwell Publishing, 2004.

Bergad, Laird W. *The Comparative Histories of Slavery in Brazil, Cuba, and the United States.* New York: Cambridge University Press, 2007.

Berlin, Ira, and Philip D. Morgan, eds. *Cultivation and Culture: Labor and the Shaping of Slave Life in the Americas.* Charlottesville: University Press of Virginia, 1993.

Berry, Diana Ramey. *"Swing the Sickle for the Harvest Is Ripe": Gender and Slavery in Antebellum Georgia.* Bloomington: University of Illinois Press, 2007.

Berry, Faith, ed. *From Bondage to Liberation: Writings by and about Afro-Americans from 1700–1918*. New York: Continuum, 2006.

Bevir, Mark. "Objectivity in History." *History and Theory* 33, no. 3 (1994): 328–44.

Blackburn, Robin. *The Making of New World Slavery: From Baroque to the Modern, 1492–1800*. London: Verso, 1997.

———. *The Overthrow of Colonial Slavery, 1776–1848*. London: Verso, 1988.

Blackett, Richard. *Building an Antislavery Wall: Black Americans in the Atlantic Abolitionist Movement, 1830–1860*. Baton Rouge: Louisiana State University Press, 1983.

Blassingame, John W. *The Slave Community: Plantation Life in the Antebellum South*. New York: Oxford University Press, 1979.

Bleser, Carol, ed. *In Joy and in Sorrow: Women, Family, and Marriage in the Victorian South*. New York: Oxford University Press, 1992.

Blight, David W. *The Civil War in American Memory*. Cambridge: Harvard University Press, 2001.

———. *Race and Reunion: The Civil War in American Memory*. Cambridge: Harvard University Press, 2002.

Blumer, Herbert. *Symbolic Interactionism: Perspective and Method*. Englewood Cliffs, N.J.: Prentice-Hall, 1969.

Bogle, Donald. *Toms, Coons, Mulattoes, Mammies, and Bucks: An Interpretative History of Blacks in American Film*. New York: Continuum, 1994.

Boles, John. *Black Southerners, 1619–1869*. Lexington: University Press of Kentucky, 1984.

Boney, Francis Nash. "The American South." *Journal of Popular Culture* 10, no. 2 (1976): 290–97.

Boothe, Demico. *Why Are So Many Black Men in Prison?* Memphis: Full Surface Publishing, 2007.

Boritt, Gabot, and Scott Hancock, eds. *Slavery, Resistance, Freedom*. New York: Oxford University Press, 2007.

Bosch, Susanna A. *"Sturdy Black Bridges" on the American Stage: The Portrayal of Black Motherhood in Selected Plays by Contemporary African American Women Playwrights*. Frankfurt: Peter Lang, 2006.

Boswell, Angela. *Her Act and Deed: Women's Lives in a Rural Southern Community, 1765–1860*. College Station: Texas A&M University Press, 2001.

Botkin, B. A., ed. *Lay My Burden Down: A Folk History of Slavery*. Rev. ed. Chicago: University of Chicago Press, 1973.

Braxton, Joanne M., and Maria Diedrich, eds. *Monuments of the Black Atlantic: Slavery and Memory*. New Brunswick, N.J.: Transaction, 2004.

Breines, Winifred. *The Trouble between Us: An Uneasy History of White and Black Women in the Feminist Movement*. New York: Oxford University Press, 2006.

Bridgewater, Pamela D. *Breeding a Nation: Reproductive Slavery, the Thirteenth Amendment, and the Pursuit of Freedom*. Boston: South End Press, 2009.

————. "Reproductive Freedom as Civil Freedom: The Thirteenth Amendment's Role in the Struggle for Reproductive Rights." *Journal of Gender, Race, and Justice* 3, no. 1 (1999): 411–32.

————. "Un/Re/Dis Covering Slave Breeding in Thirteenth Amendment Jurisprudence." *Washington and Lee Race and Ethnic Ancestry Law Journal* 7, no. 1 (2001): 11–44.

Broderick, Francis L., and August Meier, eds. *Negro Protest Thought in the Twentieth Century.* Indianapolis: Bobbs-Merrill, 1965.

Brodie, Fawn M. *Thomas Jefferson: An Intimate History.* New York: Norton, 1974.

Bronner, Simon J., ed. *Manly Traditions: The Folk Roots of American Masculinity.* Bloomington: Indiana University Press, 2005.

Brooks, Roy L. *Atonement and Forgiveness: A New Model for Black Reparations.* Berkeley: University of California Press, 2004.

————, ed. *When Sorry Isn't Enough: The Controversy over Apologies and Reparations for Human Injustice.* New York: New York University Press, 1999.

Brown, Christopher L. *Moral Capital: Foundations of British Abolitionism.* Chapel Hill: University of North Carolina Press, 2006.

Brown, Vincent. *The Reaper's Garden: Death and Power in the World of Atlantic Slavery.* Cambridge: Harvard University Press, 2008.

Browne, Katherine E. *Creole Economies: Caribbean Cunning under the French Flag.* Austin: University of Texas Press, 2004.

Brundage, W. Fitzhugh. *Lynching in the New South: Georgia and Virginia, 1880–1930.* Urbana: University of Illinois Press, 1993.

————. *Under the Sentence of Death: Lynching in the South.* Chapel Hill: University of North Carolina Press, 1997.

Burke, Peter, ed. *New Perspectives on Historical Writing.* University Park, Pa.: Polity Press, 2001.

Caldwell, Carle. "Erskine Caldwell: A Note for the Negative." *College English* 17, no. 6 (1956): 357–59.

Calomiris, Charles, and Jonathan Pritchett. "Preserving Slave Families for Profit: Traders' Incentives and Pricing in the New Orleans Slave Market." *Journal of Economic History* 69, no. 4 (2009): 986–1011.

Camp, Stephanie M. H. *Closer to Freedom: Enslaved Women and Everyday Resistance in the Plantation South.* Chapel Hill: University of North Carolina Press, 2004.

Campbell, Gwyn, Suzanne Miers, and Joseph C. Miller, eds. *Women and Slavery: Africa, the Indian Ocean World, and the Medieval North Atlantic.* Athens: Ohio University Press, 2007.

Canning, Charlotte. *Feminist Theaters in the U.S.A.: Staging Women's Experience.* New York: Routledge, 2005.

Cardyn, Lisa. "Sexualized Racism/Gendered Violence: Outraging the Body Politics in the Reconstruction South." *Michigan Law Review* 100, no. 4 (2002): 675–867.

Carey, Brycchan. *British Abolitionism and the Rhetoric of Sensibility: Writing, Sentiment, and Slavery, 1760–1807.* Basingstoke: Palgrave Macmillan, 2005.

Caron, Simone M. *Who Chooses? American Reproductive History since 1830.* Gainesville: University Press of Florida, 2008.

Carr, Edward Hallett. *What Is History?* New York: Knopf, 1965.

Carter, Everett. "Cultural History Written with Lightning: The Significance of the Birth of a Nation." *American Quarterly* 12, no. 3 (1960): 347–57.

Caruth, Cathy, ed. *Trauma: Explorations in Memory.* Baltimore: Johns Hopkins University Press, 1995.

Cash, W. J. *The Mind of the South.* New York: Vintage Books, 1941.

Catton, Bruce. *The Coming Fury: The Centennial History of the Civil War.* New York: Doubleday, 1961.

Chadwick, Bruce. *The General and Mrs. Washington: The Untold Story of a Marriage and a Revolution.* Naperville, Ill.: Sourcebooks, 2006.

Chappell, David L. *A Stone of Hope: Prophetic Religion and the Death of Jim Crow.* Chapel Hill: University of North Carolina Press, 2004.

Charron, Katherine M. *Freedom's Teacher: The Life of Septima Clark.* Chapel Hill: University of North Carolina Press, 2009.

Childs, Donald J. *Modernism and Eugenics: Woolf, Eliot, and the Culture of Degeneration.* New York: Cambridge University Press, 2001.

Chinn, Sarah. *Technology and the Logic of American Racism: A Cultural History of the Body as Evidence.* New York: Continuum, 2000.

Cleaver, Kathleen, and George Katsiaficas, eds. *Liberation, Imagination, and the Black Panther Party: A New Look at the Panthers and Their Legacy.* New York: Routledge, 2001.

Climo, Jacob, and Maria G. Cattell. *Social Memory and History: Anthropological Perspectives.* Lanham, Md.: Rowman Altamira, 2002.

Clinton, Catherine. *The Plantation Mistress: Women's World in the Old South.* New York: Pantheon Books, 1982.

Collins, Patricia Hill. *Black Feminist Thought: Knowledge, Consciousness, and the Politics of Empowerment.* 1991; New York: Routledge, 2000.

———. *Black Sexual Politics: African Americans, Gender, and the New Racism.* New York: Routledge, 2004.

———. *From Black Power to Hip Hop: Racism, Nationalism, and Feminism.* Philadelphia: Temple University Press, 2006.

Condit, Celeste M., and John L. Lucaites. *Crafting Equality: America's Anglo-African Word.* Chicago: University of Chicago Press, 1993.

Conner, Lynne. *Pittsburgh in Stages: Two Hundred Years of Theater.* Pittsburgh: University of Pittsburgh Press, 2007.

Conor, Liz. *The Spectacular Modern Woman: Feminine Visibility in the 1920s.* Bloomington: Indiana University Press, 2004.

Conrad, Alfred H., and John R. Meyer. "The Economics of Slavery in the Ante Bellum South." *Journal of Political Economy* 66, no. 2 (1958): 95–130.

Conway, M. D. *Testimonies Concerning Slavery*. 2nd ed. London: Chapman & Hall, 1865.

Conyers, James L. *Charles H. Wesley: The Intellectual Tradition of a Black Historian*. New York: Routledge, 1997.

Cook, Robert J. *Troubled Commemoration: The American Civil War Centennial, 1961–1965*. Baton Rouge: Louisiana State University Press, 2007.

Cooper, William J., and Tom E. Terrill. *The American South: A History*. Lanham, Md.: Rowman & Littlefield, 2009.

Corbould, Clare. *Becoming African American: Black Public Life in Harlem, 1919–1939*. Cambridge: Harvard University Press, 2009.

Cornelius, Janet D. *Slave Missions and the Black Church in the Antebellum South*. Columbia: University of South Carolina Press, 1999.

Cott, Nancy. *Public Vows: A History of Marriage and the Nation*. Cambridge: Harvard University Press, 2000.

Cott, Nancy F., Jeanne Boydston, Ann Braude, Lori D. Ginzberg, and Molly Ladd-Taylor, eds. *Root of Bitterness: Documents of the Social History of American Women*. 2nd ed. Boston: Northeastern University Press, 1996.

Cox, Oliver C. *Race Relations: Elements and Social Dynamics*. Detroit: Wayne State University Press, 1976.

Craig, Evelyn Quita. *Black Drama of the Federal Theatre Era: Beyond the Formal Horizons*. Amherst: University of Massachusetts Press, 1980.

Crawford, Vicki L., Jacqueline Anne Rouse, and Barbara Woods, eds. *Women in the Civil Rights Movement: Trailblazers and Torchbearers, 1941–1965*. Bloomington: Indiana University Press, 1990.

Curzon, Anne. *Gender Shifts in the History of English*. Cambridge: Cambridge University Press, 2003.

Dagbovie, Pero Gaglo. "Black Women Historians from the Late 19th Century to the Dawning of the Civil Rights Movement." *Journal of African American History* 89, no. 3 (2004): 241–61.

———. *The Early Black History Movement, Carter G. Woodson, and Lorenzo Greene*. Champaign: University of Illinois Press, 2007.

Dal Lago, Enrico, and Constantina Katsari, eds. *Slave Systems: Ancient and Modern*. Cambridge: Cambridge University Press, 2008.

David, Paul A., Herbert G. Gutman, Richard Sutch, Peter Temin, and Gavin Wright, eds. *Reckoning with Slavery: A Critical Study in the Quantitative History of American Negro Slavery*. New York: Oxford University Press, 1976.

Davis, Adrienne. "'Don't Let Nobody Bother Yo' Principle': The Sexual Economy of American Slavery." In *Sister Circle: Black Women and Work*, ed. Sharon Harley, 103–27. New Brunswick, N.J.: Rutgers University Press, 2002.

Davis, Charles T., and Henry Louis Gates, Jr., eds. *The Slave's Narrative*. New York: Oxford University Press, 1985.

Davis, David Brion. *Inhuman Bondage: The Rise and Fall of Slavery in the New World.* New York: Oxford University Press, 2006.

———. *The Problem of Slavery in the Age of Revolution.* Ithaca: Cornell University Press, 1975.

Demastes, William W. *Realism and the American Dramatic Tradition.* Tuscaloosa: University of Alabama Press, 1996.

D'Emilio, John. *Lost Prophet: The Life and Times of Bayard Rustin.* New York: Simon & Schuster, 2003.

D'Emilio, John, and Estelle B. Freedman. *Intimate Matters: A History of Sexuality in America.* 2nd ed. Chicago: University of Chicago Press, 1997.

Dennison, Stephanie, and Song Hwee Lim, eds. *Remapping World Cinema: Identity, Culture and Politics in Film.* London: Wallflower Press, 2006.

Deyle, Steven. "An 'abominable' New Trade: The Closing of the African Slave Trade and the Changing Patterns of U.S. Political Power, 1808–60." *William and Mary Quarterly*, 3rd series, 66, no. 4 (2009): 832–49.

———. *Carry Me Back: The Domestic Slave Trade in American Life.* New York: Oxford University Press, 2005.

Dillon, Merton. *The Abolitionists: The Growth of a Dissenting Minority.* DeKalb: Northern Illinois University Press, 1974.

Dixon, Chris. *Perfecting the Family: Antislavery Marriages in Nineteenth-Century America.* Amherst: University of Massachusetts Press, 1997.

Dixon, Wheeler W. *American Cinema in the 1940s: Themes and Variations.* New Brunswick, N.J.: Rutgers University Press, 2005.

———. *Visions of the Apocalypse: Spectacles of Destruction in American Cinema.* London: Wallflower Press, 2003.

Dollard, John. *Caste and Class in a Southern Town.* 3rd ed. 1937. New York: Doubleday Anchor Books, 1957.

Donoghue, Eddie. *Black Breeding Machines: The Breeding of Negro Slaves in the Diaspora.* Bloomington, Ind.: Author House, 2008.

Drain, Richard. *Twentieth-Century Theatre: A Sourcebook.* New York: Routledge, 1995.

Dreer, Herman. "What Does the Innocent Teacher Impart as History?" *Journal of Negro History* 25, no. 4 (1940): 474–83.

Drescher, Seymour. *Capitalism and Antislavery: British Mobilization in Comparative Perspective.* New York: Oxford University Press, 1987.

Dubey, Madhu. *Black Women Novelists and the Nationalist Aesthetic.* Bloomington: Indiana University Press, 1994.

Du Bois Shaw, Gwendolyn. *Seeing the Unspeakable: The Art of Kara Walker.* Durham, N.C.: Duke University Press, 2004.

Dujon, Diane, and Ann Withorn, eds. *For Crying Out Load: Women's Poverty in the United States.* Boston: South End Press, 1996.

Dunaway, Wilma A. *The African-American Family in Slavery and Emancipation.* New York: Cambridge University Press, 2003.

Dundes, Alan, ed. *Mother Wit from the Laughing Barrel: Readings in the Interpretation of Afro-American Folklore*. Minneapolis: University of Minnesota Press, 1990.

Durant, Thomas J., and J. David Knottnerus, eds. *Plantation Society and Race Relations: The Origins of Inequality*. Westport, Conn.: Praeger, 1999.

Dyer, Thomas G. *Theodore Roosevelt and the Idea of Race*. Baton Rouge: Louisiana State University Press, 1992.

Dyson, Michael Eric. *Race Rules: Navigating the Color Line*. Reading, Mass.: Addison-Wesley, 1996.

Edkins, Jenny. *Trauma and the Memory of Politics*. Cambridge: Cambridge University Press, 2003.

Eiselein, Gregory. *Literature and Humanitarian Reform during the Civil War Era*. Bloomington: Indiana University Press, 1996.

Ellis, Joseph J. *Founding Brothers: The Revolutionary Generation*. New York: Random House, 2000.

Ellis, Stephen. *The Mask of Anarchy: The Destruction of Liberia and the Religious Dimension of an African Civil War*. New York: New York University Press, 1999.

Elmore, A. E. *Lincoln's Gettysburg Address: Echoes of the Bible and Book of Common Prayer*. Carbondale: Southern Illinois University Press, 2009.

Epps, Garrett. *Democracy Reborn: The Fourteenth Amendment and the Fight for Equal Rights in Post–Civil War America*. New York: MacMillan, 2006.

Escott, Paul D. *Slavery Remembered: A Record of Twentieth-Century Slave Narratives*. Chapel Hill: University of North Carolina Press, 1979.

———. *"What Shall We Do with the Negro?" Lincoln, White Racism, and Civil War America*. Charlottesville: University of Virginia Press, 2009.

Eyerman, Ron. *Cultural Trauma: Slavery and the Formation of African American Identity*. New York: Cambridge University Press, 2001.

Fabre, Genevieve, and Robert O'Meally, eds. *History and Memory in African-American Culture*. New York: Oxford University Press, 1994.

Fairclough, Adam. *Martin Luther King, Jr*. Athens: University of Georgia Press, 1990.

———. *Race and Democracy: The Civil Rights Struggle in Louisiana, 1915–1972*. Athens: University of Georgia Press, 2008.

———. *To Redeem the Soul of America: The Southern Christian Leadership Conference and Martin Luther King, Jr*. Athens: University of Georgia Press, 2001.

Faust, Drew Gilpin. *James Henry Hammond and the Old South: A Design for Mastery*. Baton Rouge: Louisiana State University Press, 1982.

Feagin, Joe R. *Racist America: Roots, Current Realities, and Future Reparations*. New York: Routledge, 2001.

Ferguson, Harvie. *Self-Identity and Everyday Life*. New York: Routledge, 2009.

Finkelman, Paul. *Slavery and the Founders: Race and Liberty in the Age of Jefferson*. Armonk, N.Y.: M. E. Sharp, 1996.

Flannery, Kathryn T. *Feminist Literacies, 1968–75*. Bloomington: University of Illinois Press, 2005.

Fobanjong, John. *Understanding the Backlash against Affirmative Action.* Hauppauge, N.Y.: Nova Science Publishing, 2003.

Fogel, Robert W. *The Slavery Debates, 1952–1990: A Retrospective.* Baton Rouge: Louisiana State University Press, 2003.

Fogel, Robert W., and Stanley L. Engerman. *Time on the Cross: The Economics of American Negro Slavery.* Boston: Little, Brown, 1974.

Follett, Richard. *The Sugar Masters: Planters and Slaves in Louisiana's Cane World.* Baton Rouge: Louisiana State University Press, 2007.

Foner, Eric. *Reconstruction: America's Unfinished Revolution, 1863–1877.* New York: Harper & Row, 1988.

Forbes, Robert P. *The Missouri Compromise and Its Aftermath: Slavery and the Meaning of America.* Chapel Hill: University of North Carolina Press, 2007.

Ford, Lacy K. *Deliver Us from Evil: The Slavery Question in the Old South.* New York: Oxford University Press, 2009.

Foster, Frances Smith. *'Til Death or Distance Do Us Part: Marriage and the Making of African America.* New York: Oxford University Press, 2010.

Foster, Michele. *Black Teachers on Teaching.* New York: Norton, 1997.

Fox-Genovese, Elizabeth. *Within the Plantation Household: Black and White Women in the Old South.* Chapel Hill: University of North Carolina Press, 1988.

Fox-Genovese, Elizabeth, and Eugene D. Genovese. *The Mind of the Master Class: History and Faith in the Southern Slaveholders' Worldview.* New York: Cambridge University Press, 2005.

Fraden, Rena. *Blueprints for a Black Federal Theatre, 1935–1939.* New York: Cambridge University Press, 1994.

Franklin, John Hope. *From Slavery to Freedom: A History of American Negroes.* New York: Knopf, 1947.

———. *From Slavery to Freedom: A History of American Negroes.* 2nd ed. New York: Knopf, 1956.

Franklin, John Hope, and Alfred A. Moss Jr. *From Slavery to Freedom: A History of African Americans.* 8th ed. New York: Knopf, 2008.

Fraser, Rebecca. *Courtship and Love among the Enslaved in North Carolina.* Jackson: University of Mississippi Press, 2007.

Freehling, William W. *The Road to Disunion: Secessionists at Bay, 1776–1854.* New York: Oxford University Press, 1990.

Gallagher, Gary W. *Lee and His Army in Confederate History.* Chapel Hill: University of North Carolina Press, 2001.

Gardner, Sarah. *Blood and Irony: Southern White Women's Narratives of the Civil War, 1861–1937.* Chapel Hill: University of North Carolina Press, 2004.

Gaspar, David Barry, and Darlene Clark Hine, eds. *More Than Chattel: Black Women and Slavery in the Americas.* Bloomington: Indiana University Press, 1996.

Gatewood, William B. *Aristocrats of Color: The Black Elite, 1880–1920.* Fayetteville: University of Arkansas Press, 2000.

Geist, Christopher D. "In Depth: The South and Popular Culture." *Journal of Popular Culture* 16, no. 3 (1982), 1–2.

Genovese, Eugene D. *The Political Economy of Slavery: Studies in the Economy and Society of the Slave South*. Middletown, Conn.: Wesleyan University Press, 1989.

———. *Roll, Jordan, Roll: The World the Slaves Made*. New York: Vintage Books, 1974.

Genovese, Eugene D., and Elizabeth Fox-Genovese. "Slavery, Economic Development, and the Law: The Dilemma of the Southern Political Economist, 1800–1860." *Washington and Lee Law Review* 41, no. 1 (1984): 1–29.

Gibney, Mark, Rhoda E. Howard-Hassmann, Jean-Marc Coicaud, and Miklaus Steiner, eds. *The Age of Apology: Facing Up to the Past*. Philadelphia: University of Pennsylvania Press, 2008.

Giddings, Paula J. *Ida: A Sword among Lions: Ida B. Wells and the Campaign Against Lynching*. New York: Harper Collins, 2008.

———. *When and Where I Enter*. New York: Harper and Row, 1984.

Gilbert, Margaret. *On Social Facts*. New York: Routledge, 1989.

Gill, Tiffany M. *Beauty Shop Politics: African American Women's Activism in the Beauty Industry*. Bloomington: University of Illinois Press, 2010.

Glasrud, Bruce, and Laurie Champion. "'The Fishes and the Poet's Hands': Frank Yerby, A Black Author in White America." *Journal of American and Comparative Cultures* 23, no. 4 (2000): 15–21.

Glassberg, David. "Public History and the Study of Memory." *Public Historian* 18, no. 2 (1996): 7–23.

Glover, Lorri. *Southern Sons: Becoming Men in the New Nation*. Baltimore: Johns Hopkins University Press, 2007.

Glymph, Thavolia. *Out of the House of Bondage: The Transformation of the Plantation Household*. New York: Cambridge University Press, 2008.

Goggin, Jacqueline Anne. *Carter G. Woodson: A Life in Black History*. Baton Rouge: Louisiana State University Press, 1997.

Goldberg, Ann. *Sex, Religion, and the Making of Modern Madness: The Eberbach Asylum and German Society, 1815–1849*. New York: Oxford University Press, 2001.

Goldberg, Elizabeth Swanson. "Living the Legacy: Pain, Desire, and Narrative Time in Gayl Jones' 'Corregidora.'" *Callaloo* 26, no. 2 (2003): 446–72.

Goodman, Lizbeth. *Contemporary Feminist Theater: To Each Her Own*. New York: Routledge, 1993.

Goodman, Paul. *Of One Blood: Abolitionism and the Origins of Racial Equality*. Berkeley: University of California Press, 1998.

Gordon, Ann Dexter, Bettye Collier-Thomas, John H. Bracey, Arlene Voski Avakian, and Joyce Avrech Berkman, eds. *African American Women and the Vote, 1837–1965*. Amherst: University of Massachusetts Press, 1997.

Gordon-Reed, Annette. *The Hemingses of Monticello: An American Family*. New York: Norton, 2008.

———. *Thomas Jefferson and Sally Hemings: An American Controversy.* Charlottesville: University of Virginia Press, 1998.

Gore, Dayo F., Jeanne Theoharis, and Komozi Woodard, eds. *Want to Start a Revolution? Radical Women in the Black Freedom Struggle.* New York: New York University Press, 2009.

Gottheimer, Josh, ed. *Ripples of Hope: Great American Civil Rights Speeches.* New York: Basic Books, 2003.

Graff, E. J. *What Is Marriage For?* Boston: Beacon Press, 1999.

Gray, R. J. "Southwestern Humor, Erskine Caldwell, and the Comedy of Frustration." *Southern Literary Journal* 8, no. 1 (1975): 3–26.

Griffin, Farah J. "Black Feminists and Du Bois: Respectability, Protection, and Beyond." *Annals of the American Academy of Political and Social Science* 568, no. 28 (2000): 28–40.

Gudmestad, Robert H. *A Troublesome Commerce: The Transformation of the Interstate Slave Trade.* Baton Rouge: Louisiana State University Press, 2003.

Guterl, Matthew Pratt. *The Color of Race, 1900–1940.* Cambridge: Harvard University Press, 2001.

Gutman, Herbert G. *The Black Family in Slavery and Freedom, 1750–1925.* New York: Vintage Books, 1976.

Hall, Stephen G. *A Faithful Account of the Race: African American Historical Writing in Nineteenth-Century America.* Chapel Hill: University of North Carolina Press, 2009.

Hamalian, Leo. *Lost Plays of the Harlem Renaissance, 1920–1940.* Detroit: Wayne State University Press, 1996.

Hamilton, Holman. *Prologue to Conflict: The Crisis and Compromise of 1850.* Lexington: University of Kentucky Press, 2005.

Hammond, John C. *Slavery, Freedom, and Expansion in the Early American West.* Charlottesville: University of Virginia Press, 2007.

Harding, Vincent. *There Is a River: The Black Struggle for Freedom in America.* New York: Vintage Books, 1983.

Harris, Frederick C. *Something Within: Religion in African American Political Activism.* New York: Oxford University Press, 1999.

Harrold, Stanley. *The Abolitionists and the South.* Lexington: University Press of Kentucky, 1999.

———. "On the Borders of Slavery and Race: Charles T. Torrey and the Underground Railroad." *Journal of the Early Republic* 20, no. 2 (2000): 272–92.

Hartman, Saidiya V. *Scenes of Subjection: Terror, Slavery, and Self-Making in Nineteenth-Century America.* New York: Oxford University Press, 1997.

Hartnett, Stephen J. *Democratic Dissent and the Cultural Fictions of Antebellum America.* Urbana: University of Illinois Press, 2002.

Heglar, Charles J. *Rethinking the Slave Narrative: Slave Marriage and the Narratives of Henry Bib and William and Ellen Craft.* Westport, Conn.: Greenwood, 2001.

Henderson, Archibald. *Pioneering a People's Theatre.* Chapel Hill: University of North Carolina Press, 1945.

Henson, Josiah. *Father Henson's Story of His Own Life. With an Introduction by H. B. Stowe.* Boston: John P. Jewitt, 1858.

Herman, Ellen. *The Romance of American Psychology: Political Culture in the Age of Experts.* Berkeley: University of California Press, 1995.

Higginbotham, Evelyn Brooks. *Righteous Discontent: The Women's Movement in the Black Baptist Church, 1880–1920.* Cambridge: Harvard University Press, 1993.

Higman, Barry W. *Slave Populations of the British Caribbean, 1807–1834.* Mona: University Press of the West Indies, 1995.

Hill, Errol, and James V. Hatch. *A History of African American Theatre.* New York: Cambridge University Press, 2003.

Hill, Herbert, and James E. Jones Jr. *Race in America: The Struggle for Equality.* Madison: University of Wisconsin Press, 1993.

Hill, Lynda M. "Ex-Slave Narratives: The WPA Federal Writers' Project Reappraised." *Oral History* 26, no. 1 (1998): 64–72.

Hill, Shirley A. *Black Intimacies: A Gender Perspective on Families and Relationships.* Walnut Creek, Calif.: AltaMira Press, 2005.

Hine, Darlene Clark. "Rape and the Inner Lives of Black Women in the Middle West." *Signs* 14, no. 4 (1989): 912–20.

Hochschild, Adam. *Bury the Chains: Prophets and Rebels in the Fight to Free an Empire's Slaves.* New York: Houghton Mifflin, 2005.

Hodes, Martha. *White Women, Black Men: Illicit Sex in the Nineteenth-Century South.* New Haven: Yale University Press, 1997.

Hodgson, Geoffrey M. *How Economics Forgot History: The Problem of Historical Specificity in Social Science.* New York: Routledge, 2001.

Holloway, Karla F. C. *Passed On: African American Mourning Stories.* Durham, N.C.: Duke University Press, 2003.

Horsman, Reginald. *Race and Manifest Destiny: The Origins of American Racial Anglo-Saxonism.* Cambridge: Harvard University Press, 1981.

Horton, James Oliver, and Lois E. Horton, eds. *Slavery and Public History: The Tough Stuff of American Memory.* Chapel Hill: University of North Carolina Press, 2006.

Howe, Daniel Walker. *What Hath God Wrought: The Transformation of America, 1815–1848.* New York: Oxford University Press, 2007.

Huddle, Mark A. *Marcus Garvey: Black Nationalism and the New Negro Renaissance.* Chicago: Ivan R. Dee, 2012.

Huggins, Nathan Irvin. *Black Odyssey: The African-American Ordeal in Slavery.* New York: Vintage Books, 1990.

———. *Harlem Renaissance.* Updated edition, New York: Oxford University Press, 1973.

———. *Voices from the Harlem Renaissance.* New York: Oxford University Press, 1976.

Hunter, Frances L. "Slave Society on the Southern Plantation." *Journal of Negro History* 7, no. 1 (1922): 1–10.

Hunter, Tera. *To 'Joy My Freedom: Southern Black Women's Lives and Labors after the Civil War.* Cambridge: Harvard University Press, 1997.

Huston, James L. *Stephen A. Douglas and the Dilemmas of Democratic Equality.* Lanham, Md.: Rowman and Littlefield, 2006.

Hutchinson, George. *The Harlem Renaissance in Black and White.* Cambridge: Harvard University Press, 1995.

Ifill, Sherrilyn A. *On the Courthouse Lawn: Confronting the Legacy of Lynching in the Twenty-First Century.* Boston: Beacon Press, 2008.

Irons, Jenny. "The Shaping of Activist Recruitment and Participation: A Study of Women in the Mississippi Civil Rights Movement." *Gender and Society* 12, no. 6 (1998): 692–702.

Jackson, Blyden. "A Survey Course in Negro Literature." *College English* 35, no. 6 (1974): 631–36.

Jackson, John P., and Nadine M. Weidman. *Race, Racism, and Science: Social Impact and Interaction.* Santa Barbara, Calif.: ABC-CLIO, 2004.

Jacobs, Donald M., ed. *Courage and Conscience: Black and White Abolitionists in Boston.* Bloomington: Indiana University Press, 1993.

Jacobson, Matthew Frye. *Roots Too: White Ethnic Revival in Post–Civil Rights America.* Cambridge: Harvard University Press, 2006.

———. *Whiteness of a Different Color: European Immigrants and the Alchemy of Race.* Cambridge: Harvard University Press, 1998.

Jaffa, Harry V. *Crisis of the House Divided: An Interpretation of the Issues in the Lincoln-Douglas Debates.* Chicago: University of Chicago Press, 1999.

Jankowiak, William. *Romantic Passion: A Universal Experience?* New York: Columbia University Press, 1997.

Jeffrey, Julie Roy. *Abolitionists Remember: Antislavery Autobiographies and the Unfinished Work of Emancipation.* Chapel Hill: University of North Carolina, 2008.

———. *The Great Silent Army of Abolitionism: Ordinary Women in the Antislavery Movement.* Chapel Hill: University of North Carolina Press, 1998.

Jenkins, Earnestine, and Darlene Clark Hine, eds. *A Question of Manhood: A Reader in U.S. Black Men's History and Masculinity.* 2 vols. Bloomington: Indiana State University Press, 2001.

Johnson, Walter, ed. *The Chattel Principle: Internal Slave Trades in the Americas.* New Haven: Yale University Press, 2005.

———. "The Slave Trader, the White Slave, and the Politics of Racial Determinism in the 1850s." *Journal of American History* 87, no. 1 (2000): 13–38.

———. *Soul by Soul: Life Inside the Antebellum Slave Market.* Cambridge: Harvard University Press, 1999.

Jones, Jacqueline. *Labor of Love, Labor of Sorrow: Black Women, Work, and the Family from Slavery to the Present.* New York: Vintage, 1985.

Joseph, Peniel E., ed. *The Black Power Movement: Rethinking the Civil Rights–Black Power Era*. New York: Routledge, 2005.

Joyner, Charles. *Down by the Riverside: A South Carolina Slave Community*. Urbana: University of Illinois Press, 1984.

Kammen, Michael. "Public History and the Uses of Memory." *Public Historian* 19, no. 2 (1997): 49–52.

Kaplan, Carla. *The Erotics of Talk: Women's Writing and Feminist Paradigms*. New York: Oxford University Press, 1996.

Katz, Michael B., and Thomas J. Sprague, eds. *W. E. B. Du Bois, Race, and the City: The Philadelphia Negro and Its Legacy*. Philadelphia: University of Pennsylvania Press, 1998.

Kaye, Anthony E. *Joining Places: Slave Neighborhoods in the Old South*. Chapel Hill: University of North Carolina Press, 2007.

Keely, Karen A. "Poverty, Sterilization, and Eugenics in Erskine Caldwell's *Tobacco Road*." *Journal of American Studies* 36, no. 1 (2002): 23–42.

Kelves, Daniel J. *In the Name of Eugenics: Genetics and the Uses of Human Heredity*. Cambridge: Harvard University Press, 1985.

Kempadoo, Kamala. *Sexing the Caribbean: Gender, Race, and Sexual Labor*. New York: Routledge, 2004.

Kennedy, Randall. *Interracial Intimacies: Sex, Marriage, Identity, and Adoption*. New York: Pantheon Books, 2003.

———. *Nigger: The Strange Career of a Troublesome Word*. New York: Vintage Books, 2002.

Kerber, Linda K. *Women of the Republic: Intellect and Ideology in Revolutionary America*. New York: Norton, 1986.

Kimmel, M. S., and J. Fracher, eds. *Men's Lives*. New York: Macmillan, 1992.

King, Deborah K. "Multiple Jeopardy, Multiple Consciousness: The Context of a Black Feminist Ideology." *Signs* 14, no. 1 (1988): 42–72.

King, Wilma. *Stolen Childhood: Slave Life in Nineteenth-Century America*. Bloomington: Indiana University Press, 1998.

Kirby, Jack Temple. *Media-Made Dixie: The South in the American Imagination*. Athens: University of Georgia Press, 1986.

Klarman, Michael J. *Unfinished Business: Racial Equality in American History*. New York: Oxford University Press, 2007.

Klein, Herbert S. *The Atlantic Slave Trade*. New edition. Cambridge: Cambridge University Press, 2010.

Koritz, Amy. *Culture Makers: Urban Performance and Literature in the 1920s*. Bloomington: University of Illinois Press, 2009.

Kotlikoff, Laurence J., and Sebastian Pinera. "The Old South's Stake in the Inter-Regional Movement of Slaves, 1850–1860." *Journal of Economic History* 37, no. 2 (1977): 434–50.

Koven, Seth. *Slumming: Sexual and Social Politics in Victorian London*. Princeton: Princeton University Press, 2004.

Kraditor, Aileen. *Means and Ends in American Abolitionism: Garrison and His Critics on Strategy and Tactics, 1834–1850*. Chicago: Ivan R. Dee, 1989.

Krasner, David. *A Beautiful Pageant: African American Theatre, Drama, and Performance in the Harlem Renaissance, 1910–1927*. New York: Palgrave Macmillan, 2002.

———. *Resistance, Parody and Double Consciousness in African American Theatre, 1895–1910*. New York: St. Martin's Press, 1997.

Lancaster, Roger N., and Micaela di Leonardo, eds. *The Gender Sexuality Reader: Culture, History, Political Economy*. New York: Routledge, 1997.

Lassiter, Matthew D., and Joseph Crespino, eds. *The Myth of Southern Exceptionalism*. New York: Oxford University Press, 2010.

Lathrop, Barnes F. "Texas vs. Louisiana, 1849." *Southwestern Historical Quarterly* 50, no. 1 (1946): 93–97.

Lemert, Charles C. *Social Things: An Introduction to the Sociological Life*. Middletown, Conn.: Wesleyan University Press, 2008.

Lemert, Charles, and Esme Bhan, eds. *The Voice of Anna Julia Cooper*. Lanham, Md.: Rowman & Littlefield, 1998.

Levecq, Christine. *Slavery and Sentiment: The Politics of Feeling in Black Atlantic Antislavery Writing, 1770–1850*. Durham: University of New Hampshire Press, 2008.

Levine, Daniel. *Bayard Rustin and the Civil Rights Movement*. New Brunswick, N.J.: Rutgers University Press, 2000.

Levine, Lawrence W. *Black Culture and Black Consciousness: Afro-American Folk Thought from Slavery to Freedom*. New York: Oxford University Press, 1977.

Levine, Philippa. *The British Empire: Sunrise to Sunset*. New York: Pearson Longman, 2007.

Lewis, David Levering. *W. E. B. Du Bois: A Reader*. New York: Henry Holt, 1995.

———. *W. E. B. Du Bois: Biography of a Race, 1868–1919*. New York: Henry Holt, 1993.

———. *When Harlem Was in Vogue*. New York: Penguin Books, 1979.

Lightner, David L. *Slavery and the Commerce Power: How the Struggle Against the Interstate Slave Trade Led to the Civil War*. New Haven: Yale University Press, 2006.

Ling, Peter J., and Sharon Monteith, eds. *Gender and the Civil Rights Movement*. New Brunswick, N.J.: Rutgers University Press, 2004.

Link, William A. *Roots of Secession: Slavery and Politics in Antebellum Virginia*. Chapel Hill: University of North Carolina Press, 2005.

Lischer, Richard. *The Preacher King: Martin Luther King, Jr., and the Word That Moved America*. New York: Oxford University Press, 1997.

Lister, Martin, Jon Dovey, Seth Giddings, Iain Grant, and Kiernan Kelly. *New Media: A Critical Introduction*. New York: Routledge, 2003.

Logan, Rayford W. *Howard University: The First Hundred Years, 1867–1967*. Washington, D.C.: Howard University, 1968.

Long, Alecia P. *The Great Southern Babylon: Sex, Race, and Respectability in New Orleans, 1865–1920*. Baton Rouge: Louisiana State University Press, 2004.

Lowe, Richard G., and Randolph B. Campbell. "The Slave-Breeding Hypothesis: A Demographic Comment on the 'Buying' and 'Selling' States." *Journal of Southern History* 42, no. 3 (1976): 401–12.

Lowenthal, D., and C. G. Clark. "Slave Breeding in Barbuda: The Past of a Negro Myth." *Annals of the New York Academy of Sciences* 292 (1977): 510–35.

Lubin, Alex. *Romance and Rights: The Politics of Interracial Intimacy, 1945–1954*. Jackson: University Press of Mississippi, 2005.

Lystra, Karen. *Searching the Heart: Women, Men, and Romantic Love in Nineteenth-Century America*. New York: Oxford University Press, 1989.

Madison, James H. *A Lynching in the Heartland: Race and Memory in America*. New York: Palgrave Macmillan, 2001.

Malone, Ann P. *Sweet Chariot: Slave Family and Household Structure in Nineteenth-Century Louisiana*. Chapel Hill: University of North Carolina Press, 1992.

Margolick, David. *Strange Fruit: The Biography of a Song*. New York: Ecco Press 2001.

Markovitz, Jonathon. *Legacies of Lynching: Racial Violence and Lynching*. Minneapolis: University of Minnesota Press, 2004.

Marsh, Charles. *The Beloved Community: How Faith Shapes Social Justice from the Civil Rights Movement to Today*. New York: Perseus Books Group, 2005.

Mason, Matthew. *Slavery and Politics in the Early American Republic*. Chapel Hill: University of North Carolina Press, 2006.

Matterson, Lisa G. *For the Freedom of Her Race: Black Women and Electoral Politics in Illinois, 1877–1932*. Chapel Hill: University of North Carolina Press, 2009.

McBride, Dwight A. *Impossible Witnesses: Truth, Abolitionism, and Slave Testimony*. New York: New York University Press, 2001.

McCaw-Binns, Affette. "Safe Motherhood in Jamaica: From Slavery to Self-Determination." *Pediatric and Perinatal Epidemiology* 19, no. 4 (2005): 254–61.

McCrisken, Trevor B., and Andrew Pepper. *American History and Contemporary Hollywood Film*. Newark: Rutgers University Press, 2005.

McGovern, James R. *Anatomy of a Lynching: The Killing of Claude Neal*. Baton Rouge: Louisiana State University Press, 1982.

McGuire, Danielle L. *At the Dark End of the Street: Black Women, Rape, and Resistance— A New History of the Civil Rights Movement from Rosa Parks to the Rise of Black Power*. New York: Knopf, 2010.

McPherson, James M. *Battle Cry of Freedom: The American Civil War*. New York: Penguin Books, 1988.

Mda, Zakes. *Cion: A Novel*. New York: Picador, 2007.

Meier, August. *Negro Thought in America, 1880–1915: Racial Ideologies in the Age of Booker T. Washington*. Ann Arbor: University of Michigan Press, 1963.

Metcalf, Allan, and David K. Barnhart. *America in So Many Words: Words That Have Shaped America*. Boston: Houghton Mifflin, 1997.

Mills, Kay. *This Little Light of Mine: The Life of Fannie Lou Hamer.* Lexington: University of Kentucky Press, 2007.

Mills, Robert. *Suspended Animation: Pain, Pleasure and Punishment in Medieval Culture.* London: Reaktion Books, 2005.

Mitchell, Michele. *Righteous Propagation: African Americans and the Politics of Racial Destiny after Reconstruction.* Chapel Hill: University of North Carolina Press, 2004.

Moran, Rachel F. *Interracial Intimacy: The Regulation of Race and Romance.* Chicago: University of Chicago Press, 2001.

Morgan, Jennifer L. *Laboring Women: Reproduction and Gender in New World Slavery.* Philadelphia: University of Pennsylvania Press, 2004.

Morgan, Stacy I. *Rethinking Social Realism: African American Art and Literature, 1930–1953.* Athens: University of Georgia Press, 2004.

Morris, Aldon D. *The Origins of the Civil Rights Movement: Black Communities Organizing for Change.* New York: The Free Press, 1984.

Morris, Christopher. "The Articulation of Two Worlds: The Master-Slave Relationship Reconsidered." *Journal of American History* 85, no. 3 (1998): 982–1007.

———. *Becoming Southern: The Evolution of a Way of Life, Warren County and Vicksburg, Mississippi, 1770–1860.* New York: Oxford University Press, 1995.

Morris, Thomas D. *Southern Slavery and the Law, 1619–1860.* Chapel Hill: University of North Carolina Press, 1999.

Morrison, Michael A. *Slavery and the American West: The Eclipse of Manifest Destiny and the Coming of the Civil War.* Chapel Hill: University of North Carolina Press, 1999.

Morton, Mark. *The Lover's Tongue: A Merry Romp through the Language of Love and Sex.* Ontario: Insomniac Press, 2003.

Morton, Patricia, ed. *Discovering the Women in Slavery: Emancipating Perspectives on the American Past.* Athens: University of Georgia Press, 1996.

———. *Disfigured Images: The Historical Assault on Afro-American Women.* Westport, Conn.: Greenwood, 1991.

Moses, A. Dirk, ed. *Empire, Colony, Genocide: Conquest, Occupation, and Subaltern Resistance in World History.* New York: Berghahn Books, 2008.

Moses, Wilson Jeremiah. *Afrotopia: The Roots of African American Popular History.* New York: Cambridge University Press, 1998.

Mullin, Gerald W. *Fight and Rebellion: Slave Resistance in Eighteenth-Century Virginia.* New York: Oxford University Press, 1974.

Munby, Jonathon. *Public Enemies, Public Heroes: Screening the Gangster from Little Caesar to Touch of Evil.* Chicago: University of Chicago Press, 1999.

Nash, Gary B. *Race and Revolution.* Madison: Madison House, 1990.

Nash, Gary B., and Jean R. Soderlund. *Freedom by Degrees: Emancipation in Philadelphia and Its Aftermath.* New York: Oxford University Press, 1991.

Neal, Anthony W. *Unburdened by Conscience: A Black People's Collective Account of America's Ante-bellum South and the Aftermath.* Lanham, Md.: University Press of America, 2009.

Newman, Richard S. *The Transformation of American Abolitionism*. Chapel Hill: University of North Carolina Press, 2002.

Nobles, Melissa. *The Politics of Official Apologies*. New York: Cambridge University Press, 2008.

Novick, Peter. *That Noble Dream: The "Objectivity Question" and the American Historical Profession*. New York: Cambridge University Press, 1988.

Oates, Stephen B. *Let the Trumpet Sound: A Life of Martin Luther King, Jr.* New York: Harper Collins, 1982.

Okur, Nilgun Anadolu. "Underground Railroad in Philadelphia." *Journal of Black Studies* 25, no. 5 (1995): 537–57.

Painter, Nell Irvin. *Creating Black Americans: African-American History and Its Meanings, 1619 to the Present*. New York: Oxford University Press, 2006.

———. *Sojourner Truth: A Life, a Symbol*. New York: Norton, 1996.

Parent, Anthony S., and Susan Brown Wallace. "Childhood and Sexual Identity under Slavery." *Journal of the History of Sexuality* 3, no. 3 (1993): 363–401.

Parker, Philip M., ed. *Defects: Webster's Timeline History, 415 B.C.–1975*. San Diego: Icon, 2009.

Parks, Sheri. *Fierce Angels: The Strong Black Woman in American Life and Culture*. New York: One World/Ballantine Books, 2010.

Pascoe, Peggy. *What Comes Naturally: Miscegenation Law and the Making of Race in America*. New York: Oxford University Press, 2009.

Patton, Vincent K., and Maureen Honey, eds. *Double-Take: A Revisionist Harlem Renaissance Anthology*. New Brunswick, N.J.: Rutgers University Press, 2001.

Perkins, Kathy A. *Black Female Playwrights: An Anthology of Plays before 1950*. Bloomington: Indiana University Press, 1989.

Perry, Imani. *Prophets of the Hood: Politics and Poetics in Hip Hop*. Durham, N.C.: Duke University Press, 2004.

Perry, Jeffrey B. *Hubert Harrison: The Voice of Harlem Radicalism, 1883–1918*. New York: Columbia University Press, 2009.

Perry, Lewis. *Radical Abolitionism: Anarchy and the Government of God in Antislavery Thought*. Knoxville: University of Tennessee Press, 1995.

Peterson, Bernard L., Jr. *The African American Theater Directory, 1816–1960: A Comprehensive Guide to Early Black Theater Organizations, Companies, Theatres, and Performing Groups*. Westport, Conn.: Greenwood, 1997.

Peterson, Derek R., ed. *Abolitionism and Imperialism in Britain, Africa, and the Atlantic*. Athens: Ohio University Press, 2010.

Phillips, Christopher. *Missouri's Confederate: Claiborne Fox Jackson and the Creation of Southern Identity in the Border West*. Columbia: University of Missouri Press, 2000.

Phillips, U. B. *American Negro Slavery: A Survey of the Supply, Employment and Control of Negro Labor as Determined by the Plantation Regime*. 1918. Reprint, Whitefish, Mont.: Kessinger, 2004.

Pierson, Michael D. *Free Hearts and Free Homes: Gender and American Antislavery Politics.* Chapel Hill: University of North Carolina Press, 2003.

———. "'Slavery Cannot Be Covered Up with Broadcloth or a Bandanna': The Evolution of White Abolitionist Attacks on the Patriarchal Institution." *Journal of the Early Republic* 25, no. 3 (2005): 383–415.

Pinn, Anthony B., and Dwight N. Hopkins, eds. *Loving the Body: Black Religious Studies and the Erotic.* New York: Palgrave Macmillan, 2004.

Podair, Jerald E. *Bayard Rustin: American Dreamer.* Lanham, Md.: Rowman and Littlefield, 2009.

Portnoy, Alisse. *Their Right to Speak: Women's Activism in the Indian and Slave Debates.* Cambridge: Harvard University Press, 2005.

Poteet, William Mark. *Gay Men in Modern Southern Literature: Ritual, Initiation, and the Construction of Masculinity.* New York: Peter Lang, 2006.

Potter, David M. *The Impending Crisis, 1848–1861.* New York: Harper & Row, 1976.

Povinelli, Elizabeth A. *The Empire of Love: Toward a Theory of Intimacy, Genealogy, and Carnality.* Durham, N.C.: Duke University Press, 2006.

Preston, E. Delorus, Jr. "The Genesis of the Underground Railroad." *Journal of Negro History* 18, no. 2 (1933): 144–70.

Quarles, Benjamin. *Black Abolitionists.* New York: Oxford University Press, 1969.

Rabaka, Reiland. "W. E. B. Du Bois and 'The Damnation of Women': An Essay on Africana Anti-Sexist Critical Social Theory." *Journal of African American Studies* 7, no. 2 (2003): 37–60.

Raboteau, Albert J. *Slave Religion: The "Invisible Institution" in the Antebellum South.* New York: Oxford University Press, 1978.

Rael, Patrick. *Black Identity and Black Protest in the Antebellum North.* Chapel Hill: University of North Carolina Press, 2002.

Ramsey, Sonya Y. *Reading, Writing, and Segregation: A Century of Black Women Teachers in Nashville.* Urbana: University of Illinois Press, 2008.

Ransby, Barbara. *Ella Baker and the Black Freedom Movement: A Radical Democratic Vision.* Chapel Hill: University of North Carolina Press, 2005.

Ransom, Roger L. *Conflict and Compromise: The Political Economy of Slavery, Emancipation, and the American Civil War.* New York: Cambridge University Press, 1989.

Ransom, Roger, and Richard Sutch. "Capitalists without Capital: The Burden of Slavery and the Impact of Emancipation." *Agricultural History* 62, no. 3 (1988): 133–60.

Rapi, Nina, and Maya Chowdhry, eds. *Acts of Passion: Sexuality, Gender, and Performance.* New York: Herrington Press, 1998.

Rawick, George P. *From Sundown to Sunup: The Making of the Black Community.* Westport, Conn.: Greenwood, 1972.

Regosin, Elizabeth Ann. *Freedom's Promise: Ex-Slave Families and Citizenship in the Age of Emancipation.* Charlottesville: University Press of Virginia, 2002.

Rice, Alan J. *Radical Narratives of the Black Atlantic.* New York: Continuum, 2003.

Richardson, Bonham C. *Caribbean Migrants: Environment and Human Survival on St. Kitts and Nevis.* Knoxville: University of Tennessee Press, 1983.

Richardson, Riche. *Black Masculinity and the U.S. South: From Uncle Tom to Gangsta.* Athens: University of Georgia Press, 2007.

———. "Kara Walker's Old South and New Terrors." *NKA: Journal of Contemporary African Art* 25 (Winter 2010): 49–59.

Robinson, Cedric J. *Forgeries of Memory and Meaning: Blacks and the Regimes of Race in American Theater and Film before World War II.* Chapel Hill: University of North Carolina Press, 2007.

Rodriguez, Junius P., ed. *Slavery in the United States: A Social, Political, and Historical Encyclopedia.* 2 vols. Santa Barbara: ABC-CLIO, 2007.

Ross, Loretta J. "African-American Women and Abortion." In *Abortion Wars: A Half-Century of Struggle, 1950–2000,* ed. Rickie Solinger, 161–207. Berkeley: University of California Press, 1998.

Roth, Benita. *Separate Roads to Feminism: Black, Chicana, and White Feminist Movements in America's Second Wave.* New York: Cambridge University Press, 2004.

Rüsen, Jörn. "Making Sense of Time: Toward a Universal Typology of Conceptual Foundations of Historical Consciousness." In *Time and History: The Variety of Cultures,* ed. Jörn Rüsen, 7–18. New York: Berghahn Books, 2007.

Ryan, Tim. *Calls and Responses: The American Novel of Slavery Since Gone with the Wind.* Baton Rouge: Louisiana State University Press, 2008.

Salerno, Beth A. *Sister Societies: Women's Antislavery Organizations in Antebellum America.* DeKalb: Northern Illinois University Press, 2005.

Sanchez-Eppler, Karen. *Touching Liberty: Abolition, Feminism, and the Politics of the Body.* New York: Oxford University Press, 1993.

Sargent, Frederic O. *The Civil Rights Revolution: Events and Leaders, 1955–1968.* Jefferson, N.C.: McFarland, 2004.

Schechter, Patricia A. *Ida B. Wells-Barnett and American Reform, 1880–1930.* Chapel Hill: University of North Carolina Press, 2001.

Schultz, Nancy L., ed. *Fear Itself: Enemies Real and Imagined in American Culture.* West Lafayette, Ind.: Purdue University Press, 1999.

Schwartz, Marie Jenkins. *Birthing a Slave: Motherhood and Medicine in the Antebellum South.* Cambridge: Harvard University Press, 2006.

———. *Born in Bondage: Growing Up Enslaved in the Antebellum South.* Cambridge: Harvard University Press, 2000.

Scott, Daryl M. *Contempt and Pity: Social Policy and the Image of the Damaged Black Psyche, 1880–1996.* Chapel Hill: University of North Carolina Press, 1997.

Scott, James C. *Domination and the Arts of Resistance: Hidden Transcripts.* New Haven: Yale University Press, 1990.

Scott, Lawrence P., and William P. Womack. *Double V: The Civil Rights Struggle of the Tuskegee Airmen.* East Lansing: Michigan State University Press, 1992.

Seidel, Kathryn Lee. *The Southern Belle in the American Novel.* Gainesville: University Press of Florida, 1985.

Server, Lee. *Encyclopedia of Pulp Fiction Writers.* New York: Facts on File, 2002.

Shay, Frank. *Judge Lynch: His First Hundred Years.* Montclair, N.J.: Patterson Smith, 1969.

Sherrill, Robert. *Gothic Politics in the Deep South: Stars of the New Confederacy.* New York: Grossman Publishers, 1968.

Silber, Nina. *The Romance of Reunion: Northerners and the South, 1865–1900.* Chapel Hill: University of North Carolina Press, 1993.

Singer, Irving. *The Nature of Love: Courtly and Romantic.* 2 vols. Cambridge: MIT Press, 2009.

Slocum, John D., ed. *Violence and American Cinema.* New York: Routledge, 2001.

Smith, John David. "A Different View of Slavery: Black Historians Attack the Proslavery Argument." *Journal of Negro History* 65, no. 4 (1980): 298–311.

Smith, Sidonie, and Julia Watson, eds. *Before They Could Vote: American Women's Autobiographical Writing, 1819–1919.* Madison: University of Wisconsin Press, 2006.

———, eds. *Women, Autobiography, Theory: A Critical Reader.* Madison: University of Wisconsin Press, 1998.

Smith, Susan Lynn. *Sick and Tired of Being Sick and Tired: Black Women's Health Activism in America, 1890–1950.* Philadelphia: University of Pennsylvania Press, 1995.

Smith, Valerie. *Self-Discovery and Authority in Afro-American Narrative.* Cambridge: Harvard University Press, 1987.

Smithers, Gregory D. "The 'Pursuits of the Civilized Man': Race and the Meaning of Civilization in the United States and Australia, 1790s–1850s." *Journal of World History* 20, no. 2 (2009): 245–72.

———. *Science, Sexuality, and Race in the United States and Australia, 1780s–1890s.* New York: Routledge, 2009.

Snyder, Christina. *Slavery in Indian Country: The Changing Face of Captivity.* Cambridge: Harvard University Press, 2010.

Snyder, Terri L. "Suicide, Slavery, and Memory in North America." *Journal of American History* 97, no. 1 (2010): 39–62.

Soderlund, Jean. *Quakers and Slavery: A Divided Spirit.* Princeton, N.J.: Princeton University Press, 1985.

Sommerville, Diane Miller. *Rape and Race in the Nineteenth-Century South.* Chapel Hill: University of North Carolina Press, 2004.

Spalding, Henry D., ed. *Encyclopedia of Black Folklore and Humor.* Middle Village, N.Y.: Jonathon David, 1978.

Spickard, Paul R. *Mixed Bloods: Intermarriage and Ethnic Identity in Twentieth-Century America.* Madison: University of Wisconsin Press, 1989.

Spierenburg, Pieter, ed. *Men and Violence: Gender, Honor, and Rituals in Modern Europe and America.* Columbus: Ohio State University Press, 1998.

Spindel, Donna J. "Assessing Memory: Twentieth-Century Slave Narratives Reconsidered." *Journal of Interdisciplinary History* 27, no. 2 (1996): 247–61.

Stampp, Kenneth M. *The Peculiar Institution: Slavery in the Antebellum South*. New York: Knopf, 1956.

Stanley, Harrold. *The Abolitionists and the American South, 1831–1861*. Lexington: University Press of Kentucky, 1995.

Stauffer, John. *The Black Hearts of Men: Radical Abolitionists and the Transformation of Race*. Cambridge: Harvard University Press, 2006.

Sterling, Dorothy. *Black Foremothers: Three Lives*. New York: Feminist Press, 1988.

Stern, Alexandra. *Eugenic Nation: Faults and Frontiers of better Breeding in Modern America*. Berkeley: University of California Press, 2005.

Stevenson, Brenda E. *Life in Black and White: Family and Community in the Slave South*. New York: Oxford University Press, 1996.

Stewart, James Brewer. *William Lloyd Garrison at Two Hundred: History, Legacy, and Memory*. New Haven: Yale University Press, 2008.

Stuckey, Sterling. *Slave Culture: Nationalist Theory and the Foundations of Black America*. New York: Oxford University Press, 1987.

Styron, William. "Nat Turner Revisited." *American Heritage* 43, no. 6 (1992): 64–73.

Sullivan, Patricia. *Lift Every Voice: The NAACP and the Making of the Civil Rights Movement*. New York: New Press, 2009.

Sutch, Richard. "The Breeding of Slaves for Sale and the Westward Expansion of Slavery, 1850–1860." In *Race and Slavery in the Western Hemisphere: Quantitative Studies*, ed. Stanley L. Engerman and Eugene D. Genovese, 173–210. Princeton, N.J.: Princeton University Press, 1975.

Sweet, John Wood. *Bodies Politic: Negotiating Race in the American North, 1730–1830*. Baltimore: Johns Hopkins University Press, 2003.

Switala, Wilma J. *Underground Railroad in Pennsylvania*. 2nd ed. Mechanicsburg, Pa.: Stackpole Books, 2008.

Tadman, Michael. *Speculators and Slaves: Masters, Traders, and Slaves in the Old South*. Madison: University of Wisconsin Press, 1996.

Talbot, Paul. *Mondo Mandingo: The Falconhurst Books and Films*. New York: iUniverse, 2009.

Talty, Stephen. *Mulatto America: At the Crossroads of Black and White Culture*. New York: Harper Collins, 2003.

Tate, Claudia. *Domestic Allegories of Political Desire: The Black Heroine's Text at the Turn of the Century*. New York: Oxford University Press, 1992.

Tate, Gayle T. *Unknown Tongues: Black Women's Political Activism in the Antebellum Era, 1830–1860*. East Lansing: Michigan State University Press, 2003.

Taylor, Shawn. *Big Black Penis: Misadventures in Race and Masculinity*. Chicago: Lawrence Hill Books, 2008.

Temperley, Howard. "Capitalism, Slavery and Ideology." *Past and Present* 75, no. 1 (1977): 94–118.

Terrill, Robert E. *Malcolm X: Inventing Radical Judgment*. East Lansing: Michigan State University Press, 2004.

Terry, Jennifer, and Jacqueline Urla, eds. *Deviant Bodies: Critical Perspectives on Difference in Science and Popular Culture*. Bloomington: Indiana University Press, 1995.

Tetlock, Philip E. "Theory-Driven Reasoning about Plausible Pasts and Probable Futures in World Politics." *American Journal of Political Science* 43, no. 2 (1999): 335–66.

Thomas, Robert Paul, and Richard Nelson Bean. "The Fishers of Men: The Profits of the Slave Trade." *Journal of Economic History* 34, no. 4 (1974): 885–914.

Thornton, Mark. "Slavery, Profitability, and the Market Process." *Review of Austrian Economics* 7, no. 2 (1994): 21–47.

Tibbles, Anthony, ed. *Transatlantic Slavery: Against Human Dignity*. Liverpool: Liverpool University Press, 1994.

Towns, W. Stuart. *Enduring Legacy: Rhetoric and Ritual of the Lost Cause*. Tuscaloosa: University of Alabama Press, 2011.

Trouillot, Michel-Rolph. *Silencing the Past: Power and the Production of History*. Boston: Beacon Press, 1995.

Tucker, Susan. *Telling Memories among Southern Women: Domestic Workers and Their Employers in the Segregated South*. New York: Pantheon Books, 1988.

Turner, Darwin T. "Frank Yerby as Debunker." *Massachusetts Review* 9, no. 3 (1968): 569–77.

Turner, Robert F., ed. *The Jefferson-Hemings Controversy: Report of the Scholars Commission*. Durham, N.C.: Carolina Academic Press, 2011.

Tyrell, Ian R. *Historians in Public: The Practice of American History, 1890–1970*. Chicago: University of Chicago Press, 2005.

Tyson, Timothy B. *Radio Free Dixie: Robert F. Williams and the Roots of Black Power*. Chapel Hill: University of North Carolina Press, 2001.

Van Deburg, William L. *Modern Black Nationalism: From Marcus Garvey to Louis Farrakhan*. New York: New York University Press, 1997.

———. *Slavery and Race in American Popular Culture*. Madison: University of Wisconsin Press, 1984.

Vera, Hernan, and Andrew Gordon. *Screen Saviors: Hollywood Fictions of Whiteness*. Lanham, Md.: Rowman and Littlefield, 2003.

Vergne, Teresita Martinez. *Shaping the Discourse on Space: Charity and Its Wards in Nineteenth-Century San Juan, Puerto Rico*. Austin: University of Texas Press, 1999.

Vostral, Sharra L. *Under Wraps: A History of Menstrual Hygiene Technology*. Lanham, Md.: Rowman & Littlefield, 2008.

Wahl, Jenny B. "The Jurisprudence of American Slave Sales." *Journal of Economic History* 56, no. 1 (1996): 143–69.

Wald, Gayle. *Crossing the Line: Racial Passing in Twentieth-Century U.S. Literature and Culture*. Durham, N.C.: Duke University Press, 2000.

Waldrep, Christopher. *The Many Faces of Judge Lynch: Extralegal Violence and Punishment in America*. New York: Palgrave Macmillan, 2002.

Walker, Clarence E. *Deromanticizing Black History: Critical Essays and Reappraisals*. Knoxville: University of Tennessee Press, 1991.

———. *Mongrel Nation: The America Begotten by Thomas Jefferson and Sally Hemings.* Charlottesville: University of Virginia Press, 2009.

Walker, Ethel Pitts. "Krigwa, a Theater by, for, and about Black People." *Theatre Journal* 40, no. 3 (1988): 347–56.

Walkowitz, Daniel J., and Lisa Maya Knauer, eds. *Memory and the Impact of Political Transformation in Public Space.* Durham, N.C.: Duke University Press, 2004.

Wallace-Sanders, Kimberly. *Mammy: A Century of Race, Gender, and Southern Memory.* Ann Arbor: University of Michigan Press, 2008.

Walters, Ronald. "The Erotic South: Civilization and Sexuality in American Abolitionism." *American Quarterly* 25, no. 2 (1973): 177–201.

Washington, Harriet A. *Medical Apartheid: The Dark History of Medical Experimentation on Black Americans from Colonial Times to the Present.* New York: Harlem Moon, 2006.

Wasser, Frederick. *Steven Spielberg's America.* Cambridge, U.K.: Polity Press, 2010.

Watson, Peter, ed. *Psychology and Race.* 1973. Piscataway, N.J.: Transaction, 2009.

Waugh, John C. *On the Brink of Civil War: The Compromise of 1850 and How It Changed the Course of American History.* Wilmington, Del.: Rowman & Littlefield, 2003.

Weiner, Marli F. *Mistresses and Slaves: Plantation Women in South Carolina, 1830–80.* Urbana: University of Illinois Press, 1996.

Welter, Barbara. "The Cult of True Womanhood: 1820–1860." *American Quarterly* 18, no. 2 (1966): 151–74.

West, Cornel. *Race Matters.* Boston: Beacon Press, 1993.

West, Emily. *Chains of Love: Slave Couples in Antebellum South Carolina.* Champaign: University of Illinois Press, 2004.

———. "The Debate on the Strength of Slave Families: South Carolina and the Importance of Cross-Plantation Marriages." *Journal of American Studies* 33 (August 1999): 221–41.

Whalan, Mark. *Race, Manhood, and Modernism in America: The Short Story Cycles of Sherwood Anderson and Jean Toomer.* Knoxville: University of Tennessee Press, 2007.

White, Deborah Gray. *Ar'n't I a Woman? Female Slaves in the Plantation South.* New York: Norton, 1985.

———, ed. *Telling Histories: Black Women Historians in the Ivory Tower.* Chapel Hill: University of North Carolina Press, 2008.

———. *Too Heavy a Load: Black Women in Defense of Themselves, 1894–1994.* New York: Norton, 1999.

White, Hayden. *Tropics of Discourse: Essays in Cultural Criticism.* Baltimore: Johns Hopkins University Press, 1985.

White, Richard, and John M. Findlay, eds. *Power and Place in the North American West.* Seattle: University of Washington Press, 1999.

White, Shane. *Somewhat More Independent: The End of Slavery in New York City, 1770–1810.* Athens: University of Georgia Press, 1991.

Williams, Linda M., and Victoria L. Banyard, eds. *Trauma and Memory.* Thousand Oaks, Calif.: Sage, 1998.

Williams, Tennessee. *Cat on a Hot Tin Roof.* New York: New American Library, 1955.

———. *Suddenly Last Summer.* New York: New American Library, 1958.

Williams, Vernon J. *The Social Sciences and Theories of Race.* Urbana: University of Illinois Press, 2006.

Williamson, Joel. *The Crucible of Race: Black-White Relations in the American South Since Emancipation.* New York: Oxford University Press, 1984.

———. *New People: Miscegenation and Mulattoes in the United States.* Baton Rouge: Louisiana State University Press, 1995.

Wilson, Charles R. *Baptized in Blood: The Religion of the Lost Cause, 1865–1920.* Athens: University of Georgia Press, 1980.

Wolcott, Victoria W. *Remaking Respectability: African American Women in Interwar Detroit.* Chapel Hill: University of North Carolina Press, 2001.

Wood, Amy Louise. *Lynching and Spectacle: Witnessing Racial Violence in America, 1890–1940.* Chapel Hill: University of North Carolina Press, 2009.

Woodman, Harold D. "The Profitability of Slavery: A Historical Perennial." *Journal of Southern History* 29, no. 3 (1963): 303–25.

Woodroofe, Debby. *Sisters in Struggle, 1848–1920.* New York: Pathfinder Press, 1971.

Woodward, C. Vann. *The Burden of Southern History.* Rev. ed. Baton Rouge: Louisiana State University Press, 1968.

———. *Origins of the New South, 1877–1913.* 1951. Reprint, Baton Rouge: Louisiana State University Press, 1971.

Wright, George C. *Life behind the Veil: Blacks in Louisville, Kentucky, 1865–1930.* Baton Rouge: Louisiana State University Press, 1985.

———. *Racial Violence in Kentucky, 1865–1940.* Baton Rouge: Louisiana State University Press, 1990.

Wright, Michelle M. *Becoming Black: Creating Identity in the African Diaspora.* Durham, N.C.: Duke University Press, 2004.

Wubben, Hubert H. *Civil War Iowa and the Copperhead Movement.* Ames: Iowa State University Press, 1980.

Yamamoto, Eric K. *Interracial Justice: Conflict and Reconciliation in Post–Civil Rights America.* New York: New York University Press, 1999.

Yee, Shirley J. *Black Women Abolitionists: A Study in Activism, 1828–1860.* Knoxville: University of Tennessee Press, 1992.

Yellin, Jean Fagan. *Harriet Jacobs, a Life: The Remarkable Adventures of the Woman Who Wrote Incidents in the Life of a Slave Girl.* Cambridge, Mass.: Basic Civitas Books, 2004.

Yellin, Jean Fagan, and John C. Van Horne, eds. *The Abolitionist Sisterhood: Women's Political Culture in Antebellum America.* Ithaca: Cornell University Press, 1994.

Yetman, Norman, R. "Ex-Slave Interviews and the Historiography of Slavery." *American Quarterly* 36, no. 2 (1984): 181–210.

Zahedieh, Nuala. *The Capital and the Colonies: London and the Atlantic Economy, 1660–1700.* Cambridge: Cambridge University Press, 2010.

Zieger, Robert H., and Gilbert J. Gall. *American Workers, American Unions: The Twentieth Century.* Baltimore: Johns Hopkins University Press, 2002.

Zikle, Conway. "Soil Exhaustion, the Territorial Limitation of Slavery, and the Civil War." *Isis* 34, no. 4 (1943): 356–57.

Zilversmit, Arthur. *The First Emancipation: The Abolition of Slavery in the North.* Chicago: University of Chicago Press, 1967.

Zinn, Maxine Baca, and Bonnie Thornton Dill, eds. *Women of Color in U.S. Society.* Philadelphia: Temple University Press, 1994.

# INDEX

Gregory D. Smithers, associate professor of history at Virginia Commonwealth University, is the author of *Science, Sexuality, and Race in the United States and Australia, 1780s–1890s* and co-author of *The Preacher and the Politician: Jeremiah Wright, Barack Obama, and Race in America.*

The University Press of Florida is the scholarly publishing agency for the State University System of Florida, comprising Florida A&M University, Florida Atlantic University, Florida Gulf Coast University, Florida International University, Florida State University, New College of Florida, University of Central Florida, University of Florida, University of North Florida, University of South Florida, and University of West Florida.